AFTER TOCQUEVILLE

Also by Chilton Williamson Jr.

Nonfiction

The Immigration Mystique: America's False Conscience

The Conservative Bookshelf

Narrative Nonfiction

Saltbound: A Block Island Winter

Roughnecking It: Or, Life in the Overthrust

The Hundredth Meridian:
Seasons and Travels in the Old New West

Fiction

Desert Light

The Homestead

Mexico Way

The Education of Héctor Villa

Editor

Immigration and the American Future

AFTER TOCQUEVILLE

*The Promise and Failure
of Democracy*

✦ ✦ ✦

Chilton Williamson Jr.

Wilmington, Delaware

Cataloging-in-Publication data is on file with the Library of Congress.
ISBN: 978-1-61017-022-2

Published in the United States by
ISI Books
Intercollegiate Studies Institute
3901 Centerville Road
Wilmington, Delaware 19807-1938
www.isibooks.org

Manufactured in the United States of America

For John Lukacs
Mentor and Dear Friend

See, I put before you today a benediction and a curse.
—Deuteronomy 11:26

On what bridge does the present pass to the future?
—Friedrich Nietzsche, *Thus Spoke Zarathustra*

All systems, however erroneous or false, have an element of
truth, because the human intellect, being created in the
image of the divine, and made for the apprehension of
the truth, can never operate with pure falsehood.
—Orestes S. Brownson, *The American Republic*

Democracy is the word with which you must lead them by the nose.
—C. S. Lewis, *The Screwtape Letters*

Contents

✦   ✦   ✦

Preface   Two Books   xi

Part I: Democracy after Tocqueville

Chapter 1   From Tocqueville to Fukuyama   1
Chapter 2   The Momentum of Monarchy   15
Chapter 3   Democracy's Forked Road   37

Part II: Democracy and Civilization

Chapter 4   What Is Democracy?   71
Chapter 5   "Fit Your Feet"   85
Chapter 6   The King's Second Body   91
Chapter 7   The Business of Aristocracies   99
Chapter 8   Christianity: The Vital Spot   113
Chapter 9   Speechless Democracy   127
Chapter 10   Democracy and Modern Man   141
Chapter 11   Three against Democracy   167

Part III: The Future of Democracy and the End of History

Chapter 12	The Cold Monster at Bay	185
Chapter 13	The Future of Democracy	197
Chapter 14	After Democracy	221
Coda		231
Notes		233
Acknowledgments		246
Index		247

Two Books

About a decade and a half ago, a young scholar from Oxford, England, set out in the company of a lady companion named Margaret on a journey of fourteen thousand miles across France. The author of acclaimed biographies of Hugo, Balzac, and Rimbaud, Graham Robb owed his early, superficial understanding of the French language to an Algerian Berber in whose auto shop in a Paris *faubourg* he worked for a time. The couple's mode of travel was by time machine. Theirs was not the futuristic invention of H. G. Wells but a contraption already a century old: the humble perennial bicycle, powered by human muscle and breath, regulated by nothing more complex than gear ratios, critically dependent on a strong inner tube, and capable of speeds no greater than the stagecoaches familiar to readers of *The Red and the Black* and *The Charterhouse of Parma*.

Graham Robb had a wide familiarity with the history of monarchical and Republican France, of the great personages who animate the histories of that noble country that so many knowledgeable and sophisticated people have so long considered to have been the most civilized in Europe, and of its transformation during the course of the nineteenth century by revolution, war, political reform, industrialization, social reform, and centralization. Robb himself was in search of another France: the old, prerevolutionary country that had managed to survive a century and a quarter of nationalism and centralization, from 1789 until cataclysm befell Europe in 1914.

Of that country, Robb had little more than an informed apprehension. On the day the Bastille fell to the Paris mob, French was a language as incomprehensible as English or German to the nine-tenths of the inhabitants of France living outside the capital city. "It was a country that had still not been accurately mapped in its entirety" when Balzac wrote, Robb notes. "A little further back in time, sober accounts described a land of ancient tribal divisions, prehistoric communication networks and pre-Christian beliefs. Historians and anthropologists had referred to this country, without irony, as 'Gaul' and quoted Julius Caesar as a useful source of information on the inhabitants of the uncharted interior."[1]

In prerevolutionary times, "France" meant the province of which Paris was the heart. "As far as French anthropology is concerned, prehistory did not end until the Revolution. Before then, the State took no interest in the cultural and ethnic diversity of the masses." To put the matter differently: the national government in Paris left them alone. The French provincial's fatherland, his Marianne, was his *pays*; while the *pays* within the territory historically known as France were so numerous that, as late as 1937, some of them remained unknown. The *pays* (from the Latin *pagus*) was understood by Julius Caesar to be a region that a tribal entity recognized as home, often no broader than the clang of a village church bell could carry. "Some of these towns and villages were flourishing democracies when France was still an absolute monarchy," Robb observes. These communities were proud of their provinciality. Far from wishing to expand their sense of identity, they were rather concerned with straitening and deepening it. So well managed were the *pays* and the towns that formed their nuclei that crime appears to have been nearly nonexistent in prerevolutionary France. Away from the capital, almost everyone spoke a separate and distinct patois.

In the opinion of two late-twentieth-century scholars, Hervé Le Bras and Emmanuel Todd, "from the anthropological point of view, France ought not to exist." Robb asserts that, owing to the complex genetic inheritance of the Celtic and German tribes who invaded the Roman province, the same could be said from the point of view of ethnicity: "Before the mid-nineteenth century . . . France was effectively a land of foreigners." If the government of these various tribes was democratic in a rudimentary, patriarchal sense, in religion they embraced local superstition, paganism inherited from their Celtic forebears and from the Romans, and Christianity (Roman Catholicism) with substantial grafts of paganism and superstition, often tolerated by the local priest and even by his superiors, who recognized the utility of incorporating local legend with the universal Faith. Young people married their blood relations, and most people lived their entire lives in the *pays*, venturing perhaps no more than a few miles from their front doors. "Foreigners" were disliked and distrusted, to the point of being set on occasionally by the natives. There was a lively belief in witchcraft, conducive to witch burning. As travel was at best infrequent, trade between the various *pays* was uncommon, and each was therefore self-supporting, living off its modicum of land and natural resources.

Of all this, the civilized Parisian minority knew nothing, or next to nothing. Its members had little or no cause to venture into the provinces, and the roads in any case were atrocious or nonexistent. The large majority of France stretched away, as yet unmapped, between its boundaries of ocean, mountain, and plain; the many blank spaces within the territorial outline might have been inscribed "Here Be Hippogriffes." To the hippogriffes themselves—people who lived their whole lives in a small town or village—"French imperial justice [when it finally reached them] could be just as shocking and incongruous as it was to the people of colonial North Africa."

The new French Republic, in its eagerness to demonstrate national unity, fixed the new administrative boundaries with a cavalier disregard for existing tribal divisions. It was equally careless of the hundreds of tiny discrete civilizations in which the "France" of the time abounded; hence, Robb says, "modern France is not just the result of continuous traditions; it was also formed from disappearances and extinctions." In Year II (1794) of the Republic, Abbé Henri Grégoire published a report titled "The Necessity and Means of Exterminating Patois and Universalizing the Use of the French Language." Based on questions sent out to, and mailed back from, town halls across the country, Grégoire's report showed France to be a linguistic muddle of numerous *patois* and two Romantic languages—French in the north and Occitan in the south—which, on closer inspection, could be understood as having been fractured into numerous incomprehensible dialects. The situation was as Grégoire had feared, only much worse. Six million of the fifteen million "French" people, it seemed, were wholly ignorant of the language of polite Europe. Another six million could scarcely be said to speak French. Of the three million able to converse in it, a great many were incompetent to write the language. How could France plausibly call itself a nation in the absence of a national, a common language? Lacking such, the "French" people were, in the abbé's estimation, "too ignorant to be patriotic." Some of these citizens even believed that King Louis XVI still sat on his throne at Versailles.

Abbé Grégoire's report launched a national campaign to "universalize" the French language. Grégoire proposed building roads and canals, establishing schools and libraries, and simplifying the language by ridding it of irregular verbs. And he urged that the national government pay greater heed to France's border regions, where counterrevolutionaries were active. A century later, the Third Republic tackled the *patois* problem head-on with its educational policies, decreeing that children caught speaking their regional language should be subject to humiliating punishment. Eighty years after that, in 1972, President Georges Pompidou asserted, "There is no place for regional languages in a France that is destined to set its mark on Europe." The campaign for a universal French language continues today, as the Élysée Palace grapples with the arrival of peoples from North Africa, the Near East, and Asia.

Further, postrevolutionary governments adopted a conscious policy of erasing the immemorial divide between north and south, which they viewed as irrational as well as divisive, in ways having nothing to do with geography. The first step toward this end was the creation of *départements*—administrative units that ignored natural boundaries in favor of an approximate equality of size that ensured their administrative centers were no farther than a day's journey from any location subject to their jurisdiction. "The idea," Robb writes, "was that timeless, natural logic should prevail over the old feudal and tribal traditions. . . . In this way, 'prejudices, habits and barbaric institutions consolidated by fourteen centuries of existence'" would be swept away. Language barriers were explicitly ignored, despite objections from some councils—like that of Saint-Malo on the borders of Brittany—that they would be forced to work with people who spoke 'languages predating Caesar's conquest.'" By such means, the peoples of France were shorn of their particular collective names and reduced to a single category—"the French"—while "provincial" became the equivalent simply of "peasant."

"For all its practical virtues," Robb suggests, "the division of France into *départements* helped to create a process that can best be described as the opposite of discovery. Ignorance of daily life beyond the well-connected cities and familiarity with the monuments and personalities of Paris would be signs of enlightened modernity." For the central government, this process of autoamnesia was essential to the formation of the new French nation. Yet the former life, lived in what Graham Robb so poignantly describes as the old "suffering land of fragmented village states," had been no dark chaos of formlessness and unreason but an intensely human way of existence, piquantly evoked in a plenitude of fine detail by the modern historian.

The processes of nationalization and centralization at work in nineteenth-century France were linked inevitably with, and depended on, the expansive growth of the country's transportation infrastructure—its roads, waterways, and railroads—and of its industrial base. Just as inevitably, nationwide development entailed harmful effects together with the beneficial ones. Those regions of the country most directly served by the improved transport arteries certainly found themselves better connected to the rest of France than they formerly had been, but towns, villages, and entire regions bypassed by the main arterial systems were left still more disconnected and remote than ever. The result was not simply what Robb calls "the contraction of space and the gravitational pull of Paris"; it amounted to what Victor Hugo saw as the slow disappearance of France. The rail companies, which brought prosperity to some cities, such as Marseille, ruined others, like Beaucaire, a town situated on the Rhône whose fortunes were tied to the international fair it had hosted for centuries. By degrees, the metropolis on the Seine was colonizing the rest of France—by military fortresses, like Napoléonville in the rebellious west; by economic development; by the industrialization of the French countryside; by speculative industrial agriculture (exemplified by the disastrous silkworm bubble); by ecological havoc (the deforestation of the Alps and the Pyrenees, for instance); and by suburbanization. "Everyone knows that the nineteenth century was an age of change," Robb adds, " but for many people of the time, roads, railways, education and sanitation were trivial innovations compared to the complete and irreversible transformation of their physical world."

The "discovery of France," as Robb calls it, involved all these things and more, among them the exploitation and destruction of national treasures, many of them acquired from the sale of properties confiscated from the Roman Catholic Church and from the châteaux of the aristocracy. "No sooner did poets and art lovers learn of this magical land [undiscovered France] than they found it in ruins"—despite the best efforts of the novelist Prosper Mérimée, appointed inspector general of historic monuments in 1834, to save it.

After 1815, British tourists flocked to France. Tourism increased apace throughout the nineteenth century as the English and the Americans were joined eventually by Parisians venturing outward from the capital to encounter "the wonders of France," both the cultural and the natural varieties. And yet, Robb notes, "Never before had it been possible to cross the country in such a state of blissful ignorance. As early as the 1850s, the great roads from Paris were being drained by traffic from the railways."

Certainly *not* among the wonders of France was French provincial cuisine, which was nearly meatless and relentlessly dull. This did not prevent tourists from discovering what they fancied to be regional specialties, notwithstanding the fact that these dishes were often unrepresentative of the region. Quite frequently, indeed, they were available chiefly in Paris itself—from which they might even have originated. This was only one aspect of the growing cult of French "diversity," imagined to be nourished and protected by the same connoisseurs in the capital who were pillaging provincial towns of their finest artwork, which they conscientiously removed to Paris. In these and other ways, what was offered as being distinctively French became, essentially, simply Parisian.

By midcentury, village locals, though still conversing in patois, spoke of modern topics rather than of age-old concerns, while the French bourgeois who sped past them on their way to somewhere else continued to regard them almost as prehistoric relics. "Politics has arrived with conscripts and migrants, postmen and railroad engineers, apostles of socialism sent from the central committee in Paris, and traveling salesmen who sell manifestoes instead of magic spells," Robb observes of this period. Thirty years later, the progressives began a campaign to nationalize the youth of France. "The fatherland," wrote Ernest Lavisse, a professor at the Sorbonne and author of a series of teachers' manuals, "is not your village or your province. It is all of France. The fatherland is like a great family." Hence the Third Republic's assault on patois, through punishment meted out to schoolchildren who insisted on speaking the language of their earliest childhood.

Small wonder that a nostalgic memoir of a provincial French boyhood enjoyed a smashing success one year before the outbreak of the Great War, which nearly destroyed France while transforming it forever. *Le Grand Meaulnes*, by Alain-Fournier, recounts the author's life as a boy in the rural Bourbonnais. It provided at the time, and does still today, what Graham Robb calls "a tantalizing sense of *la France profonde* as a distant but familiar place, a little world full of simple things that spoke of another age."

Mr. Robb's book implies a question of crucial importance for modern times. Even if we suppose the France of the present day to be a stronger, wealthier, happier, and altogether "better" country after two centuries of nationalization, centralization, and social equalization, is it really a more "democratic"—or, at any rate, a *freer*—country, affording its citizens a greater liberty, together with a larger measure of personal authority and dignity, than it was before the Revolution? The question is relevant not only to France but to many other countries in the modern democratic world, including especially the United States: the nation that inspired Alexis de Tocqueville to predict, in his seminal work *Democracy in America* (1835), that democracy was the future of the West.

One hundred seventy-three years after Alexis de Tocqueville and his friend Gustave de Beaumont landed at Newport, Rhode Island, in 1831, the editors of the *Atlantic Monthly* proposed to Bernard-Henri Lévy, the celebrated French *philosophe* and man of the Left, that he retrace the steps of his illustrious compatriot in America and write up his experiences for their magazine.

Lévy admits to having held the distinguished author with whose texts he was extensively unfamiliar in low esteem. Like most of his contemporaries, he had regarded Tocqueville as "an old-fashioned hiccupping aristocrat, an adept of lukewarm thinking and happy mediums, a quibbling, overscrupulous dilettante, a moaning sensitive, a sad Narcissus, a boring, reactionary public intellectual, a sententious activist, a man of wit who amused himself by posing as a writer, a failed politician, a pale imitator of Montesquieu, a lightweight version of his uncle Chateaubriand (who seemed to have preempted the entire gamut of attractive roles). . . . For people like us [the sixties radicals], ignorance of Tocqueville, this [estimation of the] moderating spirit straddling the Old World and the New, the Orléans and the Bourbons, resignation to democracy and fear of revolution, was, I'm afraid, commonplace."[2]

In the end, Lévy agreed to undertake the *Atlantic*'s somewhat vulgar project. He read up on Tocqueville, flew to the United States, rented cars and purchased plane tickets, and traveled widely across the nation, exceeding by thousands of miles his predecessor's itinerary throughout a young republic less than half the size of the present continental colossus. His purpose (he explains at the start of *American Vertigo*, the book that Lévy developed from the magazine assignment) was also Tocqueville's purpose: to evaluate the stage of development of his own democratizing society by comparison with the form of a realized democracy created by "democratic revolution"; to search out the origins of this democracy in the New England states; and to discern, in Tocqueville's words, the alternate paths leading "to slavery or freedom, to enlightenment or barbarism, to prosperity or wretchedness."

M. Lévy had as well another concern, possibly an ulterior one. After citing Goethe's remark that the United States allowed Europeans to view their own history recapitulated in America, he notes that American democracy is essentially a European idea. America therefore, in Europe's moment of doubt, is "the only tangible proof that its own supranational dream is neither a piece of nonsense nor an unattainable ideal." Were democracy in the United States somehow to fail, Europe would stand to "lose a little of its reasons for belief, and, hence, a little of its motivating force: its famous constitutional patriotism, its aim of adding to everyone's national feeling the liberating allegiance to an Idea." So the question weighing heavily on Bernard-Henri Lévy's mind as he traveled around the United States was, "What *is* the present state of democracy in America?"

America and Americans are greatly changed since 1831–2. So are French intellectuals. Tocqueville would be shocked and scandalized by the United States today—as indeed he would be by his native France and by the England he so greatly admired. It is impossible, really, to imagine him at home in the modern democratic world. Bernard-Henri Lévy, by comparison, is the consummate postmodernist, thoroughly comfortable within the milieu that created him and that has rewarded him with worldly success and influence far beyond those with which Tocqueville himself was favored. What disturbed Lévy on his American journey were the things that typically shock men of the Left: the persistence of poverty and of capital punishment; prison conditions; the physical separation of rich and poor; fundamentalist and evangelical Christianity; "racism"; and military adventurism. The displacement, by secularism and moral relativism, of traditional morality rooted in Christian doctrine fails to alarm, much less offend, him; rather, he approves of the phenomenon. Lévy is hardly inclined to perceive the indispensable connection between religious belief and democratic government on which Tocqueville insists throughout *Democracy in America*.

Lévy's impressionistic, on-the-run portrait of the United States of America in the first years of the twenty-first century is finally an unpleasant one, although the author himself appears not to see it that way. The French count, coming so many years before him, did not, it is true, extend his sociological investigations to taverns, gambling dens, and brothels—the nineteenth-century equivalents of the casinos, gay bars, strip clubs, and lap-dancing joints that Lévy describes in fairly graphic detail in *American Vertigo*. In his determination to assess the validity of the prevalent European stereotype of the obese American, he visited a weight-loss clinic in California and finally concluded from direct observation that the percentage of grossly overweight Americans is no greater than that of the inhabitants of an ordinary French village. The obesity quest, however, furnishes Lévy with a metaphor for American society as a whole: "A social obesity. An economic, financial, and political obesity . . . A global, total obesity that spares no realm of life, public or private. An entire society that, from the top down, from one end to the other, seems prey to this obscure derangement that slowly causes an organism to swell, overflow, explode." America, M. Lévy thinks, is a nation "that has strayed from, or broken, that secret formula, that code, that prompts a body to stay within its limits and survive."

"Obesity" is one of several "derangements" Lévy observed during his travels in the United States. Another is what he calls "the chopping up of American social and political space," the nation's "differentiation" amounting to "tribalization—the transformation of America into a plural nation, a mosaic of communities, a rhapsody of ethnic groups and collectivities that makes increasingly problematic the realization of the venerable problem . . . inscribed in the motto of the country: *E pluribus Unum*." And a third is "the derangement of the mechanisms of memorialization" in America, typified for Lévy by the Baseball Hall of Fame in Cooperstown, New York, an institution based on a mythic history of baseball that is known publicly to be a myth—more frankly, a hoax—while being celebrated widely as truth. Later, this "myth" connects in the author's mind with the Kennedy myth: the accepted view that John F. Kennedy was a secular saint, an aristocrat, and a great statesman—all so contrary to historical fact that sophisticated Americans recognize these propositions to be demonstrably false. The American public's determination to live in a world of dreams conjured by sentimentality, publicity, and a willingness to be gulled by "truths" it knows, or at least suspects, to be untrue disturbs and even angers M. Lévy—no doubt aware that what Sir Henry Sumner Maine in the late nineteenth century called "the most difficult form of government" requires a firm public grip on reality in order to survive.

Lastly, Lévy ponders the identity of the American nation, which he denies is determined by any particular race, or a soil that is particular or fixed itself. Rather, he says, American identity is based on an abstract "Idea" and a dedication to personal autonomy, self-realization, and even self-reinvention. He quotes President Clinton, who affirmed in his first inaugural address that it is for each generation of Americans to decide for itself what America is, and adds: "I want myself to say that [America] is nothing else, when all is said and done, but a prodigious yet mundane machine whose purpose is to produce more Americans—a magnificent illusion, an Idea again . . . one of [Nietzsche's] 'useful errors,' one of those 'tall tales,' that allow a human being, whoever he may be, to represent what he is and what he has become in order to survive."

Graham Robb's *The Discovery of France* calls into question whether the French centralized democracy of the twenty-first century is really more free and "democratic" than the far more loosely organized constitutional monarchy of Tocqueville's day. (The same might be asked of the United States, which in the early 1830s was predominantly an agricultural and frontier society whose population had little, if any, contact with the powers that dwelt in Washington, D.C., or even those in their respective state and territorial capitals.) Similarly, *American Vertigo* invites the reader to consider a question critical to the present time, to the future age, and to the book you are holding: Does the United States, as Bernard-Henri Lévy described it a century and three-quarters after Tocqueville's sojourn there, resemble a polity, a society, that in its structure, mind, and soul is still conducive to democratic government, to democratic freedoms, and to liberty itself?

How one answers this question depends, as we shall see, on how one understands the words *democracy, freedom, liberty*—and, above all perhaps, *liberalism*, which claims to embrace all three things within its own, increasingly ample bosom.

Part I

Democracy after Tocqueville

✦   ✦   ✦

1

From Tocqueville to Fukuyama

Historians have debated for nearly two centuries whether Alexis de Tocqueville's political sympathies were fundamentally liberal or essentially conservative. Hugh Brogan, Tocqueville's most recent biographer, maintains that the youthful enthusiast of *Democracy in America* was not the same man who wrote the *Recollections* or the final work, *The Old Regime and the French Revolution*, left unfinished at the time of Tocqueville's death (at age fifty-four), from consumption.[1] No one, on the other hand, has challenged the French aristocrat's reputation as a political prophet. "A great democratic revolution," he wrote in *Democracy in America*, "is taking place in our midst; everybody sees it, but by no means everybody judges it in the same way. Some think it a new thing and, supposing it an accident, hope that they can still check it; others think it irresistible, because it seems to them the most continuous, ancient, and permanent tendency known to history."[2] Tocqueville belonged, unequivocally, to the latter party. The future of western Europe and North America, he insisted, belonged, for good or ill, to democracy. And that future, he believed, was sanctioned by the blessing of God.

Alexis de Tocqueville was no hidebound aristocrat, but an aristo he was born and an aristo he remained until the end of his life. It is true that he departed from family tradition in religion (he lost his

Catholic faith before he reached adulthood and remained a deist until his death), in marriage (his wife was an English Protestant, of middle-class origins, and a commoner), and in politics (he refused to adhere to legitimist principles). Even so, "When I talk to a *gentilhomme*," he once remarked, "though we have not two ideas in common, though all his opinions, wishes, and thoughts are opposed to mine, yet I feel at once that we belong to the same family, that we speak the same language, that we understand one another. I may like the *bourgeois* better, but he is a stranger." Really, the sentiment does Tocqueville credit. Had he felt otherwise, he might have been, like so many of his republican contemporaries, a mere ideologue rather than the liberal-minded man he was, a savant of true understanding, of prophetic genius. For Tocqueville, a republican world would be an altered, certainly, yet still a familiar world, replete with familiar things, institutions, people, and relationships—not an unrecognizable, unprecedented, and threatening false utopia, the old world turned upside down and inside out.

Alexis de Tocqueville was descended on both the paternal and maternal sides from aristocratic families. The Clérels (later the Tocquevilles) were an old Norman family, ennobled since 1452 or perhaps earlier, whose manor house is situated in the Cotentin, not many miles east of Cherbourg. Alexis's grandfather Bernard, the second comte de Tocqueville, married into the Damas family and in this way acquired the funds sufficient to make the house over into a château. Hervé, Tocqueville's father, wed Louise de Rosanbo, a granddaughter of Chrétien-Guillaume Lamoignon des Malesherbes, scion of one of the greatest families of the *noblesse de robe* and a reform-minded minister of Louis XVI's who later offered his services to the monarch as the king's chief counsel during his trial by the Convention and was himself executed, together with numerous members of his family. Hervé and Louise were imprisoned in Port-Libre for ten months and released only after the execution of Robespierre. Among Alexis's earliest memories was of an incident that occurred in his fourth year, when the Tocquevilles and their near relations the Rosanbos and the Chateaubriands gathered before the fire to sing a royalist song about the suffering and death of Louis XVI.

Brogan claims that it was not until Tocqueville, as a young man, read Adolphe Thiers's *History of the Revolution* that he began to understand the French Revolution as having been something more than the work of Freemasons or of the Duke of Orléans. He also credits a series of lectures delivered by François Guizot in Paris in the months before the July Revolution with having drawn Tocqueville's attention to the fact that a process of democratization had been in train for centuries, and leading him eventually to the conclusion that democracy was the future of his civilization. The following year, in early April 1831, Tocqueville and his friend Gustave de Beaumont, who like Tocqueville was a legal apprentice at the *parquet* at Versailles, from which the two men had been granted leave to research a report on prison reform in the United States, sailed from Le Havre for Newport, Rhode Island.

It would be an exaggeration to say that Alexis de Tocqueville arrived in America prepared, even predisposed, to admire its democratic system of government and its relatively egalitarian society. Brogan speculates that he was encouraged in his political attitudes (as well as in his decision to visit America in the first place) by his uncle François-René de Chateaubriand, the celebrated author of *Atala*, *The Natchez*, and *Voyage to America*. As a young man during the early stages of the Revolution, Chateaubriand had traveled in North America, where for a time he managed to evade the contradiction between his liberal politics and his loyalty to the old France. Tocqueville, who had taken the oath to support the new monarch (thus renouncing his allegiance to the Bourbons), might plausibly have taken a cue from his illustrious relative. Brogan suggests that germs of *Democracy in America* are perceptible in *Voyage to America*. However that may be, by the time he and Beaumont left New York City, Tocqueville had his theme. "We are traveling," he wrote, "towards unlimited democracy, I don't say that this is a good thing, what I see in this country convinces me on the contrary that it won't suit France; but we are driven by an irresistible force. No effort made to stop this movement will do more than bring about brief halts."

"It won't suit France." Tocqueville was ever at pains to remind himself, as well as readers of *Democracy in America*, that the subject of his book was *American* democracy, not democracy as a generalized system of government and society. (Rather surprisingly, he draws few, if any, comparisons with the supposedly democratic states of the ancient world.) Early in his sojourn in the United States, he learned, from a conversation with John Quincy Adams, the enormous importance of the country's *point de départ*, its formative circumstances and particularities. The formal statement of this understanding is found in volume 1, part 2, chapter 9 of *Democracy in America*, titled "The Main Causes Tending to Maintain a Democratic Republic in the United States."

Alexis de Tocqueville was a prophet—perhaps the foremost prophet—of democracy in his time. But in predicting democracy to be the future, Tocqueville seems to have regarded the future, in this respect, as open-ended. For how long did he suppose democracy would, or could, last? Did he expect democracy to represent, in Francis Fukuyama's famous phrase, "the end of history"? After nearly two centuries, Tocqueville's future is our historical past. Yet democracy still exists. Or does it? If so, how much future remains to a system based on free societies and institutions of popular government developed over two and a half millennia of speculative political and social theory?

Most Americans would be surprised to learn that democratic government, whether actual or potential, was widely disparaged by the majority of philosophers and political thinkers before World War II. That changed after the defeat of the Axis powers, when democratic governments appeared to have been vindicated everywhere in the world. And yet, as early as the 1950s many liberals, even in America, scorned Western "democracy," denying that any such thing had been achieved; a decade later, it was popular to denounce democracy as essentially fascistic by writers like Herbert Marcuse of the Frankfurt School and their followers in Students for a Democratic Society (SDS) and other left-wing student organizations. People forget, but "democracy," whether considered in its domestic or in its international application, did not begin to acquire its present mystique until Ronald Reagan's forcefully pro-"democratic" administrations and the collapse of the Soviet Union. At that, the mystique prevailed mainly in the United States: in France, the inheritor of the revolutionary tradition and the universal rights of man, an antidemocratic (though certainly not authoritarian) school was already forming on the Left Bank, as we shall see. Even so, during the past two decades democracy has been appraised far more enthusiastically than at any other time in its history, owing, significantly, to the efforts of those literary and political activists known as the neoconservatives, of whom Francis Fukuyama is among the most influential.

In 1992, Fukuyama published *The End of History and the Last Man*, a book whose claims for a democratic future make those of *Democracy in America* appear like an exercise in intellectual timidity. Democracy, Fukuyama declared, is the "end point of mankind's ideological evolution," the "final form of human government"—the "end of history." "While some present-day countries might fail to achieve stable liberal democracy, and others might lapse back into other, more primitive forms of rule like theocracy or military dictatorship, the *ideal* of democracy [can]not be improved on."[3]

In the two decades since *The End of History*'s appearance, Francis Fukuyama has had to defend his thesis against misinterpretation, in particular objections raised by obviously dense readers that substantial historical events, such as the Iraq war or the rise of Vladimir Putin, continue to unfold. His meaning, Fukuyama patiently replied, was that what had come to an end was not "the occurrence of events" but rather "History: that is, history understood as a single, coherent, evolutionary process, when taking into account the experience of all people in all times"—history as Hegel and Marx had understood the term, ending, respectively, with the liberal democratic state and communist society. This process does not move in a straight line or operate, perhaps, to man's ultimate benefit or pleasure, Fukuyama reiterated, but it is neither random nor unintelligible.

Fukuyama explained his historical process by referencing the development of technology made possible by modern science, which in turn opens up a "uniform horizon of economic production possibilities," facilitating the accumulation of "limitless" wealth and the expansion of unbounded human desires. In this way, history at once requires and guarantees the eventual homogenization of all human societies, no matter their histories and inherited cultural differences. Still, neither scientific and technological advance nor economic development, by itself or in combination with the other, ensures the creation of liberal democracy. An added third element, Hegel's historical principle of the "struggle for recognition" has helped to set an end to history. Men's insistence that they should be recognized as human beings, endowed with all of the rights that human status entails, including the right of "universal and reciprocal recognition" (that is, equality), combined with scientific and economic tendencies, has lifted human history to its culminating point—and its close. Of all the political and social systems devised (or, rather, evolved) by men, liberal democracy comes closest to compounding the humanly liberating benefits of technique, modern economics, and democratic politics in the nearest thing to utopia of which humanity is capable. The process is equivalent with that of modernization itself. Liberal democracy is fully satisfying not only to the citizens of a particular state but also to liberal democratic states in their mutual relationships with one another.

It was Francis Fukuyama who popularized the neoconservative mantra that democracies do not make war on one another and that universal peace has consequently become, for the first time in history, something more than a wishful vision. True, Fukuyama conceded, modern democracies suffer from many problems, including homelessness, drug abuse, environmental destruction, and "frivolous" consumerism. Yet none of these faults, he contended, signals a "contradiction" in liberal democracy comparable to the fatal contradictions that brought about the collapse of communist societies toward the end of the twentieth century. For Fukuyama, history as it remains to be experienced by the human race may be summed up by the familiar, but timelessly elegant, Gallic aphorism *Plus ça change, plus c'est la même chose,* to which his theory seems to give universal meaning.

Decades before Fukuyama's book, in the 1950s, another Hegelian, Alexandre Kojève, had argued substantially the same thesis in predicting the end of art and philosophy. True to his own vision, Kojève ceased to write books and give lectures and took a job as a bureaucrat in the European Economic Community, which he hailed as the very model of the End of History.[4]

Unlike Francis Fukuyama and Alexandre Kojève, Alexis de Tocqueville was not a theorist but an empiricist and a historian who based his predictions for the future of democratic government in Europe on what seemed to him the undeniable will of the majority of the Western peoples for representative government, and, in the case of the United States, on a boundless enthusiasm for democracy as well as conditions that were particularly conducive to maintaining and advancing it. In *Democracy in America,* Tocqueville arranges these conditions according to three general categories: "the peculiar and accidental situation in which Providence has placed the Americans," American laws, and American mores (*moeurs*) and habits.

The first category includes America's geographic isolation (ensuring freedom from proximate enemies), territorial extent, and natural bounty. Tocqueville writes: "It was God who, by handing a limitless continent over to [the Americans], gave them the means of long remaining equal and free." The second pertains to the federal form of government, "which allows the union to enjoy the power of a great republic and the security of a small one"; communal (that is, secondary) institutions that restrain majoritarian despotism while developing the skills necessary for self-government; and the organization of the nation's judicial power to check democratic excess. The third points not only to "the habits of the heart" but also to what Tocqueville described as "the various notions possessed by men, the various opinions current among them, and the sum of ideas that shape mental habits"—in short, "the whole moral and intellectual state of a people," the *point de départ* that allowed the French visitor to "see the whole destiny of America contained in the first Puritan who landed on these shores, as that of the whole human race in the first man."

Although Tocqueville considered the geographical situation of the United States to be of less consequence than its laws to a democratic future, and the laws in turn less important than its mores, this last category effectively comprises the first two. ("In the United States not legislation alone is democratic, for Nature herself seems to work for the people.") At any rate, it is interesting, from the vantage point of the twenty-first century, to see what struck Tocqueville as those American characteristics most likely to perpetuate the American republic.

Among the first to attract Tocqueville's notice was the fact that the United States has no great capital city. This may strike the modern reader as odd, but for Tocqueville, who feared and deplored the process of centralization in France that had located all significant powers in Paris, "the preponderance of capitals" posed a serious threat to representative government. It had, he believed, destroyed the republics of antiquity.

Next, he lists the Americans' religious faith, which Tocqueville considered essential to democratic government. "From the start, politics and religion [in America] agreed, and they have not ceased to do so. . . . One can say that there is not a single religious doctrine in the United States hostile to democratic and republican institutions"—very much including, he believed, Catholic doctrine. Although religion in

America did not directly influence the laws and political system of the United States, it did shape and direct American mores and so, by regulating the lives of individual families, helped to order the larger family, American society itself. Tocqueville considered religion "the first of [the Americans'] political institutions."

The third condition of American democracy is that the first American colonists were the products of a great civilization, arriving "completely civilized" on the shores of North America with "no need to learn, it being enough that they should not forget." And the fourth is that nearly every inhabitant of the republic is descended from the same stock, speaks the same tongue, and prays to God "in the same language." From this, Tocqueville concludes, "It is their mores, then, that make the Americans of the United States, alone among Americans [that is, the North and South Americans taken together], capable of maintaining the rule of democracy; and it is mores again that make the various Anglo-American democracies more or less orderly and prosperous."

Tocqueville did not draw from this conclusion the lesson that democracy could not arise in other countries and flourish in them. His great hope was that France—and after it, every European nation in its turn—might find its way to a variant of the American democracy that would best suit its national character, position in the world, and national aspirations. Tocqueville was describing American democracy only, and identifying those of its endowments that seemed to him necessary to its survival as a (so far) successful human experiment and an example to the world. Still, he was a close observer—and a realist. "Why," he mused, thirty years before the War between the States, "in the conduct of [American] public affairs, is there something so disorderly, passionate, and, one might almost say, feverish, by no means presaging a long future?"

No modern reader who considers Tocqueville's "main causes tending to maintain a democratic republic in the United States" can fail to notice that not one of the conditions he mentions persists today, including the religious faith of the American public, which is everywhere under assault by real or virtual secularists, a significant number of whom identify themselves as believers and even churchgoers. This quite obvious fact is not a concern for agnostic universalists like Francis Fukuyama, who regard fixed identities as liabilities rather than assets for democratic societies. But Alexis de Tocqueville would probably be appalled by the monopolization of political power, opinion, and culture by Washington, New York, and Los Angeles in the United States of the present day.

There is, of course, the possibility that Tocqueville was simply wrong in his condemnation of centralization in a democratic nation—and in other things. (I am uncertain, for instance, whether he truly understood the American judicial system he admired so greatly.) Also, as brilliantly perceptive as Tocqueville was as an observer, a writer, a thinker, and a prophet, his work is characterized by vast and unsupported generalizations that seem often more like inspired impression and philosophical elaboration than the political "science" he helped to pioneer.

Even so, American conservatives (such as Pat Buchanan) and left-liberals (Kirkpatrick Sale) alike have complained for generations that the American republic is a republic no longer and that the American federal democratic system is being wrecked and delegitimized by political and administrative centralization, bureaucracy, the imperial presidency, judicial tyranny, the erosion of civil liberties, the growth of a police state, corruption in government, the influence of interest groups and of lobbies, the power of money in electoral politics, and the irresponsibility of the two-party system. Moreover, they maintain that American society is being progressively undone by the decay of religious belief and by moral rot, by cultural illiteracy and incoherence, by public indifference to serious issues of public concern, and by the decline in educational standards. The "God-given" North American continent is being despoiled and polluted, and the United States has made mortal enemies of countries overseas whom the Atlantic and Pacific Oceans no longer suffice to hold at bay. Throughout its history, America has served as a beacon for democrats around the world.

Should the salt lose its savor, American democracy falter or fail, the effect on popular governments everywhere would be tremendous.

Tocqueville, despite his sympathy and controlled admiration for the young American democracy, was never blind to its flaws and expressed reservations (in *Democracy in America*, volume 2, especially) about the future of democratic institutions and society in the United States—and, by extension, the future of every country that might commit its fortunes to the democratic experiment.

He has much to say in *Democracy in America* about the overbearing power and threatening tyranny of the majority and about the intellectual conformity so apparent in the United States. "The majority has enclosed thought within a formidable fence. A writer is free inside that area, but woe to the man who goes beyond it. Not that he stands in fear of an *auto-da-fé*, but he must face all kinds of unpleasantness and everyday persecution. A career in politics is closed to him, for he has offended the only power that holds the keys. He is denied everything, including renown. Before he goes into print, he believes he has supporters; but he feels he has them no more once he stands revealed to all, for those who condemn him express their own views, while those who think as he does, but without his courage, retreat into silence as if ashamed of having told the truth." Tocqueville presses further: "Princes made violence a physical thing, but our democratic republics have turned it into something as intellectual as the human will it is intended to constrain. Under the absolute government of a single man, despotism, to reach the soul, struck clumsily at the body, and the soul, escaping from such blows, rose gloriously above it; but in democratic republics that is not at all how tyranny behaves; it leaves the body alone and goes straight to the soul."

In passages such as these Tocqueville anticipates the iron grip of political correctness and the self-censorship that so powerfully constrain debate today. The fact is that the America Alexis de Tocqueville admired was the Federalist Party's America—that Tocqueville, in company with the Founders, viewed the United States as a republic governed by the educated and the propertied classes while they held the poor, the ignorant, and the violent orders of society in control. Hugh Brogan believes that Tocqueville, in writing *Democracy in America*, had a definite aim in mind: to propose a new kind of liberalism and have a hand in directing it, not as an author simply but also as a member of France's active elite, an ambition that was to dominate and shape the course of his subsequent life.

In 1839, Tocqueville was elected to the Chamber of Deputies from Valognes (Department of the Manche, the province on the northern coast of France where the Tocqueville estate was located) and sat there until 1851. He served also as general counselor of the Manche in 1842 and as president of the department's general counsel (*conseil général*) from 1849 to 1851. In the revolution of February 1848, he was elected a member of the Constituent Assembly, and he had a part in drafting the Constitution of the Second Republic, while advocating universal suffrage as a means to bring the conservative countryside to bear against the Paris revolutionists. Under the Second Republic, Tocqueville supported the Party of Order (*parti de l'Ordre*) against the socialists and the workers, and he supported General Cavaignac's repression of the June Days revolt. He served briefly as foreign minister in Odilon Barrot's government, and, as a supporter of the Bourbon Restoration, he departed political life after Louis Napoleon's coup in 1851. Brogan supposes that Tocqueville would have enjoyed greater success as a politician had he been capable of accepting the exigencies of party politics, which he abhorred. For the mob, he had the greatest contempt, remarking that although there might have been wickeder revolutionaries in history than those of 1848, he did not believe that there had been stupider ones. Seven years earlier, he had expressed his political credo in compact formula. "I like democratic institutions with my head, but I am an aristocrat by instinct, that is to say I despise and fear the mob. I passionately love liberty, legality, respect for rights, but not democracy. . . . Liberty is the first of my passions. There is the truth." He might have added that he was inseparably attached to property as well, but what is important to grasp here is that, for Alexis de Tocqueville, democracy was a political phenomenon, never a faith.

After 1848, Tocqueville saw the French Republic becoming a means—a means to the socialism that soon replaced democracy as the European political ideal—rather than an end, and he wanted none of it. It is as if, believing the republic of the American Federalists too good to be true, he expected the republican future to be of short duration. From the beginning, Tocqueville had had a keen awareness of the self-destructive tendencies of democracy, developing from its dual nature. "On the one hand," he had written in *Democracy in America*, "democracy's project is unrealizable, because it is contrary to nature. On the other, it is impossible to stop short of this democracy and go back to aristocracy. This is because democratic equality also conforms to nature. . . . To affirm and will democracy insofar as it is in conformity with nature, to limit it insofar as it is contrary to it, such is the sovereign art on which depend the prosperity and morality of democracies."

For nearly two hundred years, Alexis de Tocqueville has been both prophet and symbol of a democratic future, first for "Christendom," later for the world. Is it possible that this future may become, in a relatively few years, the past, and that the new future—the future after Tocqueville—may be claimed by a postdemocratic age? If so, Tocqueville might have been disappointed by history's great turn. He would scarcely, I think, have been surprised by it.

2

The Momentum of Monarchy

One very good reason Alexis de Tocqueville has been so widely considered democracy's prophet is that, in his time, democratic government had so few friends among the intellectual, political, and even the artistic classes of nineteenth-century Europe.

"Kings never die," wrote Blackstone in the *Commentaries* in 1765. The reference was to the doctrine of "the King's two Bodies," which appears to have originated with a cleric known as the Norman Anonymous, who maintained, in a series of tracts written around A.D. 1100, that the power of the king and the power of God are identical, distinguished from each other by the fact that God's power is in His nature while the king holds his power by an action of God's grace. Therefore, the Anonymous argued, "whatsoever [the king] does, he does not simply as a man, but as one who has become God and Christ by grace."[1]

From that idea, the English developed a "royal Christology," differing from the Continental "theology of kingship" and based on the application of Christ's teaching in respect of the *Corpus Mysticum* (the church) to the whole of human society, as well as on another Christian doctrine, the hypostatic union, by which the divinity and the humanity of Christ are united in one Person. Elizabethan judges held that the king "has not a body natural and distinct and divided by itself from the Office and Dignity royal, but a Body natural and a Body politic together indivisible; and these two bodies are incorporated in one person, and make one Body and not Divers, that is the body corporate in the Body natural, *et e contra* the Body natural in the Body corporate. So that the Body natural, by this conjunction of the Body politic to it (which Body politic contains the Office, Government, and Majesty royal) is magnified, and by the said Consolidation hath in it the Body politic."[2] Hence, according to one Justice Brown in the *Plowden Reports*, "King is a name of continuance" for as long as the king's people shall continue.[3] "Long live the king!" then. For indeed the king, this man of two bodies, can never die.

Nearly a half century after the publication of *Democracy in America*, the English jurist Sir Henry Sumner Maine noted that, a mere century earlier, the claim that democracy was inevitably the future of the Western world would have been received as "a wild paradox." Before the French Revolution, the history of two millennia seemed to confirm the prejudice against democracy as an exceedingly fragile institution by comparison with, for example, the French monarchy and the Venetian oligarchy, both of them long lived. Maine considered the brief Athenian democracy to have been, in fact, a new aristocracy that succeeded in replacing the old one. Italian commonwealths, feudal estates, and parliaments all gave way, Maine argued, to tyrannies and military despotisms, while monarchy prevailed. The reason is that that institution was in the highest degree popular, capable indeed of inspiring all the enthusiasm of a modern radical for "democracy"—even in England, where the Commonwealth and the Protectorate were never popular at all.[4]

"From the reign of Augustus Caesar to the establishment of the United States," Maine wrote, "it was democracy which was always, as a rule, in decline, nor was the decline arrested until the American Federal Government was founded, itself the offspring of the British constitution."[5] The history of the British and American Constitutions during the past two centuries, and they alone, offered evidence of the durability of democratic government. Moreover, in Sir Henry's estimation, democracy in the nineteenth century, so far from being "inevitable," was the result of a long series of accidents, mostly unrelated. Maine conceded, however, that "if a large number of Englishmen, belonging to classes which are powerful if they exert themselves, continue saying to themselves that Democracy is irresistible and must come, beyond all doubt it would come." This was scarcely a firm prophecy, or ringing endorsement, on his part.

Naturally, Americans have always had a fond appreciation for the French aristocrat who responded so warmly to their young republic. This has a good deal to do with the contrast between Tocqueville's openness to the United States and the scorn, amounting to disgust, expressed by the greater part of European visitors stateside. Without doubt, *Democracy in America* is by far the most sympathetic volume among a list of chiefly hostile accounts by European travelers to the United States during the same period.

Mrs. Frances Trollope, the mother of Anthony and herself a novelist, arrived in the United States four years before Tocqueville landed at Newport and lived in the country for three and a half years, for a stay about three times the length of Tocqueville's sojourn. Mrs. Trollope, unlike the French count, had little interest in political issues and arrangements. *Domestic Manners of the Americans*, which appeared in 1832, the year of Tocqueville's return to France, was written with the deliberate aim of comparing American society with that of Great Britain, very much to the disadvantage of the former. The British Constitution, Mrs. Trollope felt assured, was the source of all that was sensible, gracious, and intelligent in her native land; its New World counterpart was the direct cause of the rudeness and social chaos that resulted naturally from the Founders' supposed determination to place the American national government in the hands of the great mass of the people. She was, indeed, a most uncompromising critic. "I do not like [the Americans]," she wrote on an early page of her book. "I do not like their principles, I do not like their manners, I do not like their opinions." Mrs. Trollope noted that, as a woman and a stranger, she would not add to this indictment her dislike of their government as well. It suited them, she admitted, but was unworkable for any other people.[6] Tocqueville had arrived at the same conclusion in respect to the French people (one wonders whether, at home in France, he bought a copy of *Domestic Manners*), but this assessment, coming from Mrs. Trollope, was unambiguous.

Where Tocqueville was impressed (however reservedly) by the Americans' obsession with politics and the press, Mrs. Trollope was appalled. "And I'd like you to tell me," she quotes one solid citizen as protesting, "how we can spend [time] better [than in reading the newspapers]. How should freemen spend their time, but looking after their government, and watching that them fellers as he gives office to, does their duty, and give themselves no airs?" Worse, this man, unknowingly echoing Dr. Johnson, admitted that the tavern stool was the seat of a democrat's felicity—"but I do say," he added, "that I'd rather my son drunk three times a week, than not look after the affairs of his country."

Unlike the international company she was accustomed to meeting in London and Paris, the Americans, Mrs. Trollope complained, failed to make conversation, or even communication, easy. "It is less necessary, I imagine, for the mutual understandings of persons conversing together, that the language should be the same, that their ordinary mode of thinking, and habits of life, should, in some degree, assimilate; whereas, in point of fact, there is hardly a simple point of sympathy between the Americans and us." The slightest criticism of their form of government, or doubt expressed regarding its future, she found to be bitterly resented. (Tocqueville, too, noted what he called the "irritable patriotism" of Americans.) Still, "As long as they can keep down the preeminence which nature has assigned to great powers, as long as they can prevent respect and human honor from resting upon high talent, gracious manners, and exalted station, so long may they be sure of going on as they are." Mrs. Trollope witnessed with disdain the local reaction to a frank account, by her compatriot Captain Basil Hall, of America and the Americans when the American edition came off press. "They cannot believe in the sincerity of the impressions he describes," she noted. Rather, rumors circulated that Captain Hall was a spy dispatched by the British Treasury for the purpose of fomenting anti-American sentiment in Britain, and with express orders to take objection to whatever in America seemed to him worthy.

One thinks of *Reflections on the Revolution in France*, published in 1790 (three years before the execution of Louis XVI), as the supreme indictment of political equality, at least in its revolutionary form. In fact, Edmund Burke, though his original plan for the book included a section on democracy, in the end omitted any discussion of the subject. It is true, of course, that *Reflections* defends the French monarchy and aristocracy under the Old Regime and deplores the revolutionary government's treatment of the Gallican church. Yet Burke believed, as Tocqueville was to do, that an increase in the democratic element in politics and society was inevitable in the Europe of the future. What outraged and alarmed him, and what he represented powerfully in his great work, was the spectacle—in France, in 1789—of the thoughtlessly deliberate and wantonly violent destruction of the other harmonizing elements in society in the interest of deifying one of them— Equality. Regarding the so-called Rights of Man, Burke remarked: "The pretended rights of these theorists are all extremes; and in proportion as they are metaphysically true, they are morally and politically false." As for the theorists themselves, "This sort of people are so taken up with their theories about the rights of man that they have totally forgotten his nature." The restraints placed on men, Burke believed, are as much "rights" as the liberties entrusted to them, and both kinds of rights depend on and reflect a given historical time and historical circumstances: they are not absolute rights but contingent ones. "A perfect democracy," he concluded, "is the most shameless thing in the world. As it is the most shameless, it is also the most fearless."[7]

John Stuart Mill remarked that democracy had won the day against the wishes of the intellectual class. A modern historian, Roland N. Stromberg, has noted that the student of the intellectual history of democracy soon finds that the vast majority of intellectuals have been antidemocratic. "Not theory, but experience, on the whole, produced democratic regimes." His explanation for this phenomenon is both simple and obvious: "Nobody who is sure of the truth will think it sensible to leave it to an election."[8] "No artist," the twentieth-century painter, novelist, and critic Wyndham Lewis said, "can ever love democracy." (His statement admittedly requires qualification today, the contemporary artist having learned to manipulate the democratic art market as, in former times, his predecessor managed his aristocratic patron.)

Stendhal, the (qualifiedly) anticlerical author of *The Red and the Black* and *The Charterhouse of Parma*, admitted that he had come at last to "subject myself to my aristocratic tendencies after having railed for ten years, and in good faith, against any aristocracy."[9] Other social novelists of the period—Dickens, Gaskell, and Kingsley, not just the unforgiving Mrs. Trollope—disapproved of popular democracy. "The masses, sheer numbers, are always stupid," Flaubert wrote in a letter to George Sand. Proudhon thought democracy the greatest fraud of the nineteenth century, worse in some respects than tyranny. Coleridge opposed the Reform Act of 1832, which enfranchised a portion of the British middle class, and so did Hegel, who described the modern state as absolutized democracy. (I do not recall Fukuyama quoting this assessment of Hegel's in *The End of History*.)

Thomas Macaulay predicted that universal suffrage would be "fatal to all the purposes for which government exists; utterly incompatible with the very existence of civilization," and Comte and Taine both warned against the perils of democracy. Ernest Renan urged that Europeans "cure ourselves of democracy." Civilization, he said, began as an aristocratic project, and its preservation is an aristocratic project as well. His ideal aristocracy would amount to "the incarnation of reason; a papacy of true infallibility," in whose hands power could not fail to benefit society. Émile Faguet opined that democracies depend on either their ability to produce aristocracies or their allowing aristocracies to perpetuate themselves. Thomas Carlyle wrote that he prayed to Heaven daily for a new hierarchy and a new aristocracy, and appealed to the "dire necessity," in a world "not yet doomed to death," for nature to bring forward "her ARISTOCRACIES, her BEST, even if by forcible measures." It was true, he conceded, that men needed to relieve themselves of their "Mock-Superiors," yet that act would do no more than confront them with the "grand problem" of procuring government by their "Real Superiors." That the mass of men required guidance, Carlyle was certain—but how were they to find it? The question was for him imperative, as he, like Tocqueville, was convinced that democracy was the inexorable demand of the time, what Cavour called a "predestined revolution."

The antidemocrats' objection to democracy was at once cultural, intellectual, social, political, practical, moral, and religious. Carlyle perceived in its rejection of heroism and heroic virtue an atheism he found fundamental to the democratic movement, which scorned the great "Heroes" he regarded as "the visible Temples of God." Should England fail to learn to reverence its heroes, he warned, by distinguishing them from its "Sham-Heroes and Valets and gaslighted Histrios," and if England were not prepared to cry out to them, "Be ye king and Priest, and Gospel and Guidance for us," it would find itself condemned to the continued worship of "Quackhood" in ever-renewed form, and pay eventually for its obdurate want of respect with its very existence.

The greatest and most thoroughgoing of the religiously minded enemies of democracy, which he called republicanism, was Joseph de Maistre, whom the historian Faguet described as "a fierce absolutist, a furious theocrat, an intransigent legitimist, apostle of a monstrous trinity composed of Pope, King and Hangman, always and everywhere the champion of the hardest, narrowest, and most inflexible dogmatism, a dark figure out of the Middle Ages, part learned doctor, part inquisitor, part executioner" whose "Christianity is terror, passive obedience, and the religion of the State." In point of fact, Maistre's *Considerations on France*, published in France in 1797 (seven years after *Reflections of the Revolution in France* and in the year of Burke's death), accused his country of having demoralized all of Europe by abandoning its divine mission to Christianize the Continent. Every institution of strength or duration can be shown to rest on a divine idea, Maistre argued. In the case of France, that idea was "*liberty through the monarchy.*" The French Republic had no roots—unlike the monarchy, which had been rooted in history. In creating that republic, the Revolution had destroyed all dignity in France by its destruction of the sovereignty of the monarchy, whose foundations, established in extreme antiquity, came from God, not from man.

Kierkegaard remarks somewhere that the same people who demand "freedom" hardly ever make use of the freedom they have— freedom of thought, for instance, for which freedom of speech is a form of compensation granted by the state. Skeptics of democracy in the early democratic age doubted the ability of the common man to comprehend the meaning of "freedom" and "liberty" in individual and personal terms, and therefore to find satisfaction in those freedoms democracy promised to bestow on him. Carlyle wrote, "The true liberty of a man, you would say, consists in his finding out, or being forced to find out the right path, and to walk thereon. To learn, or to be taught, what work he actually [is] able for . . . to set about doing the same. . . . If liberty be not that, I, for one, have small case about liberty." On this point, Matthew Arnold was to agree. And beyond it lay the existential issue: emancipation from all men does not equal emancipation from oneself—or the Devil. Lastly, liberty in its modern social and economic aspects concerned Carlyle and other critics. "The liberty especially which has to purchase itself by social isolation, and each man standing separate from the other, having 'no business with him' but a cash-account: this is such liberty as the Earth seldom saw;—as the Earth will not long put up with."

Decades later, the prophecies of this crusty and bellicose Scotsman were amplified to a frenzy of poeticized philosophy (or philosophic poetry) by that most lucid of madmen, Friedrich Nietzsche: the John the Baptist to the Übermensch who complained that, in the marketplace, "nobody believes in higher men." Nietzsche perceived, as he said, more idols than realities in the world of the nineteenth century, of which the greatest were Christianity and the bourgeois democracy he believed Christianity's "slave morality" had created. In fact, Nietzsche's challenge to men to transcend themselves through the transfiguration of values bore some resemblance to the democratic desire to better the situation of one's class, which became, in the second half of the twentieth century, a quest for individual self-fulfillment. But Nietzsche expected his Overman to arise from a small minority of superior men, not from the masses themselves. "Once the spirit was God, then he became man, and now he even becomes rabble."

The world has given Friedrich Nietzsche, postmortem, the only gift he could perhaps have appreciated: the gift of being read and despised at the same time, owing largely to his undeserved connection with Adolf Hitler, an enthusiast of Nietzsche's friend Richard Wagner and his music dramas. But Nietzsche is worth reading in his own right, not only as a highly original poet, of course, but also as a ferocious critic of modernity, of which democracy is but a part; he is among the first in a long line of subsequent critics and poets that includes T. S. Eliot, Wyndham Lewis, James Joyce, and Marcel Proust. His apothegms endure. "Life is a well of joy, but where the rabble drinks too, all wells are poisoned." "Mob above and mob below!" Both rich and poor had become confounded in the mob, and through it in the "mob-sadness" that much of Eliot's poetry dramatizes. The modern world has become a place where everyone wants the same thing, wants to be and live alike, and "whoever feels different goes voluntarily into a madhouse." The mob cannot distinguish greatness, whether of soul or anything else; it is dishonest and crooked; it always lies, if only because it cannot perceive the truth. Anticipating Camus's evocation of modern man as a creature "who fornicates and reads the newspapers," Nietzsche dismissed the mob as "all diseased and sick with public opinion." Christianity demands slave thinkers, and modern society requires slave workers: "Slave morality is a morality of utility." Nietzsche's "Last Man" is an existential version of Ortega's mass man of the 1930s, and his writings, taken together, are Nietzsche's *Die Götterdämmerung* in prose, the ne plus ultra in modern prophecy, the work of one of the greatest of the "great despisers" who were, for Nietzsche, also the "great reverers"—being, indeed, one and the same category of superior people.

Nineteenth-century dissenters from the democratic project were as much concerned with practical objections as they were with philosophical and moral concerns. Thomas Carlyle deplored what he called "the perpetual nomadic and even ape-like appetite for change and mere change." Sir Henry Maine, a comparative historian as well as a jurist, agreed. In his book *Popular Government*, a classic treatise on democracy that appeared in 1885, he attacked the notion of progress itself—a word, he claimed, of which he had never read a definition. For centuries Englishmen had enjoyed government infused with a popular element that had evolved, two hundred years before, into a government that was almost unqualifiedly popular; yet the forefathers of Englishmen living at the end of the nineteenth century had fought for the historical Constitution of the past, not some imaginary one in the future.

Maine attributed the desire for change for change's sake to what he called the enthusiasm for legislative activity, beginning with autocratic government as it had been established in revolutionary France. "The popular expectation is that, after the establishment of a democracy, there will be as much reforming legislation as ever." Democracy, Maine saw, is perpetually restless, continually legislating for the sake of legislation, tireless in the effort to reform the reform and build on it.

The British Parliament, like government bodies in the predemocratic era, including the classical one, had legislated scarcely at all before the appearance of Jeremy Bentham—who, however, had been concerned with legal, not political, reform. Instead, members of Parliament had devoted themselves to matters of diplomacy and justice. But in 1832 the First Reform Act initiated, on the Continent as well as in Great Britain, a period of continuous reform whose end was nowhere in sight. "Neither experience nor probability afford any ground for thinking that there may be an infinity of legislative innovation at once safe and beneficent," Maine thought. In any event, history showed that legislative change, so far as it went, had been more often accomplished by powerful monarchies than by other forms of government.

Maine was careful to distinguish between popular justice, of which he approved, and popular government, of which he was deeply skeptical. What he called the old adjudicating democracy had begun in England with the institution of the jury system; modified and improved with time, it had been well cultivated to produce "Popular Justice." Maine understood modern governing democracy to be a somewhat modified version of the old adjudicating one, yet he perceived that it was tending toward unmodified democracy grasping for a hold on the management of public affairs. The resulting demand for perpetual change, he feared, being contrary to human nature, must result in popular disappointment leading to political disaster.

At bottom, Sir Henry's distrust of popular democracy was really more practical than theoretical. Refusing to take an ideological view of this political phenomenon, he insisted on treating it (as Tocqueville had done) simply as another form of government among a number of possible ones, entrusted with the basic functions and responsibilities common to the alternative forms. "If the choice has to be made, and if there is any real connection between Democracy and liberty, it is better to remain a nation capable of displaying the virtues of a nation than even to be free."

Maine was convinced that democracy lacked these virtues and was incapable of realizing them. Democracy, he said, was the most difficult form of government, particularly in respect of large and complex societies. Among its greatest infirmities is that, under popular government, "liberty is power cut into fragments." That, however, was not, for him, the principal argument against democracy. Bentham had urged that power be placed in the hands of the people so that they might employ it in their interests and to their own ends. Maine countered him by questioning whether the people saw clearly enough to recognize and understand those interests. Here he could quote the great democrat Jean-Jacques Rousseau himself for an authority: "The general will [Rousseau had written] is always right, but the judgment which guides it is not always clear"—as if Rousseau lent him standing to confront the "vulgar assumption" that the popular mass is capable of resolving for itself the great issues of the day. The belief that it had that capability, and that democracy is a form of government superior to every other, had hardened into one of the chief tenets of a faith that could be understood only as a religion, rooted in a state of mind that was essentially religious rather than political, and therefore extraneous to politics and political debate.

Maine found confirmation in his view of democracy as religion in the fact that democrats never take democratic failure as proof that democracy is unworkable; they react exactly like the Millerites in America, who, having congregated one night to witness the end of the world, concluded the following morning that God had postponed the event by twenty-four hours. Wherever democracy had previously been tried, Maine asserted, it had produced "monstrous and morbid forms of government by the One, or government by the few." Maine did nevertheless perceive one exception to the general rule, and that was the success of the United States of America under the Federal Constitution. The history of that country, he thought, represented democratic government's one success in the world, its sole beacon cutting through the mists of confusion. The chaotic record of failure and disappointment convinced him that the march toward democracy was distinctly less inevitable than the human march toward death, as he sardonically remarked.

Burke had praised the British Constitution ("our political system") as being in a symmetrical and just correspondence with "the order of the world" and well suited to a corporation at once permanent and transitory: never old, nor middle-aged, nor young. Walter Bagehot, the English political economist who was also the finest writer of discursive prose in Victorian England, put the thing rather differently. "An ancient and ever-altering constitution," he wrote in *The English Constitution* (1867), "is like an old man who still wears with attached fondness clothes in the fashion of his youth; what you see of him is the same; what you do not see is wholly altered."[10]

The choicest parts of Bagehot's great work are the chapters on the British monarchy and the British aristocracy, both of which he defended as valuable, indeed necessary, institutions helping to uphold the traditional polity of Great Britain. But Walter Bagehot, a cofounder of the *National Review*, an editor of *The Economist*, and the author of a brief volume about the Lombard Street money market, was a liberal: an advocate of reforming the House of Lords and a supporter of the first Reform Act. He was, however, no democrat, as his reservations regarding popular government show. Bagehot considered electoral reform to have been necessary and prudent, yet not without its dangers. He thought the electorate before 1832 had been competent to decide questions set before it by the higher classes, and no more. But the newly enfranchised electorate was in need of greater guidance than the old, and Bagehot thought it not at all clear whether it would defer to wealth and rank, which he called "the higher qualities of which these are the rough symbols and the common accomplishments." The great threat, to his mind, was a political combination of the lower classes determined to use the suffrage to create a "poor man's paradise," organized and cried on by their irresponsible betters—"well-taught and rich men"—for the political advantage of the latter. In this way, *vox populi* was certain to become *vox diaboli*. "The wide gift of the electoral franchise will be a great calamity to the whole nation, and to those who gain it as great a calamity as to any." There was but one way around that calamity, Bagehot thought, and that was through responsible statesmanship in selecting the great questions to be put before the country while pushing aside issues likely to excite the lower orders, and presenting them in a truthful and honorable manner in Parliament and on the hustings.

Tocqueville explained that he wrote *Democracy in America* because he wished to illuminate the enormous pitfalls that equality sets in the way of human independence. As a pragmatic thinker, he believed that political theory that cannot be put into practice has no lasting value. For Tocqueville, American democracy was a crucial experiment, a sort of laboratory in which modern governmental theory was tested or refined—or refuted.[11]

Alexis de Tocqueville, to repeat, was a republican rather than a democrat—in American terms, a Federalist, not a Jacksonian. Like Madison and Bagehot, he feared the power of the majority to dominate and even to enslave the minority, for him the superior part of political and civic society. Tocqueville did not regard political constitutions as clockwork oranges—engineering marvels whose precise instrumentation and calibration made them foolproof against breakdown or abuse—and he believed that the "rare and brief exercise of [the people's] free choice . . . will not prevent them from gradually losing the facilities of thinking, feeling, and acting for themselves, and thus gradually falling below the level of humanity."

Tocqueville's thought, as I have noted, combined the eighteenth-century belief in public virtue with the aggressive democratic insistence on the will of the people, whether virtuous or otherwise. Like the Abbé Emmanuel-Joseph Sieyès (a prominent theorist and actor in the French Revolutionary period and the First Empire) before him, he distinguished between civil rights, which all men rightly deserved to possess, and political rights, which ought to be reserved to the relative few. "The principle of equality," he thought, "may be established in civil society without prevailing in the political world." Sieyès himself had expressed the same idea at greater length: "The difference between *natural and civil rights* and the *political* rights of citizens consists in the fact that natural and civil rights are those for whose preservation and development society is formed; and political rights are those by which society is formed. For the sake of clarity, it would be best to call the first ones passive rights, and the second ones active rights."

Although men living in democratic societies valued their independence, nevertheless independence was eclipsed in their minds by the impossible and dangerous ideal of equality. Democrats, Tocqueville thought, needed to cultivate a secure sense of individuality that transcended their sense of sameness in equality: "Among democratic nations, men easily attain a certain equality of condition, but they can never attain as much as they desire. It perpetually retires before them, yet hiding itself from their sight, and in retiring draws them on. At every moment they think they are about to grasp it; it escapes at every moment from their hold. They are near enough to see its charms, but too far off to enjoy them; and before they have fully tasted its delights, they die." Lasting inequality reflects the fact that, in a democracy, power is rearranged, not equalized.[12] Tocqueville explained this reallocation of power by appealing to a sort of informal law of human endowments, the greatest of them being birth, wealth, and knowledge, which can be shared only by the few. These goods—"aristocratical elements," Tocqueville called them—are common to every society, past and present; by a natural process, they are to be found in the hands of the well-connected social elites, which, together with their respective governments, form the basis of a strong and lasting aristocracy, and of civilization. "He who seeks in liberty anything other than itself," Tocqueville asserted, "is made for servitude." He understood that, although taking responsibility for one's own affairs is necessary to human dignity, no one has the right to be entrusted with affairs lying beyond his sphere of competence.[13] This explains why Tocqueville not only opposed universal suffrage but also considered the suffrage principle to be inessential to the democratic one.

Tocqueville's devotion to property rights and his abhorrence of socialism did not prevent him from recognizing, and deploring, the concentration of property and power in progressively fewer hands in France in the 1840s. He feared that collective individualism strengthened the appeal of the socialist program, warned against the new industrial aristocracy ("the most selfish and grasping of plutocracies"), and was partial to a saying of Alphonse de Lamartine's that "*laissez-faire and laissez-passer* mean nothing less than *laissez-souffrir* and *laissez-mourir.*" As Tocqueville wrote in *The Old Regime and the French Revolution* and *The Social and Political Condition of France before the Revolution*, the advancing centralization that had plagued the country since the seventeenth century had created a wall between the aristocracy and the French people and between one class and another, while thwarting democratic development in France. The French nation, he said, was once again divided against itself, as it had been under the ancien régime. This time, however, it was not the nobility against the bourgeoisie but the propertied against the propertyless, the middle class against the working class, who opposed one another on "the great field of battle." Physiocracy, the economic doctrine that land is the basis of natural wealth, had produced administrative socialism, and socialism, if successful, would do the same, thus reestablishing the tyranny that had been broken in 1789. Tocqueville, it seems, never answered for himself the question of whether prosperity creates liberty, or the reverse. Influenced apparently by the legitimist economist Alban de Villeneuve-Bargemon, he did agree with Smith and Malthus, and against Ricardo and Duchâtel, that political economy is a branch of moral, political, and religious inquiry and not a science in its own right.[14]

Tocqueville thought the revolution of 1830 that put Louis-Philippe on the throne of France resolved a long, often bloody contention between the French middle class and the aristocracy. Yet he was distressed by what he considered the torpidity of public life induced by the triumph of individualist thinking. He deplored what was to him the elite's neglect of the political education of the lower classes in favor of a devotion to their own interests. Still, he feared the dangerous enthusiasm of the people, which, to his mind, could be restrained only by extending political power to them by "different degrees of election" that kept pace with the progress they made in political enlightenment under the direction of their tutors.[15] Eighteen years later, the revolutions of 1848 shocked him profoundly while strengthening his conviction that France was trapped in a fatal circle, in which repression and domination alternated with periods of bloody anarchy. Although he despised the socialist principles that underlay the events of 1848, Tocqueville could not blame democracy for a catastrophe that found no counterpart in Great Britain or the United States. The explanation, he argued, had to do with traditions of local and self-government in England and America, and also the relative openness of the Anglo-American upper class to talent and ability from below. After 1848, Tocqueville never lost faith entirely in the possibilities for a democratic future, but he disapproved more strongly than ever of the democratic tendency to "think," as he had written in *Democracy in America*, "of the government as a sole, simple, providential, and creative force."

"In Europe," said Montesquieu, "the last sigh of liberty will be heaved by an Englishman."

One contemporary historian has considered Alexis de Tocqueville in the context of the "inquiétude" prevalent among liberal republicans in the late eighteenth and early nineteenth centuries who, following the French Revolution, looked to Montesquieu and Rousseau to alleviate their political doubts in a strange new era. Among these was Tocqueville, who shared their concerns for the nature, and the future, of modern liberal commercial republics.

Rousseau believed anxiety the natural state of mind of man in society, and he expected the development and progress of civilization (science and culture, commerce and economic growth) to exacerbate inquiétude by stimulating the self-love that arises naturally from personal rivalry. Montesquieu, in *Considerations on the Romans and Universal Empire*, described the French Continental Empire as the successor to the Roman Empire, both of which he compared unfavorably with the English domestic republic and its empire overseas. The French Empire, Montesquieu predicted, was fated to destroy itself, as the Roman Empire had done, whereas Britain, the modern Carthage, possessed the political stability required for survival. But stability could not protect England from the inquiétude to which men living in liberal commercial societies were susceptible, a malaise that left them subject to fears great enough to tempt them to seek shelter in despotism. Even so, Montesquieu hoped, and dared expect, that the rivalry between the English executive and legislative powers would excite a jealousy of government power sufficient to channel anxiety toward a spirit of manly resistance to oppression. The future of English liberty depended on the government's ability to resist the temptation to make its citizens economically reliant on it, and equally on the people's strength of character in resisting government patronage. The best liberal-commercial republics of the day, Montesquieu argued, furnished their citizens with what he described as "political liberty in its relation to the constitution," whereby "no one will be constrained to do things that the law does not require or prevent them from doing those which the law permits them to do." Yet these republics, being devoid of secondary powers capable of checking the central government, were unable to provide the people with the calm and security necessary to their peace of mind that Montesquieu called "liberty in relationship to the citizen."

Tocqueville agreed in part with both Rousseau and Montesquieu on the subjects of inquiétude, the bourgeois malaise, and the necessity of secondary institutions in free and peaceable societies. But he suspected that the state lacked the restraint to avoid meddling in economic matters, whereas the development of the arts and sciences seemed to him as desirable as they were inevitable. As for inquiétude, he thought it a fundamental and inalienable characteristic of democratic society, so insistent on equality of condition. Because

Tocqueville was certain that democracy and social equality were the inevitable future, the way forward was unclear to him. His chief fear was that democratic individualism would engender selfishness and a materialist spirit in the people, who would in time resort to the state as their ally in the quest for riches. This alliance would promote the centralization of government, and centralized government, in turn, would lead to rule by a mandarin bureaucratic class and eventual paralysis in the state.[16]

To the extent that Alexis de Tocqueville was the prophet of democracy, he was clearly not a prophet of democracy as it developed in the twentieth century. He was not even, really, the prophet of democratic tendencies in his own time, which was the liberal period lasting, roughly, from 1830 to 1870. Finally, it is debatable whether, considered in either of these contexts, Tocqueville was a democrat at all. In America, his closest political analogues were the Federalists, who had, as a party, disappeared by 1830. Among European democrats, he is best understood as one of a small group of "aristocratic liberals" that included his close friend John Stuart Mill, Jacob Burckhardt, Walter Bagehot, George Eliot, and Gustave Flaubert.[17]

The classic philosophers regarded virtue as a static quality and equated mutability in human nature and human affairs alike as a form of corruption. Renaissance authors never came up with an answer to the conundrum presented by this understanding of history. During the Renaissance, Francesco Guicciardini and other Italian political theorists proposed that the object of political life was to promote virtue and nobility among the citizens in order that they might be capable of honorable actions. Unlike Machiavelli, who credited all men with that capability, Guicciardini supposed only the best of them to be so endowed. The Florentine civic humanists, however, introduced what has been described as a "sociology of liberty," based on the concept of a negative ideal of liberty defined as freedom from the domination of other people.

This method of analysis of human liberty survived into the Enlightenment, was adopted by both the English and the American democrats, and became an essential element in the modern humanism that provided the basis for aristocratic liberalism, which, in its thoroughgoing historicism, accepted change as a necessity and possibly even a good. Modern humanism provided aristocratic liberalism, which was indebted as well to the civic humanism carried over from the classics, with its basic values and tenets; the aristocratic liberals added the concept of positive liberties to the idea of negative ones, and added to this humanism a teleological dimension reflecting its conviction that liberty, individuality, and diversity were necessary to human thought and action, to the possibility of progress through change, and to the mental and moral benefits of education, which it was willing to accept as an effective substitute for classical virtue. Yet aristocratic liberalism's inclination was always essentially conservative. Although acknowledging the nearly universal demand for democratic equality, it wished, first and foremost, to protect and defend liberty against the forces that threatened liberty in its own name. "I have," Tocqueville said, "but one passion, the love of liberty and human dignity." Aristocratic liberalism envisioned a society that would be at once free, ordered, and, in the classical European sense of the word, civilized.

"This," Jacob Burckhardt explained in his *Historical Fragment*, "is European: the expression of *all* powers, in sculpture, art, and word, institutions and parties, up to the individual—the development of the intellect on all sides and in all directions—the striving of the mind to express *everything* within it, not, like the Orient, to silently surrender to world monarchies and theocracies."

European yes, but hardly democratic, even when judged by the standards of the nineteenth century. The aristocratic liberals wanted constitutional government, limited suffrage, decentralization, and active local government. Beyond that, they favored a political education for the people—the electorate especially—that was basically aristocratic in outline. Yet none of these men was convinced that the values that had shaped their philosophy were of universal appeal, or anything like it, to a liberal democratic society. Although avid to build a society that *would* find the values appealing, they were at a loss to imagine what such a society might be like, let alone how to realize it through democratic political effort. Mill held that the chief role of government should be to act as an educative agency, while Burckhardt devoted his career to the preservation of the old, humane, liberal-aristocratic ideal. Yet neither was there popular acceptance of that ideal nor was the human material available by which to realize it.

Tocqueville and the rest were not pessimists, but they considered the return of despotism to be a perennial possibility (Mill thought the United States a "collective despotism"), and they felt that time was not on their side. They were right about that. Compared with popular and influential liberals between 1830 and 1870, they were much less optimistic, they had a more restrictive view of the state, and they worried more about class hostility; moreover, they could never overcome their innate distaste for the commercial bourgeoisie. All of Tocqueville's books were read and respected by educated and influential people, in England and on the Continent. But, in the estimation of one historian, "their practical effects in their own times were almost nil"—a shocking thought, perhaps, for generations of readers of *Democracy in America*. "Aristocratic liberalism," Alan S. Kahan argues, "was condemned to the sidelines because it refused to link its particular elitism to any of the elite or the aspiring elite groups that might have given it power, refused to make any the bearer of its values."[18]

Although perhaps *refused* is the wrong word. When were the aristocratic liberals given the opportunity of refusing anyone?

3

Democracy's Forked Road

M odern scholarship tends toward the view that the ancient "democracies" of the classical world had little in common with those democracies that trace their development from late medieval and modern Europe. One argument holds that the citizens of Athens in the fifth and fourth centuries B.C. were indeed self-governing but that what they understood by "democracy" was a complex institutional arrangement that should not be understood as the ancient equivalent of modern democratic government. "When any modern state claims to be a democracy it necessarily misdescribes itself," says the British political theorist John Dunn.[1] Although the early history of democratic government is beyond the scope of the present book, two observations regarding democracy's origins must be made here. The first is that democratic thought arose from the long struggle between church and state in Europe. The second is that Western democracy is a specific product of the wider civilization in which that conflict occurred. Taken together, these two facts suggest the truth of Tocqueville's remark (in *The Old Regime and the French Revolution*) that "it is to the religious revolutions that one must compare the French Revolution, if one wishes to understand it by the aid of analogy." In America, he noted, one is liable to meet a politician when he thinks he is meeting a priest.

The nineteenth-century American political philosopher Orestes A. Brownson attributed despotism to man's temptation to mistake himself for God by setting himself up as his own final authority. "It is not monarchy or aristocracy against which the modern spirit fights, but Loyalty"—loyalty to one's country, loyalty to one's government, loyalty to the Deity Who alone confers legitimacy on governments.[2] The political history of medieval Europe is substantially the story of the attempts by kings and princes first to deny and then to free themselves from the secular authority of the papacy, and of the ensuing struggles of the burghers in their cities and towns to wrest a list of rights, liberties, and powers from the kings, who had substantially succeeded in defying the temporal authority of Rome. Necessarily, though perhaps at first unconsciously, their assertion of civic freedom was equally an assertion of freedom against the authority of the Roman Church in particular and later, more broadly, against the authority and claims of Christianity itself. In its origins, then, democracy was the rival of religion and inherently its enemy.

Yet the church played a significant role in the creation of the nation-state, which, as the French political philosopher Pierre Manent has pointed out, was the solution to the ancient conflict between Guelphs and Ghibellines, between city and empire, to which European civilization is so enormously indebted. "The entering wedge of the nation-to-be was the Christian king," Manent argues. "The European nation came into being through obedience to the Christian king." The logic of popes, kings, and history itself is plain.[3]

Christian kings showed the Roman Church greater possibilities than the governors of city-states and the heads of empires had previously offered it. As Christians, these monarchs owed spiritual fealty to the pope; in their kingly role, they were responsible for the defense of their Christian nations (and of Christendom itself) not only against barbarian invasions—but also against the Holy See when papal demands were overbearing. In this context, the Reformation—a thoroughgoing revolt against authority, temporal as well as spiritual—may be understood as the "nationalization of Christianity," or its appropriation, a process hugely facilitated by the rendition of the Latin Bible into the vulgates of Europe. "Only through the crystallizing of the nation can Christian liberty coincide with Christian obedience," Manent explains. "At that time, Christendom was broken apart and the 'commonwealth of Christian subjects,' the Christian nation, was born." During the following two centuries, these Christian nations evolved steadily into sovereign and religiously neutral states, and their Christian subjects developed a self-identity that was increasingly national and less religious.[4]

When nationalist consciousness evolved into democratic consciousness and self-assertion, the Age of Revolutions commenced, founded on what Orestes Brownson called "the right of insurrection," invoked by democrats to defend insurgents and revolutionists. "The established government that seeks to enforce respect for its legitimate authority and compel obedience to the laws, is held to be despotic, tyrannical, oppressive, and resistance to it to be obedience to God, and a wild howl rings through Christendom against the prince that will not stand still and permit the conspirators to cut his throat." Brownson attributed such a catastrophe to "political atheism," the attempt to create a state on professedly secular principles. In his view, civil society requires both movement and stability, the first of which is supplied by human action, the second by supernatural agency. Only a political doctrine, therefore, that recognizes divine authority working through the people is able to realize these two elements so essential to a legitimate and effective polity. Yet, Brownson noted, "For nearly two centuries the most popular and influential writers on government have rejected the divine origin and ground of civil authority, and excluded God from the state."[5]

Democratic government is a product of the progressive European rebellion against religious and civil authority from late medieval times down to the modern era. It is, equally, a fruit of the European genius for theological and philosophic thought, for art, for science, for society (a sense of civility, gentility, charity, tolerance, and mutual accommodation), and, in Great Britain especially, for constitutional government, all of them elements of the specifically Christian genius. Alexis de Tocqueville thought that the Christian religion and Christian civilization, taken together (and, so far as the thing is possible, separately), constitute the ground for democratic government and the necessary condition for its success. Democracy, as with so many things, is in the eye of the beholder; what passed for democracy assumed multiple forms in Tocqueville's time, and has since. In the United States, for several generations after Tocqueville, democracy, for all practical purposes, was one big thing; in Europe, for as long or longer, it was an array of differing smaller things, most of them inconsistent, or at dagger's point, with one another. As he considered democracy's prospects, Tocqueville feared two principal dangers. The first was socialism. The second was democratic *ideology*, a word invented early in the nineteenth century by the French philosopher Baron Destutt de Tracy. It was in his fears, perhaps even more than in his hopes, that the author of *Democracy in America* proved himself to have been a man of deep intuition and a true prophet of history.

In the wake of the French Revolution, what Henry Sumner Maine described as a longing for liberty and a revulsion toward the barbarities of the revolutionary period encouraged the Continental countries to look to constitutional monarchy, which had proved so great a success in Britain, for their political salvation. In France, which had nearly destroyed its aristocracy, and elsewhere the result was a century-long attempt to reconcile the restored monarchy with the new democracy.[6] Monarchy, Maine perceived, had traveled a great distance from the ancien régime of the Bourbons: "It may now be affirmed of the civilized monarchies, what was formerly said of republics alone, that they are a government of laws, not of men."[7] Maine understood democracy as being, simply, monarchy inverted—a description that he claimed reflected the actual historical process by which modern republics had developed. Although French and English political theory between them dominated the political thought of Europe after 1815, Maine rightly noted that modern popular democracy originated only in England. France was not England, nor was England France. Tocqueville thought England's great advantage was the openness of the English aristocracy to talent and success from below. On a visit to England in the 1840s, he reflected that the English had perfected the aristocratical system, with incalculable benefits to the country as a whole. Still, aristocratic liberalism of the sort that he—and, he believed, the English aristocracy—represented had few takers, and no natural constituency at all.

Although the nationalist impulse, both on the European Continent and in the United States, has flourished alongside some form of egalitarian politics from 1848 down to the present day, socialist democracy in this period has, generally speaking, been the European temptation; following the War between the States especially, a growing passion for aggressive ideological democracy has been America's weakness. Thus Tocqueville, as a prophet, seems to have had it both ways (not that he would have taken pleasure in the accomplishment). How this came about is an interesting question for debate. It has been suggested that the hand of the French state—and also that of other European governments—lay more heavily on its citizens than the American government ever weighed on its own people.[8] It is possible also that the idea of democracy as the representation of an "order of equality" (asserted by the French revolutionaries Babeuf and Buonarroti) was more compelling for European democrats than the fundamentally aristocratic "order of egoism" (which made equality an equivalence of standing, beyond offense by political condescension) established by the U.S. Constitution in 1789 and effectively unchallenged in the United States until the twentieth century.[9]

Or perhaps the nature and origin of socialism hold the answer. Socialism, Claude Polin (another contemporary French political philosopher) maintains, owes its birth to the nature of Western man. Socialism, according to this argument, although not of the essence of

Western civilization, is a temptation entirely natural to it. Christianity is the soul of the West, and socialism is a restatement of the Christian message in secular terms. "A revolution is at hand; the intercession of a savior makes the revolution possible; the revolution is complete when the last are the first," Polin says.

Catholicism—though not, until recent times, the institutional church—has been particularly susceptible to socialist ideas since the beginning of the monastic movement at the end of the Roman Empire. Usually these ideas have appeared as a type of heresy: the Carthusians, the Beguins, the socialist utopia of Campanella in the early 1600s. France was still a Catholic country in the nineteenth century, and it was in France that several of the most influential socialist communities were founded, including that of Saint-Simon and his "New Christianity."[10] In any case, French democrats, before and after Marx, were wont to argue that citizenship confers an entitlement to a never-ending claim on society. In this way, Polin claims, "socialism has revealed itself as the truth—the hidden truth—of French democracy."[11]

On the other side of the Atlantic, by contrast, "pessimistic idealism," rather than equality, formed the basis of American democratic society and of democratic idealism itself, understood as a willingness to tolerate other people's freedoms, enterprises, and prejudices in exchange for the toleration extended to one's own. Democracy in its American form was obviously antisocialist in its insistence on tolerating whatever inequalities might result from the unequal material success of certain individuals relative to that of others.[12] This deeply rooted popular antipathy to socialism allowed and encouraged the federal government to proceed with a nationalist, expansionist, and, finally, imperialist version of democracy that encouraged those aspirations of national glory that Tocqueville had thought to be more typical of aristocracies over the equality of condition sought by socialist nations. And nationalism, it has been well said, was the first collectivism.[13]

Tocqueville recognized in the revolutions of 1848 a more or less coordinated socialist aggression against individualism, private property, and civilization that shocked him profoundly. Although he lived for seven years after, he never recovered the optimistic, if reserved, enthusiasm for democracy that had made his book and himself famous. Pierre Manent describes the period from 1848 to 1968 as the "Marxist democratic period," followed by a Tocquevillian interlude characterized by an explosion of what Tocqueville called "democratic mildness" that produced a comprehensive critique of totalitarianism in favor of a gentler version of Marxism, and, through the influence of its own variety of "soft totalitarianism," brought about the collapse of the Soviet Union. According to this historical schema, democracy commenced in 1776 at the start of the American Revolution and by 1820 was sweeping everywhere. The year 1848 appeared to give the lie to Tocqueville's definition of democracy as equality of conditions, since, manifestly, a more politically democratic Europe remained far from achieving any such equality. Hence, the period stretching from that *annus horribilis* to the riotous student rebellions of 1968 developed, and finally exhausted, the "social question," which was replaced by "an interrogation of democracy" in the spirit of Tocqueville that has continued into the twenty-first century.[14]

And yet, throughout these successive variations, democracy—as a percipient historian, Roland Stromberg, has noted—was hardly ever considered an end in itself; instead, it was a means to another end, most often liberalism, socialism, or nationalism.[15] This observation holds for Europe in the nineteenth century—but not for the United States during the same period, or for Great Britain, where, almost until the next century, political agitators on behalf of democratic reform were really extremists who demanded a complete makeover of society and its institutions but were willing to leave practical democratic legislation to Conservative politicians like Benjamin Disraeli.[16] French positivism replaced romantic democracy in Europe after 1848; it was matched across the Channel by utilitarianism, both of them reflecting the power of the new commercial and industrial bourgeoisie. This appropriation of liberal reformism (which in Britain passed as "radicalism") by the middle class alienated the European artistic and intellectual classes from the working classes, which thereafter looked to conservative statesmen like Cavour in Italy, Bismarck in Germany, Napoleon III in France, and Disraeli for "democratic" reforms.[17] (Just two years after the Reform Bill of 1886, the British Conservative Party commenced its unbroken reign of twenty years in office. "I am an out-and-out inegalitarian," said Mr. Gladstone to John Ruskin.)[18] In the 1870s, following the abdication of Napoleon III, liberalism and democracy made peace with each other, and by century's end the plutocracy, on the one hand, and the Roman Catholic Church, on the other, acquiesced in the Republic, for which no replacement could be imagined and which seemed the least divisive political system available at that time to France.[19]

Inevitably, democratic republicanism was compromised in the eyes of European radicals by the relative ease with which the bourgeoisie accepted it. (Georges Sorel thought democracy was "the greatest error of the past century.") Yet it had been the revolutions of 1848 that distanced not only the aristocratic liberals but also the broad middle classes and the intellectuals from the lower orders. "Man can be democratic," said Mallarmé, "but the artist goes his own way and ought to remain an aristocrat." European artists, in their disenchantment, turned from romantic politics first to the romantic aestheticism of art for art's sake, next to the notion of art for the artist's sake, and, finally, to a deliberate artistic and moral perversity. By the end of the nineteenth century, Stromberg says, "This generation's brilliant crew of writers and artists was marked above all by an almost hysterical rejection of democracy in the sense of popular culture and majoritarianism. . . . The Italian futurist Marinetti described popularly elected parliaments as 'noisy chicken coops, cow stalls, or sewers.'" For these people, democracy was the political face of the imperial-bourgeois-scientific-industrial project, and they wanted none of it. Even so, many agents of that same project shared their distaste for democratic government.[20]

Writing in the early 1880s, Henry Sumner Maine noted the obvious association in the popular mind between "political innovation" and the advance of science. The new Promethean science, however, benefited nationalist and socialist innovations to a far greater extent than it did liberal-democratic ones. Benjamin Kidd and Karl Pearson in England, Gustave Le Bon in France, and Friedrich Naumann in Germany advocated a form of national socialism, of which the nationalist component was the more significant part. Darwin's theories regarding natural selection and the survival of the fittest, taken together with the scientific development of increasingly destructive weaponry, suggested that corrupt and inefficient democracies were unaffordable in an age in which nations possessed the capacity to wipe each other from the map, as the Prussians had come close to destroying France in 1870–71.

The efficient alternative to liberal democracy was therefore totalitarian democracy, led by a charismatic strongman. Ferdinand Lassalle, a German socialist who described himself as a democrat, despised parliamentary government and sought an agreement with Bismarck to promote the creation of a "social monarchy" based on an alliance between the proletariat and the aristocracy to restrain the bourgeoisie and put it in its proper place. Moreover, the new "science" of sociology seemed to offer evidence of the incapacity of the common people for self-rule, and of the related necessity for social-scientific managerial "experts," working pro bono as progressive politicians in the United States were doing, to replace venal elected politicians in public affairs. Lastly, a suspicion was growing that democratic government could work only under the restraint of patrician leadership and a deferential electorate, as Maine and Bagehot argued.

This suspicion, this skepticism regarding democracy-all-the-way, had real substance behind it. "It is hard not to see," Stromberg suggests, "the great era of Gladstone and Disraeli (roughly 1865–90) as the golden age of parliamentary politics in Great Britain, marked by leaders of intellectual distinction, significant partisan issues, high public interest, and exciting elections. Significantly, it coincided not with a complete democracy but with a half-way one." This "half-way" democracy is precisely "the aristocratic balance" Lord Robert Cecil—later Lord Salisbury, the Tory prime minister—sought successfully to preserve at the time of the Second Reform Act of 1867, a strategy that allowed aristocracy to survive in England concurrently with the formation of bourgeois democracy.[21] Thus at the end of the nineteenth century, popular disillusionment below was rife while, above, the educated classes perceived a crisis of liberal democracy—which was, in the years leading up to the Great War, an object of strenuous criticism by everyone from Sorel and Charles Maurras to James Bryce and the English Distributists Hilaire Belloc and G. K. Chesterton (who, as orthodox Catholics, also rejected socialism as heresy).

Democracy, so maligned before 1914, was almost wholly discredited by the war that seemed to many people at the time to have wrecked European civilization. The German invasion of Belgium and immediate subsequent events were greeted with a huge and horrible enthusiasm by the peoples of every one of the warring nations. An immediate, all-pervasive thrill was perceptible, an electric excitement at the prospect of national communities fraternally united in full equality on behalf of a common heroic effort. The late French historian François Furet thought that four years of total warfare had created the mass-democratic nation-states of modern Europe. But after the armistice, despite the very real democratization that had occurred everywhere since 1914, postwar democracy seemed a tremendous letdown—almost as much a fraud as democracy's prewar instauration had been. Liberal democracy had been tried and found wanting by the horrific conflict that had so brutally ended an era of unprecedented material progress enlightened by the doctrine of materialism and the historical optimism with which that doctrine had been inseparably associated. After such horrors as world war entailed, life itself appeared to great numbers of people (and to the popular imagination itself) as the cruel denial of a beautiful illusion. (Juliet Nicolson, in her book *The Great Silence*, shows how fully Great Britain, and, by extension, the rest of Europe, comprehended the irreparable damage the war had wreaked on their civilization, and also the human soul.)[22] Socialism, on the other hand, had never been realized, or even conscientiously attempted, despite the enthusiasm for it since 1848; unlike democracy and liberalism, it had no record to have been compromised. And one could not say of socialism, as was said of democratic liberalism, that it had been complicit with capitalism—another institution discredited by the war.

Not just the classes, but the European masses as well, sensed the extent to which the old prewar societies had been destroyed and replaced by looser, less comfortable, and more uncertain ones. The intellectuals, for whom the postwar world was a type of betrayal, were particularly sensitive to what Harold Nicolson deplored as a Woolworth world dominated by a cheap and cheapening mass culture, for which the new democracy was chiefly responsible. Oswald Spengler claimed that the late medieval period had marked the zenith of Western civilization, from which, infected by liberalism and democracy, it had declined ever since. "What is best worth having," André Siegfried commented in 1928, "can be enjoyed only by a cultural aristocracy." It is hardly surprising that writers and artists should have looked back to what in retrospect seemed the golden decades of the prewar period for ideas susceptible of creative refurbishment. Roland Stromberg writes: "Postwar totalitarianism picked up its storehouse of ideas from pre-1914 writers: from aspects of Nietzsche, Sorel, Barrès, Maurras, Le Bon; Darwinists, futurists, Wagnerians, D'Annunzians; poets like Stefan George and William Butler Yeats, and many others whose common denomination was disgust with democratic (mass) culture and democratic (parliamentary) politics. They projected a sense of a gigantic crisis of civilization or authority, a feeling of 'all security gone,' as . . . Jacob Burckhardt had put it in 1878."[23]

Democracy's debased reputation allowed the two ideals that survived the political holocaust of war intact—socialism and nationalism—to be cannily yoked in a political persuasion—national socialism—that became the sole popular and efficient political system in the interwar period. Paradoxically, its success was facilitated by Germany's and Italy's early adherence to basic democratic practice and even democratic form. This made it possible to view national socialism as really another type of democracy, an alternative to the Anglo-Saxon variety with its parliaments and elections—a tribal organicism that looked back to the premodern communities Rousseau had praised and of which the ancient Nordic communities were examples.[24] At this point in the history of the twentieth century, however, a complicating political development in the history of democracy reappeared, one that had actually begun in Europe following the Age of Revolutions.

In the 1920s, the German National Socialists were popularly known as Nazi-Sozis. But it was not long before the "Sozi" element was overwhelmed by the "Nazi" one. This development crystallized a broader trend that had begun in Europe in the latter part of the previous century, one that was evidenced in what the historian John Lukacs has noted was a series of "wars between nations rather than struggles between classes." The nationalist aspect of the democratic urge that from the beginning had characterized democracy in America thus asserted itself within the European nations as well. Bismarck both understood and exploited this aspect, of which Marx had never dreamed, but it was Adolf Hitler who recognized that socialism, to succeed, must have a national, rather than an international, basis, reflecting the fact that sentiments related to national identity were stronger in the popular mind than resentments arising from class distinctions. (This truth had belatedly dawned on the Left during the Great War, when the proletariat chose enthusiastically to take up arms against the enemies of their country in preference to attempting to overthrow their governments and the ruling classes that comprised them.) For this reason, Hitler's nationalism was more attractive to the German peoples and to peoples outside Germany than was his socialism. "It was populist and popular," Lukacs noted. "It was thus that nationalists and populists in many countries and states rallied to Hitler's side both before and during the Second World War—at times against their own governments' struggles to maintain independence from Germany." The chief example of this was Austria. The alliance between nationalism and socialism that preceded World War II also succeeded it, while the continuing appeal of intense nationalist feeling today has brought about that strange phenomenon, the internationalist nationalist movement.[25]

The decade that followed World War II experienced no reaction against democracy comparable to that which came after the Great War. To the contrary: the mass democratic socialist system that during the interwar years replaced the liberal democracy of the pre–World War I era appeared to have been vindicated by its triumph over premodern democracy of the tribal sort. Nationalism, on the other hand, was almost fatally compromised among the states of western Europe by the hypernationalism that was blamed for the war (a war started by one man: Hitler), the terrors of the Third Reich, and the seedy criminality of Mussolini's regime.

Following the collapse of the Soviet Union, the opposite has been the case with the liberated countries of eastern Europe and western Asia, where the nationalist spirit has been both fervent and, owing to their unhappy history of subjugation by Moscow, unabashed. But in western Europe, the institutional embodiment of this reaction against nationalist enthusiasm, national loyalty, and the nation-state itself was achieved a little more than a decade after V-E Day, with the founding of the European Economic Community (EEC) by the Treaty of Rome in 1957. The EEC was the precursor of the European Union, established by the Maastricht Treaty of 1993, from which the peculiar notion of "democracy without nations" gradually arose.

Bertrand Russell agreed that America was an exceptional country, at least to this degree: unlike the nations of western Europe—England in particular—the United States, he thought, lacked strong institutions, descended from medieval times and forming the foundation of its freedoms.

Liberal Protestantism is in some sense a reversion to ancient Judaism; certainly the Jews' belief in themselves as the Chosen People is reflected in the Puritans' self-understanding as the divinely appointed founders of a "City upon a Hill."[26] The historian Perry Miller spoke of the "uniqueness of the American experience." Yet the Puritans in America were still Englishmen, natives or transplants from East Anglia or Holland, who sought only a remote home where they might practice their sectarian Christianity at a distance, beyond the reach of the Crown and the Church of England.[27]

Similarly, Hector St. John de Crèvecoeur was hardly the "new man" he has been said to have been, but a French aristocrat who returned from America eventually to live on his ancestral demesne in France. The American "revolutionists" justified their "revolution," if such it really were, by appealing to wholly English principles developed over centuries during the Glorious Revolution and the English, Scots, and French Enlightenments, and incorporated into English common law. Before 1865, most Americans were descended from British stock. On his visit to the United States, Tocqueville conceived his well-known maxim that the character of a people is more important than its institutions. Other visitors to America, chiefly from the British Isles, during the same period remarked that the Americans remained essentially British, though they seemed Britons of a ruder type. And the settlement of North America by the English, French, Spanish, and Dutch is a significant part of European, as well as American, history.

Mindful of all this, the British academic and journalist Godfrey Hodgson, a man who has lived many years in the States and written several books on American topics, recently wrote another about the basic unexceptionalism of America. The American colonists, he reminds us, belonged to a transatlantic world that had in common many intellectual, cultural, political, and social interests and preoccupations. When, a century and a half after the founding of Plymouth Colony, Tom Paine asserted that "the cause of America is in great measure the cause of all mankind," he was making a statement that was truly revolutionary in the context of British colonial history. The notion caught the fancy of the Revolutionary era, but it scarcely survived it: after winning independence, the colonists turned their attention largely to commercial enterprise, in which they seemed, even to themselves, not so exceptional at all. At least, they no longer talked about their exceptionalism so much. Following the War between the States, the idea of American exceptionalism enjoyed something of a revival; it flourished throughout the twentieth century, before merging with a still more expansive universalist ideal. But the concept of American exceptionalism has always been essentially a pleasant fiction, soothing to a portion of the American public and an inspiration (as well as a temptation) to certain of its more idealistic politicians. "An exceptionalist tradition," Hodgson concludes, "has exaggerated the differentness, the solipsistic character has been overstressed."[28]

Paradoxically, as Hodgson notes, to the degree that America ever *was* exceptional, it was so during the relatively idyllic republican period between the Revolution and the Age of Jackson, when Americans really did experience something like political and economic equality. But with incipient industrialism and the formation of an urban working class and a wealthy capitalist one, that began to change. After the war between North and South, the United States came rapidly to approximate the nations of Europe, as headlong industrialization produced the same social stratification, inequality of income, and class warfare that had always characterized Old World societies. America's will to empire, emerging about the middle of the nineteenth century, hastened and completed the convergence between the Old World and the New. The history of the United States between 1900 and 1950 (Hodgson argues) was "exceptional" only insofar as the country had been spared invasion by foreign armies and widespread destruction of the homeland between the two wars. So far from emerging from these conflicts with its economy in ruins—the fate of the European powers and of Japan—the United States realized a profit from President Wilson's war to make the world safe for democracy, and it wrested economic and military domination on a global scale from Franklin Roosevelt's war.

Finally, American exceptionalism has been insufficiently exceptional to withstand humanity's ages-old fascination with royalty. Benjamin Franklin supposed that "there is a natural inclination in mankind to kingly government." Franklin himself detoured from the Low Countries to London in September 1761 to witness the coronation of King George III, whose reign, he predicted at the time, would be happy and glorious. Nearly three decades later he repeated, on the floor of the Constitutional Convention, his belief in a natural human inclination to monarchy: "It sometimes relieves [men] from Aristocratic domination. They had rather have one tyrant than five hundred. It gives them more of the appearance of equality among citizens, and that they like."

The Founding generation was far more sympathetic to monarchy than their calculated denunciations of the British king suggested. John Adams thought that "limited monarchy is found in nature" and admitted that "Americans are particularly unfit for any Republic but the Aristo-Democratical Monarchy." Benjamin Rush predicted that the corruption of the people would probably make absolute monarchy necessary in the United States in a hundred years' time. Tom Paine considered Louis XVI of France a progressive agent, a "republican monarch," and thought kingly sovereignty to be compatible with republican government. George Bancroft reminded readers, in his highly popular *History of the United States (1864–75)*, that "neither Franklin, nor Washington, nor John Adams, nor Jefferson, nor Jay had ever expressed a preference for a republic. The voices that rose for independence, spoke also for alliances with kings. The sovereignty of George III was renounced, not because he was a king, but because he was deemed a tyrant." The men who drafted the U.S. Constitution may have paid little attention to the long struggle between King George and his ministers, which ended in a significant reduction of the royal power. Perhaps from neglect of this constitutional development, the Founders devised a plan of government that granted a good deal more power to the chief executive than the contemporary king of Great Britain enjoyed (a fact duly noted by the American Anti-Federalists). Indeed, many nineteenth-century observers (including Walter Bagehot and Henry Sumner Maine) on both sides of the Atlantic concluded that the United States was actually an elective monarchy disguised as a republic, while Great Britain had evolved into a republic concealed by the elaborate dress and ritual of monarchy.[29]

As early as 1793, the year of the regicide in Paris, Americans had laid aside much of their antipathy to George III; almost thirty years later, his death provoked considerable sympathy in the former colonies. Tocqueville, during his time in America, noted, "One scarcely encounters an American who does not owe something of his birth to the first founders of the colonies, and as for the offshoots of the great [English] families, America seems to me to be entirely covered with them." In the Jacksonian era, egalitarianism and universal suffrage induced second thoughts about the virtues of democracy among upper-class and cosmopolitan Americans. But it was the ascension of Victoria to the British throne in 1838 that produced a monarchical fever in America that reached its apogee in the reign of Edward VII, coincident with the heyday of the American plutocracy and the presidency of Theodore Roosevelt, who once described his office as that of an "elective king." Yet Victoria's appeal for Americans was of a very different sort from that of her son's. "The Queen's genius was to enhance the monarch as a symbol of constitutional rectitude, while associating royalty with the prevailing middle-class sentiments of the age," Frank Prochaska writes in *The Eagle and the Crown: Americans and the British Monarchy*. "Her religious upbringing accommodated the pieties of the day, and she was identified with the practical morality that was such a feature of the mid-nineteenth century in both Britain and America."[30]

After the Great War, the American passion for the royals entered a slow decline, owing in part to the fact that Americans descended from British stock were no longer the majority of the population. Still, the Duke and Duchess of Windsor, before and after the abdication, were great favorites in the United States, and King George VI's and Queen Elizabeth's state visit to the States in 1939 (the first by a reigning monarch) was welcomed as a major national event. In 1953, Queen Elizabeth's coronation equally enthralled the American public. By the time of the Prince of Wales's marriage to Lady Diana Spencer in 1981, however, American enthusiasm for the royal family had been significantly compromised by the cult of international celebrity, to which the phenomenon of Princess Di mania may be realistically attributed. Still and all, "No community worships hereditary rank and station like democracy"—as the novels of American writers from Mark Twain to Sinclair Lewis suggest.[31]

Americans' self-image as an exceptional people entrusted with an exclusive moral destiny and endowed with a rich material future has tended to inoculate them against the socialist virus. And so has socialism's internationalist character, unattractive or positively offensive to a proudly nationalist people whose nationalism has always been an expression of its sense of exceptionalism and the individualist form of democracy it embraces. Richard Hofstadter once remarked that the fate of the United States was not to have an ideology but to be one. If that were really so, ideology—"the American political tradition," as Hofstadter understood it—was a latecomer to American history, an idea that began to take form and substance in the United States after World War II, owing mostly to the efforts of liberal intellectuals like Professor Hofstadter himself. (In fact, Hofstadter's "American political tradition" is hardly seamless and continuous as he imagined it, but rather fractured and incoherent.)[32]

Right from the beginning, the nationalist impulse strove with the spirit of Washington's Farewell Address for dominance in the early American Republic. Thomas Jefferson declared in 1806 that "our constitution is a peace establishment—it is not calculated for war," yet Jefferson's unconstitutional Louisiana Purchase, only three years before, has been called the death knell of republicanism. On the eve of the War of 1812, President James Madison, concerned about the centralization of power, worked to restrict the government's war-making prerogatives. "John Adams wrote Jefferson that Madison's administration was glorious," the essayist J. O. Tate observes, adding that the historian Gordon S. Wood "insists that [Madison's] conception of war and government, whether we agree with it or not, might help us understand better the world we have lost."[33] "All. All dead," Jefferson himself wrote in 1825. "And ourselves left alone amidst a new generation whom we know not, and who know not us." The Founders in their later years were painfully conscious that their time had passed into history and that the classically virtuous republic they had created was rapidly growing into something different.

But democracy, even in early nineteenth-century America, was more popular than republicanism. The War of 1812 was popular everywhere outside New England, and a pugnacious nationalism, carrying a frontier chip on its shoulder, pervaded the country. Jacksonian democracy had an undeniable messianic strain that included socialist aspects, however much these were overemphasized by Arthur Schlesinger Jr. in *The Age of Jackson*. Yet no socialist party of national, or even regional, importance developed before the War between the States, despite the number of working-class associations that viewed American politics in terms of European class warfare.[34]

Clyde Wilson, an American historian and Calhoun scholar, proposes that "the history of national politics up to 1861 is largely the history of a holding action against the 'American System'"—against the federal government's promotion of a program of corporate welfare intended to generate private profit through the establishment of bank charters, tariffs, and grants.[35] But opposition to that system was offered on republican and democratic, free-enterprise, capitalist, and regional principles—not socialist ones. The suffrage was extended to all adult white males during Andrew Jackson's presidency, a period in which the nation as a whole was preoccupied with the nationalist project of territorial expansion in the South and West. Indeed, the national government, anticipating Mexico's hostile reaction and the possibility of economic retaliation by Great Britain, annexed the young Republic of Texas with some reluctance.

The term *manifest destiny* was coined by a newspaper editor in the summer of 1845, during the debate on adding Texas to the Union, and popularized, along with the slogan "Fifty-Four Forty or Fight," some months later in the course of Washington's dispute with Britain over the disposition of the Oregon Territory. After the Mexican War, the Treaty of Guadalupe Hidalgo, concluded in 1848, added the present states of California, Nevada, Arizona, and Utah, and also parts of Wyoming, Colorado, and New Mexico, to the United States. These new states plus Texas, to which Mexico ceded all claims north of the Rio Grande, amounted to a total of 1,193,061 square miles. In the 1850s, expansionists made unsuccessful attempts to annex Cuba, and Commodore Perry persuaded the Japanese to establish trade relations with the United States. Expansionism was not primarily an ideological project, but it was in certain ways a substitute for one. And it engaged the enthusiasm of the young democracy, partly for reasons of nationalist sentiment but also, more important, on account of the opportunities it offered a burgeoning population: opportunities for land, for entrepreneurship, and for simple adventure. American democracy before 1861 felt no need for a theoretical "order of equality" when the very real "order of egoism" offered—and produced—benefits for almost everyone. What is more, the vast, wide-open expanse of suddenly available territory alleviated demographic, social, and political pressures in the old cities of the East, thus relieving tensions of the sort that encouraged radical democratic and socialist ideas in the great European capitals.

After 1865, the reunited nation faced the tasks of settling, securing, and developing the vast territories it had acquired before Fort Sumter and of expanding the industrial base and transportation system it had developed during the war years. All this was to be the country's chief preoccupation for the next three decades. The expansionist period, for the time being, had largely ended; now a more self-consciously nationalist one commenced, strengthened and enlarged by a spirit of triumphant patriotism engendered by the restoration of the continental Union after a catastrophic civil war. The victory of the Union forces in the field was presented as a triumph for democracy as well as for union, and so was the tremendous industrial expansion that had defeated the Confederacy. American politics in the era of Reconstruction and during the Gilded Age horrified the Northern radicals of the Civil War period and before. They had expected to see slavery give way to democracy at last; instead, they were forced to witness the ugliness of the new industrial capitalism and the corruption of politics by a rising plutocracy. But if an American democrat found nothing to boast of in the economic or the political state of his country, he could take pride at least in the burgeoning wealth and power of the new Prometheus unbound. Henry Adams and Mark Twain were appalled by the new nation; Horace Greeley was thrilled.

After 1865, the hegemony of the Grand Old Party had four great consequences. First, owing to the postwar constitutional amendments, the states, which for Jefferson had been "the best bulwarks of our liberties," had ceased to be subsovereignties within the federal system, endowed with the authority to defend their citizens against encroachments by the newly empowered federal government. Second, the government in Washington was transformed into a dynamo designed for the transfer of wealth from the American people to vast capitalist enterprises whose captains preferred ententes cordiales and flagrant bribery of government officials to rugged individualism and fair competition—a resurrection, enhancement, and refinement of the antebellum American System. (John D. Rockefeller referred to free-market economists as "academic Know-Nothings.") Third, American political discourse devolved from rough public argument and frank congressional debate into lofty moralistic abstractions and vulgar slogans for consumption by a mass electorate, devised by government literary hacks.

Finally, there was the spoils system, exponentially expanded since 1865. Distracted by the Indian wars on the frontier and the dramatic events associated with the settlement of the western territories, American democrats—indeed, most Americans—failed to perceive how, under a regime of industrialism and government by plutocracy, the United States was becoming, in terms of economic, social, and political equality, increasingly like Europe. This convergence had partly to do with the growing interdependency of America and the European

powers. England, by itself, underwrote the bulk of American industrial development in the latter half of the nineteenth century, in particular the extension of the western railroads. Nevertheless, between
1865 and 1917, the altered conditions of American life were effectively obscured by the gilded myth of American freedom and popular
democracy. This myth, promoted by nationalist aggression and the
beginnings of empire, helped to hold socialism at arm's length in the
United States, despite the waves of immigrants who arrived to form
a new, vast, and importunate labor force for the new corporate state,
depressing industrial wages.[36] "Gilded Age politics induces pertinent
despair about democracy," Jack Beatty writes in *The Age of Betrayal: The
Triumph of Money in America, 1865–1900*.[37] Beatty's subject, by impli-
cation, is as much the new gilded age at the start of the twenty-first
century as it is Mark Twain's. In the late nineteenth century, however,
the despair to which he refers was characteristic less of the burgeoning
American proletariat than of the upper-middle, and largely professional, classes.

Werner Sombart, a distinguished German economist and sociologist of the period, asserted flatly that socialism failed to take hold in
the United States. The Populists are a case in point. The People's (or
Populist) Party reached its political peak in the 1890s, electing members of Congress and state legislators largely from the Great Plains, the
South, and the West, but the party declined rapidly after the first two
failed presidential candidacies of William Jennings Bryan of Nebraska.
Populists have been described as socialists of a sort, but in fact they
were no such thing. Populism—an agrarian, not an industrial, movement—wished to re-create the rough equality of economic and social
conditions that had existed in the early years of the Republic—from
1789 until the 1830s, which, as we have seen, was the only period in
the history of the United States when the country may actually have
been in some sense exceptional among the nations of the world.

The Socialist Party of America was founded in 1901, five years after
Bryan's most famous campaign for the presidency. But socialism—or
perhaps one should say the idea of social democracy—in the United

States was developed not from a revolutionary movement or even a working-class one but rather from a spirit of ethical reform cultivated by the upper-middle class.[38] Unlike European socialism, Progressivism (so quintessentially American in nature) was a nationalist movement, not an internationalist one; indeed, it never really thought of itself as "socialist" at all. The lead-up to the Spanish-American War prompted widespread debate in the United States on the question of whether forcibly imposing democracy on a foreign nation was a defensible act on the part of a great democratic nation. In the end, Theodore Roosevelt (a personally great man whose determination to reinvent the United States of America in the image of himself ensured a disastrous political legacy) got his war with Spain, and President William McKinley's administration acquired Guam, the Philippines, and Puerto Rico for the United States. As president, Roosevelt engineered Panama's independence from Colombia and proclaimed the Roosevelt Corollary to the Monroe Doctrine, declaring that the United States had the right to interfere in the Western Hemisphere where it perceived "chronic wrongdoing" or hurtful "impotence." In this way, Roosevelt mobilized the powerful internal state created by Lincoln and consolidated in the decades since the War between the States to establish an American imperial presence overseas.

Almost twenty years later, President Woodrow Wilson's social-democratic-progressive administration had no moral scruples (it did have a few political ones) in committing the United States to a European war for the stated purpose of making the world safe for democracy. Shortly after his election in 1912, Wilson had explained to the chairman of the Democratic Party that God Himself had made him president of the United States. In that divinely appointed role, Wilson worked to strengthen and expand the reach of the federal government through the Sixteenth Amendment (Lincoln had imposed the first federal income tax) and the Seventeenth Amendment, which, by introducing the direct election of U.S. senators, greatly reduced the power of the state legislators to influence congressional politics, thereby further weakening the federalist principle.

In foreign policy, Wilson showed his hand early in his presidency when he stated, "Since trade ignores national boundaries and the manufacturer insists on having the world as a market, the flag of his nation must follow him, and the doors of the nations which are closed against him must be battered down. Concessions obtained by financiers must be safeguarded by ministers of state, even if the sovereignty of unwilling nations be outraged in the process. Colonies must be obtained or planted, in order that no useful corner of the world may be overlooked or left unused." In 1914, Wilson, adopting a somewhat more idealistic tone, announced, "It is America's duty and privilege to stand shoulder to shoulder to lift the burdens of mankind in the future and show the path of freedom to all the world. America is henceforth to stand for the assertion of the right of one nation to serve the other nations of the world." To that end, the president went as far as he could toward striking down the First Amendment, made government censorship legal by means of the Espionage Act of 1917 and criticism of himself and his war illegal under the Sedition Act the following year. H. L. Mencken, a passionate enemy of Wilson's ("the perfect model of a Christian cad," he called him), concluded that democracy must be a self-devouring, as well as a self-limiting, phenomenon: "One cannot observe it objectively without being impressed by its curious distrust of itself—its apparently ineradicable tendency to abandon its whole philosophy at the first sign of strain."[39]

The peacetime reaction in America to the Great War, though superficially similar to that in Europe after the armistice, in fact differed substantially from it, mainly in the reaction of disillusioned artists and intellectuals (Gertrude Stein's "lost generation") in the twenties and Marxist ones (chiefly the same people, after taking a political step or two to the Left) in the thirties. Many of the lost generation moved to Europe, where Hemingway discovered that the American malaise was a phenomenon endemic to the West (he planned *The Sun Also Rises* as a pastiche of "The Wasteland"). Others stayed home—including Mencken, who professed to enjoy the ludicrous but nevertheless invigorating spectacle of democracy, which he defined as "the theory that the plain people know what they want, and deserve to get it good and hard." "All the [democratic] paradoxes," he claimed, "resolve themselves into thundering paradoxes, many amounting to downright contradictions in terms. The mob is competent to rule the rest of us—but it must be rigorously policed itself. There is a government, not of men, but of laws—but men are set on benches to decide finally what the law is and may be. The highest function of the citizen is to serve the state—but the first assumption that meets him, when he essays to discharge it, is an assumption of his disingenuousness and dishonor."[40]

For the rest, the armistice, so far from discrediting representative democracy and industrial capitalism in the view of the American public, vindicated and exalted them as the two institutions that, between them, had defeated the Central Powers, rescued democracy from the Old World Order, and elevated the United States to the status of superpower. Americans understood this "democracy" to mean not socialism, nor even liberalism, but American nationalism, a native-grown answer to the forms of national socialism ascendant in Europe. With the onset of the Great Depression, American democracy converged in some degree toward the British variant of social democracy—but, in the mind of the average citizen, in practice only, not in theory. This example of collective split-mindedness explains how President Franklin D. Roosevelt succeeded in imposing his thoroughgoing democratic-socialist agenda on the country. Yet it explains as well why not even the fraternal patriotic solidarity engendered by the New Deal and World War II succeeded in transforming the individualistic American people into enthusiastic, conscious, and professing socialists.

From 1945 down to the second decade of the twenty-first century, the socialist-democratic versus nationalist-ideological divide between the European countries and the United States has widened—never mind that America, in the past half century, has confirmed its essentially socialist nature without having ever admitted doing so. During the Cold War and throughout the Vietnam War, the United States maintained a passive-aggressive attitude of containment. Beginning, however, with Ronald Reagan's first administration and continuing with the consolidation of his neoconservative advisers' influence in his second one, defensive democracy evolved into offensive democracy. Three presidential administrations later, George W. Bush refurbished offensive democracy as messianic democratism—modified by a strain of virulent nationalism embodied in the Bush Doctrine, which asserted the right of the United States to launch a preemptive military attack anywhere in the world.

Developments in America have been paralleled on the eastern side of the Atlantic by the socialization of the European nations and by their integration into the European Union (EU). From the beginning, the EU was inspired by more or less conventional socialist principles, ideas, and politics—most of all, perhaps, by socialist bureaucracy. But whereas its architects frequently describe the union as a political and economic counterbalance to the United States, European nationalism is hardly its operative principle, but rather the opposite. The EU is the institutional embodiment of the European elites' profound ambivalence toward the historical identities of their respective countries, in their minds fatally compromised by the Continental dictatorships of the 1930s and the ensuing global war. "Pure" democracy, European politicians have concluded, can be conscientiously realized only through supranational bureaucracy, untainted by national, ethnic, and cultural peculiarities and prejudices. Yet, as Pierre Manent inconveniently but correctly points out, abstractions like "democracy" are meaningless when removed from the historic contexts that produced them. "Pure" democracy has nothing to do with democracy at all. It is nothing but a static and impotent bureaucracy based on a code of rights and regulations, powerless to engage in the active and effective political life it would deny.

In the United States, the champions of global democracy tied to the hegemonic status of America are prepared, for the sake of realizing their ideological dream, to deprive the American people of what remains of their living democracy at home. In Europe, the proponents of democratic socialism busy themselves with a project that would achieve the destruction of the European democracies by destroying the nation-states that gave rise to them.

Since the Second World War, the United States and the nations of Europe have converged in their domestic policies—as the United States has become a progressively socialized society—while diverging in their foreign policies, as American nationalism has intensified and the European countries have sought to banish or bury nationalist identities. If today we in the West are all socialists now, the American people stand forward as the First World's most aggressive nationalists. Their hypernationalism has two causes. The first is the cherished belief that they and their country are indeed something new under the sun. The second is that "democracy" is the highest social, political, and moral good, and that it is, therefore, a thing of universal value and application throughout the world.

Thomas Paine thought that "the cause of America is in a great measure the cause of all mankind." Lincoln called the United States "the last, best hope of earth." And Thomas Jefferson spoke of the enlarging United States as "an empire of liberty." During the early history of the country, democracy was thus identified variously with political independence, with nationalism, and with empire. The next and final step was to identify it with universalism. In the past several decades, that step has been taken, the threshold crossed. But America's is a form of universalism that is founded on, and propelled by, a kind of nationalist mania.

During the nineteenth century the United States enjoyed, without having to work for it, an influence on Europe generally, and Great Britain in particular, that impressed on foreign observers at a distance, as well as foreign imitators, a sense of democratic destiny in some ways more coherent even than the Americans' own conviction of an inevitable democratic future.[41] Victorian England, seemingly so complacent, beneath its even surface was an unstable society seething with conflicting social standards and competing classes, each of which, from top to bottom, understood very well the significance of the exemplary New World democracy three thousand miles to the west.[42] This was true especially during Andrew Jackson's presidency, when English conservatives attributed the Reform Act of 1832 directly to the extension of universal suffrage in the young American republic.[43] Sir John Morley, a Gladstonian Liberal, in his refutation of Maine's *Popular Government* noted that the "success of popular government across the Atlantic has been the strongest incentive to the extension of popular government here."[44] Eighty years later, Wyndham Lewis, the English painter, novelist, and critic, stated: "The influence America has exerted all along upon England is enormous; a fact that is generally forgotten. England would not be the place it is today had there been no America. Almost certainly there would be no social-democratic government at this time—no Mr. Atlee or Mr. Bevin—but some regime such as the Dutch still have, or like that obtaining in Hungary prior to the war."[45] In 1917, President Wilson took an infinitely long step away from the principle of national influence through distant example by embracing the principle of force at a distance instead. Following World War II, the United States, while invoking the power of example, scarcely bothered to conceal the fact that another, more direct, power stood in waiting behind it.

The Cold War made the word *democracy* a household term.[46] Because the recent global conflict had been billed in the West as a struggle between "undemocratic" totalitarianism and liberalism, "liberalism" in the postwar era was synonymous with "democracy," despite the fact that certain of the postwar dictatorships claimed to be "people's democracies" themselves.[47] In this way "democracy" became a highly charged as well as an overly familiar word, and both the Soviet Union and the West were at pains to present the Cold War as a confrontation between representative democracy and communist democracy. Hans Morgenthau and George Kennan (also Kennan's friend and admirer, the young historian John Lukacs, a refugee from communist Hungary) deplored American politicians' insistence on viewing in ideological terms what was essentially a classic balance-of-power rivalry. Their protests went largely unheeded. Democratic nations have typically leaned toward a moralistic foreign policy that disdains international power politics, with its pursuit of national interest, as an aristocratic game, and so these men's realistic understanding of the politics of the Cold War failed to appeal to an aroused American public, while falling considerably short of supplying the political stimuli and emotional cues their government required. So it was that the apocalyptic view of the standoff between East and West remained largely unchallenged.

In reference to the forty-year period between 1960 and 2000, Godfrey Hodgson argues, the public philosophy of Americans evolved to reflect the character of their exceptionalism. From the 1950s on, Hodgson suggests, Americans learned to regard their supposed commitment to capitalist economics as a crucial element in whatever it is that makes them exceptional. Thus the American public has come to accept material prosperity, military strength, and national prestige as being not only as important as freedom but actually identical with it.[48] Hodgson's view agrees with "order of egoism" critique of Western democracy since the French Revolution, which holds that the "order of equality" has been steadily overwhelmed and finally defeated by selfish individualism.

During the 1950s, a widening divide developed between the confident—even propagandistic—assertion of the value of democracy put forward by Western governments (the American government especially) and the increasingly uncertain commitment to modern capitalist democracy among the intellectual class, many of whom believed, as the Columbia philosopher Charles Frankel expressed it, that "all human social ideals have been rendered irrelevant" by a rationalist, mass technological society. Establishment liberal intellectuals—"his Majesty's dogs at Kew"—like Arthur M. Schlesinger Jr. and John Kenneth Galbraith were almost entirely comfortable and at ease with what Schlesinger called "the vital center," even if the order of egoism evolved around that center.

Many other liberals, perhaps less egocentric than they, were less comfortable. "In the past," Frankel wrote (in a book intended as an explicit defense of democracy), "the United States was a contagion. The distinction, the quality that set it apart, was that it was a society moved by its prospects. The sense that American democracy has a prospect—that its future does not consist simply in rolling with the punches of its adversaries or in expanding the present source of afflu-ence still further—is most obviously absent from the present scene."[49] Modern society, Professor Frankel thought, is "an experience in dissatisfaction, a wager on the benefits of discontent."[50] Only a few years after his book appeared in 1962, quiet skepticism regarding the accomplishment of liberal democracy was overwhelmed by the cul-tural and political tsunami set in motion the New Left, which, fifty years later, has still not entirely subsided from the immense territory it flooded and drowned. The New Left was—it still is, insofar as it survives as an element of advanced liberalism and the multicultural-ist ideology—ferociously antidemocratic in thought and in practice. Although in its Gallic incarnation it failed in 1968 to bring down the government of President Charles De Gaulle, in America it succeeded in routing two presidential administrations and changing American politics forever. Nevertheless, Washington, though rocked by the physical and emotional violence of the antiwar movement, was too committed to both its millenarian mission and its imperial ambition to abandon either of them.

Before President Richard Nixon's retreat from Vietnam, Ameri-can foreign policy had been a combination of defensive and aggressive elements, more or less in equal parts and representing hegemonic real-politik and democratist idealism in about equal measure. That changed during the presidency of Jimmy Carter as the administration veered in the opposite direction by adhering to an internationalist policy that proudly eschewed the pursuit of any strictly national interest abroad at all.[51] But, after four years of failure—the most spectacular of which was the hostage fiasco in Iran—Carter's Quakerish millenarianism was reversed by the newly assertive, often aggressive, and occasionally ideological policies of President Reagan and his ambassador to the United Nations, Jeane Kirkpatrick.

Reagan's determination abroad has been widely credited with achieving the collapse of the Soviet Union more than a decade after he was elected president in 1980. That is a great oversimplification of a huge, and hugely complex, historical event. It is clear, on the other hand, that Reagan's toughness and the demise of the USSR inspired the development of evangelical democracy through three successive presidential administrations, beginning with George H. W. Bush's New World Order, continuing with Bill Clinton's military counter-crusade in the Balkans, and culminating in George W. Bush's catastrophic attempts at nation building in Afghanistan and Iraq and his conflation of democratist ideology and ultranationalist patriotism. (The most striking example of this was the second President Bush's declaration that democracy is a human right whose global reification is not simply a priority of American foreign policy but the destiny of America itself, the revealed reason for its historical existence.)[52]

In the wake of the attack on the World Trade Center on September 11, 2001, global democracy was transformed from "a heraldic value" to "a key political weapon," according to John Dunn.[53] That may be, perhaps, an extreme statement—but only in the sense of being an extremely fair one. In an address to the National Endowment for Democracy in Washington, months after he ordered the invasion of Iraq, Bush asserted, "The advance of freedom is the calling of our time; it is the calling of our country. From the Fourteen Points to the Four Freedoms, to the Speech at Westminster, America has put our power at the service of principle. We believe that liberty is the design of nature; we believe that liberty is the direction of history. We believe that human fulfillment and excellence come in the responsible exercise of liberty. And we believe that freedom—the freedom we prize—is not for us alone, it is the right and capacity of all mankind."[54] "We need," wrote William Kristol—the editor of the neoconservative

Weekly Standard and a staunch supporter of the Bush administration's foreign adventures—"to err on the side of being strong, and, if people want to say we're an imperial power, fine."[55] Thus modern American nationalism is compatible, even interchangeable, with the cause of internationalism, provided only that the American imperial power is a benign one.

Europe's approach to extending democracy throughout the world, by comparison with American activism, is "quietist," yet its aim is similar: the promotion of democratic world empire. "We do not reflect enough," Pierre Manent observes, "on the singular fact that we [Europeans] are the first people who wish to submit all the aspects of the world to a single principle. Even though this principle is that of liberty, the project itself nonetheless has something tyrannical about it."[56]

Can liberty really be a single principle, and still be liberty? That is the great question for our own, hyperdemocratic time.

Part II

Democracy and Civilization

✦ ✦ ✦

4

What Is Democracy?

For Francis Fukuyama, liberal capitalist democracy is the high-est, most humanly fulfilling, and historically favored form of gov-ernment, likely to endure in fact and as ideal so far as the prophetic eye can see. Of course, democracy's worth can be evaluated only by comparison with the virtues inherent in those other possible forms of government, which appear to be limited. Walter Bagehot listed four: the parliamentary, the presidential, the hereditary, and the dictatorial, or revolutionary, systems. To these we may add the modern corpo-rate state, exemplified by China and Russia and toward which the United States seems to be tending, and ideological totalitarianism, which Hannah Arendt called the last political form of government to have been devised since nationalism. Of his four types of government, Bagehot clearly considered the first two to be democratic in essence. But what *is* democracy?

The question is unanswerable: there is no longer (if indeed there ever were) an agreed-on definition or description of this historically odd political system that began as an ideal, developed into an idol, and has now become an international commodity of sorts. During the past two centuries, the word *democracy* has grown increasingly elastic: ever more subjective, relativistic, and impressionistic, until today it is really a sort of Rorschach blot. Most recently, it has fallen victim to the verbal dishonesty Orwell condemned when he warned that, when words lose their meaning, men lose their freedom. What has happened to *democracy* is the same thing as has befallen the word *marriage*: both nowadays are applied in a manner that ignores, even defies, the original intended meaning of the term. Democracy is perhaps most easily defined by what it is not; yet what it is not is very often what it is called. Bertrand de Jouvenel thought democracy to be so indefinite a term as to make every attempt to define it futile.[1]

"Democracy," said G. K. Chesterton, "is the enthronement of the ordinary man; if it is not that, what is it?" C. S. Lewis reduced democracy to the practice of voting. The twentieth-century French philosopher Jacques Ellul argued that the word was meaningless if not based on a notion of "complete individual liberty." Samuel P. Huntington followed Joseph Schumpeter in thinking that democracy is basically procedural (though Schumpeter also dismissed it as rule by the politician); for the American scholar Robert Dahl it is a matter of contestation and participation. Christopher Lasch called democracy a description of the therapeutic state. "Populism," he added, "is the authentic voice of democracy." The political scientist and sociologist Alan Wolfe understands democracy as individual self-fulfillment, facilitated by government. The British political theorist John Dunn defines it as political authority wielded through the persuasion of the larger number and observes that Athenian democracy was heavily dependent on that political art. An American Europeanist, Roland Stromberg, holds that modern democracy amounts to an insistence on personal liberties, or what in the nineteenth century was called liberalism. The eminent political scientist Kenneth Minogue associates it with what he calls "politico-moral" thinking in search of collective social salvation, and a transforming ideal of social life. And the late philosopher John Rawls insisted that political liberty, or "democracy," depends on each citizen's enjoying a fair opportunity to hold public office and to exert an influence in political decisions.[2]

A problem, noted by Pierre Manent, is that the principle of democracy fails to specify an operational framework for itself. Hence, the question is whether democracy indicates a type of government or simply a set of political values, or whether it might be considered a secondary result of other, nonpolitical, activities. One might conclude either that democracy is an expression of modernity or that the two are the same thing. (Father John Courtney Murray in the 1950s described communism as political modernity pressed to its logical conclusion, however unintentionally.) I suggest that "democracy" has become a never-ending attempt, based on the conviction that the politically impossible is actually being realized, to square the circle. "Democracy," really, is no longer a political concept at all; it is shorthand for universal human bliss. So *democracy* today is simply a synonym for *utopia*.

Original definitions, being root definitions, are significant. Plato meant by democracy "a state in which the poor, gaining the upper hand, kill some and banish others, and then divide the offices among the remaining citizens equally, usually by lot." Aristotle described it as a perversion of government of the many, in which the constitution or polity had been diverted from a concern for the general welfare to a sole regard for the wants and interests of the needy. After the ancient philosophers, the classical republican statesmen and writers are worth consulting on the matter—in particular the American Founders, who agreed with James Madison that a democracy is the political constitution established by a society few enough in numbers to allow each member of the polity a direct and personal voice in deciding public questions, and confined to a commensurate territorial jurisdiction. Hence, according to the Founders' understanding, the government they sought to establish was a republic and not a democracy at all. (Owing to their deliberate intent to exclude the majority of ordinary people from fully democratic participation in the affairs of government, the Constitutional Convention was, in truth, more Aristotelian than it is usually given credit for being.)

In the end, no one, perhaps, has better defined or described democracy in terms more widely acceptable to the average democrat than James Bryce, the British scholar and warm advocate of democratic government, as it existed in North America in the late nineteenth and early twentieth centuries especially. "Where the will of the whole people," he wrote, "prevails in all important matters, even if it has some retarding influences to overcome, or is legally required to act for some purposes in some specially provided manner, that may be called democracy."[3] (Bryce's description of the democrat himself is touching in its simplicity: "a person of a simple and friendly spirit and genial manners, 'a good mixer,' one who, whatever his wealth or status, makes no assumption of superiority and carefully keeps himself on the level of his poorer and less eminent neighbors.")[4] One is tempted to add "and where the freedom of every citizen is preserved from abuse of power," yet the theoretical and historical grounds for the extension do not exist. Montesquieu warned against the error of confusing the power of the people with the liberty of the people, and he was right to do so. Jouvenel thought that the confusion between the two lay at the root of modern despotism. For democracy, of itself, is neither liberal nor conservative. It is perfectly possible for the democratic state to frame an illiberal society, as was the case with Germany under the Third Reich, when "democracy" was for German Aryans only. This is but one reason why *freedom* and *democracy* are today almost meaningless words.

The ultimate definition of democracy, I believe, is that it is a false religion—a proposition I shall consider at length further on in this book. For now, we note simply that "democracy" is a form of government based on faith. "The sole fact that liberalism is against what it recognizes as religious," the contemporary scholar J. Budziszewski notes, "need not prevent it from being a religion—provided that it does not perceive what it is."[5]

✦　　✦　　✦

Is democracy the best possible form of government? The answer depends, of course, on what one means by "best," and the extent to which this "best" is actually attainable.

A contemporary writer observes that liberals, socialists, and conservatives today alike recognize the "implausibility" of constructing a regime the principles of which would have offended the men who made the French Revolution.[6] One might argue that the "order of egoism" that inspires every Western regime today would be offensive to those revolutionaries, but it is certainly true that no Western politician, and few outside the West, dare insult the democratic ideal in whatever form it has assumed within their respective societies. Yet many democrats (though hardly ever politicians), understanding that democratic institutions are of less value than the broader elements that comprise civilized society, recognize democracy as a means, not an end. Roland Stromberg has suggested that nobody could approve the establishment of evil by democratic consensus, or hesitate to establish good by undemocratic means, in circumstances in which everyone understood the meaning of these two things.

Orestes Brownson aptly perceived that to every true philosopher there is something divine in the state—no God, no politics, he thought—and so the question regarding the "best" government is, fundamentally, a theological one.[7] This is not to say that there is a single "correct" answer to the question. Brownson believed that all systems, as constructs of human beings who are themselves creatures of God, necessarily contain an element of truth; further, he thought it impossible to identify a constitution fit for all peoples in every time. Pitirim Sorokin, the Russian-born American sociologist, writing from the standpoint of the Second World War, denied that any human institution—whether capitalism or socialism, communism or totalitarianism, private or commonly held property, individualism or collectivism, aristocracy or democracy, centralism or federalism—has absolute value, maintaining that each of these things, in turn, might, in certain historical circumstances, be valueless and even socially harmful.[8] Monarchy is ordinarily assumed to be antidemocratic, yet many monarchies, including the British monarchy, have been highly developed democracies, just as modern democracies, such as the United States, as we have seen, have functioned as informal monarchies.

It is unreasonable and unrealistic to suppose that there is but one form of government by which to govern a people aptly and fairly, as it would be unreasonable to argue that there is one way only to compose a symphony, or to compose a novel or a poem, or to write this book. The right government, Brownson argued, must arise from the general conditions of a people, as Tocqueville thought the American federal government had—if only the people will allow themselves to be guided by Providence.

Still, general conditions and circumstances are determinative, and wise statesmen will regard them as such. Establishing democratic government in Russia is a difficult task. Equally difficult, as Walter Bagehot recognized, is the work of founding a deferential nation among a people for whom social deference is not a habit and a tradition. Yet Bagehot believed a country of "respectful poor" far better suited for cabinet government (in his opinion, the best kind) because, in a respectful country, the polity makes use of the best classes, whereas, in a country in which every man considers himself the equal of every other, the worst alone are available for the practical purpose of governing. Bagehot admitted that, under deferential rule, the poor are less happy. He believed also, however, that the lower classes in England did not blame their misery on the English political system, which, combined with a hierarchical social order, provided them with "the theatrical show of society." The royal court was in part the people's entertainment but also something far more profound. Bagehot called it visibility. "Royalty," he wrote in a famous passage, "is a government in which the attention of the nation is concentrated on one person doing interesting actions. A Republic is a government in which that attention is divided between many, who are all doing uninteresting actions. Accordingly, so long as the human heart is strong and the human reason weak, royalty will be strong because it appeals to diffused feeling, and Republics weak because they appeal to understanding."[9]

Even after the Reform Bill of 1832, British suffrage was hugely restricted by comparison with that of the United States, where universal suffrage (white males twenty-one years of age or older) was realized during Andrew Jackson's presidency. Yet Britons, in other respects, were as free as Americans, thanks to the same tradition of the rights of Englishmen in whose name the colonists had fought the crown—and freer than any other people in Europe, enjoying liberties in respect of meeting and association, the press (though with restrictions), free speech, habeas corpus, the assumption of the inviolability of a man's home, and so forth.

The terms *republic* and *democracy* are often conflated. In reality, they are so far from being synonymous that Claude Polin argues that, from the classical point of view, the two things are actually opposites, a republic being properly understood as "the unity of a diversity," striking a balance between private and public, local and central, interests. Republican citizens are not shareholders in their society; they are more than the sum of their own private interests. They are truly independent, yet they do not value their individual freedom more than their membership in the community. A republic is a middle-class society founded on an agrarian tradition that does not hold one man's living at the expense of another man. A republic is a city or community on the small scale, limited to a size that permits its citizens familiarity with one another. Lastly, a republic is characterized by minimum government, in whose actions the citizens consent without necessarily participating directly in public decisions; whose organization is spontaneous; and whose governors are morally and intellectually prominent people. Clearly, such a polity cannot reasonably be equated with what we moderns, from the time of the French Revolution, have called democracy.[10]

Today the American Old Right wishes a return to the republican form of government that prevailed at the Founding and for a generation thereafter. Do free and civilized alternatives to the mass democracies of modern times really exist? "A people," Bagehot observed, "*never* hears censure of itself." Short of historical catastrophe, a democracy will never cede what it has managed to acquire through long struggle, or the struggle of its self-proclaimed leaders.[11] Democracy, among democrats, is overwhelmingly assumed to be just. But is it so in fact? The New Left always insisted otherwise, but not the New Left alone. "The idea of justice," John Dunn suggests, "and the idea of democracy fit very precariously together."[12]

Democracy has benefited greatly from having long been regarded as the equivalent of liberalism and, through that connection, equated with the idea of social justice. In the nineteenth century, it was possible to be, like Tocqueville and the other aristocratic liberals, a good liberal without being a democrat as well. Since World War I, however, liberalism has been conflated with democracy, which in the process has been transformed into the ideology of democratism. There is now simply no recognized distinction between the two, yet it is actually the first which has succeeded in appropriating the other. One can have democracy without liberalism, surely. But can one have liberalism without democracy?

This was once an interesting speculative question; in the present era of what has been called "advanced liberalism," the question has been answered.[13] And that answer is plain to see. If the project of global democracy should ever be realized, the result will really be the establishment of global liberalism, which is only a reassuring term for global tyranny of a kind that no country—not the British Empire, not the Soviet Union, not the United States of America—has ever succeeding in imposing on humanity.

The modern liberal state is identical with the managerial society, whose rise was first described and analyzed by James Burnham in *The Managerial Revolution*, published in 1941. As Burnham recognized, and as his astute student the late Samuel T. Francis has explained at length, managerial liberalism is not a coherent political philosophy but rather the ideology of a distinct class of men invested with multiple self-seeking interests. It is, further, the product and expression of the social and political arrangements underlying modernity—of the modern scientific and technological world, and of the realities of mass democracy. More fundamentally, it lies at the heart of the Faustian project aimed at subjugating and controlling the natural world, human nature, and human society by means of scientific technique in particular and rationality generally, while uprooting custom and banishing religion to the wholly private realm to which it and other superstitious and irrational relics are, under the new dispensation, consigned. In the past three decades, managerial liberalism has been supplanted by advanced liberalism, for which power is the supreme good, the measure of every social and human value. "How can an order be liberal . . . in which social planners reconstruct morality, or democratic, if government reconstitutes a people it finds lacking?" asks James Kalb. "Nonetheless, such transformations have been brought about by the same principles that have always made liberalism what it is."[14]

Those principles reinforce, and justify, the inevitable development of what Jouvenel called simply "Power." By this process Power, no matter its social basis and ideology, seeks to extend and aggrandize itself in the quest for total power, up to the point where it is destroyed from within by one of the power cells that have been growing within the body of the Beast—following which the process begins all over again. Power, Jouvenel noted, has experienced good times and bad, yet its advance has been steady, as its resources, its military power, and its legislative capacities have expanded enormously throughout the past two centuries in Western history. Every revolution, he argues, whatever the intent of the revolutionists (Cromwell, Napoleon, Stalin), ended by increasing Power's strength and scope. The modern omnipotent state represents "the *ancien régime*'s urge to rule erected into a doctrine and a system. In other words, the modern state is no other than the king of earlier centuries: it continues triumphantly his relentless work of suppressing all local liberties; it is, like him, leveler and standardizer."[15]

Power accomplished this feat by using the king, allied with the people, to destroy the mediating aristocracies that had previously resisted the encroachments of Power. In time, the assemblies or legislatures that had been created to assure popular participation in government conceived the "novel" idea that they were intended to represent the nation as a whole rather than certain interests; thus they came to aspire to the role that had formally been reserved to the king. Hence "Parliament [became] the king's successor as the representative of the whole; it had taken over his mission and his requirements. Unlike him, however, it no longer had representatives of diversity to deal with, mandatories of particular interests to take into account."[16] In this way, a body that had been entrusted with protecting private citizens charged itself with advancing the public good, assuming legislative powers the king himself had never enjoyed. So the principle of individual liberty was used to justify committing that principle into the hands of a "parliamentary aristocracy" to interpret and act on as the parliament saw fit. The mass of the people, gratified by the dispossession of the old aristocracy, applauded this usurpation, and allied themselves gladly with the new political structure. ("The passion for absolutism is, inevitably, in conspiracy with the passion of equality," Jouvenel said.)[17]

As the state defeated the landed aristocracy, and the industrial capitalists subordinated what remained of it, so the statocracy is presently engaged in destroying the capitalists. After this, Jouvenel predicted, the state itself will be destroyed by the statocracy it created, and the process will begin over again. From beginning to end, the driving principle is simply this: "all command other than its own, that is what irks Power. [And all] energy, wherever it may be found, nourishes it."[18] The state is at war with all the intermediary institutions of society that Hannah Arendt, equally with Tocqueville, praised as barriers to tyranny. One thinks of the blind, predatory, and voracious sea slug that Edmund Wilson, in his famous introduction to *Patriotic Gore*, took as a metaphor for the postrepublican, imperial United States in the 1960s.

The nature of Power is the same in whatever form of government it is located, yet liberal government especially agrees with that nature, and with Power's aims. It is probably true, as James Kalb holds, that Power alone is an insufficient explanation for the development of liberalism, in the West and elsewhere, and its success. Half a century ago, the political scientist Kenneth Minogue asserted that from the moment the germ of liberalism is introduced into the traditional body politic, that body is doomed to death. And its death leaves Power standing alone above the brittle shell and its defunct contents.

Two of liberalism's most dangerous characteristics are stealth, by which it creates the illusion that issues either unpleasant or embarrassing to it were illusory to begin with, and its fundamental quality of invisibility.[19] These characteristics are entirely expectable in a pseudophilosophy emanating from a moral and intellectual delusion that fatally misconstrues reality, which it almost violently denies even as it revolts against that reality. Power is required to defy the universe, and since the nineteenth century modern and advanced liberalism have availed themselves of plenty of Power, in its social, cultural, and political forms. Advanced liberalism in particular requires constraint without the illiberal semblance of it. "Power is to be maximized [in a liberal polity], but it is also made so equal and so devoted to human satisfactions that it seems to disappear," Kalb notes.[20] (His observation confirms Tocqueville's intimation of democratic tyranny disguised by "democratic mildness.") Such constraint implies not state police and state jails and detention camps but a managerial regime supported by a vast administrative bureaucracy whose function is to assert, impress, and finally enforce the metaphysical illusion that contradicts everything human beings, before liberalism, ever thought or believed. To accomplish this, liberalism depends on a certain kind of human being, a type it must either create or extend, if necessary by eliminating uncooperative types.

Liberalism claims to aim at a completely free, rational, and neutral political and social order, yet advanced liberalism itself is fundamentally unfree, irrational, and biased. Liberalism is inspired by faith in a specific view of human nature to which it is irrationally wedded, a view that requires closing certain lines of inquiry on the assumption that they are beyond debate. Liberalism for this reason should be recognized as "a new religion, a system of moral absolutes based on a denial that moral truth is knowable, [which] consists in nothing less than the deification of man," according to Kalb. Like most organized religions, the liberal state in our time is limited by its refusal to question its own creed or tolerate any challenges to that creed. "What presents itself as enlightened and limited government becomes in practice obscurantist tyranny."[21]

Unlike James Kalb, who emphasizes the power of liberalism, James Burnham stressed liberalism's weakness. Although Burnham, too, noted the basic irrationality of liberalism—or rather the unreasonableness of its rationality—he understood liberalism as "the ideology of western suicide," a rationalization of the contraction and destruction of the Western world. Burnham did not accuse liberalism of causing that contraction, for which, he suspected, the decay of religious belief, material luxury, and simple exhaustion were ultimately responsible. Nevertheless, like Kalb, he recognized modern liberalism—universalist, relativist, secularist, materialist, moralistic, antitraditionalist, and endlessly reformist—as the natural enemy of the civilization that gave it birth: "Quite specifically, [what the West needs is] the pre-liberal conviction that Western civilization, thus Western man, is both different from and superior in quality to other civilizations, and non-civilizations. . . . [Also] it requires a renewed willingness, legitimized by that conviction, to use superior power and the threat of power to defend the West against all challenges and challengers."[22] Neither the modern liberalism typical of his day nor the advanced liberalism of our own possesses any such conviction or willingness; rather, the old liberalism was content to see the West perish, while the new liberalism is eager to engineer its death. Yet the democracy to which both liberalisms are professedly committed was a product of Western civilization, and depends for its future on that civilization's survival.

Democratic government is indisputably the creation of the advanced Western civilization which shaped it, and within which it developed. But are democratic institutions compatible with the modern mass democracies that differ so greatly in almost every respect from the nineteenth-century democracies that developed within simpler societies built to a vastly smaller scale? Are they compatible as well with mass technological societies dominated by scientific expertise and bureaucratic management, by mass electronic communications systems, and, increasingly, by the new transnational institutions and arrangements for which the word *globalization* is shorthand? The question is not whether democracy can exist without traditional Western societies; the rise of democracy in the early nineteenth and twentieth centuries signaled the end of tradition in the West. It is whether democracy could survive the destruction of the modern West that produced it and that is, arguably, engaged in a process of self-destruction both heedless and deliberate.

5

"Fit Your Feet"

This book began by considering whether the modern French nation is a more "democratic" and more "free" society than the variegated, decentralized France of the first half of the nineteenth century and earlier—or not. Similar consideration needs to be extended to the other Western democracies of the present time, taken separately and together.

Enthusiasts will argue that modern social democracy agrees with the modern mind, which views the world as a complex set of interrelated problems needing to be resolved in the interests of "progress," a process that assures that the future will always be an improvement on the present so long as citizens achieve sufficient enlightenment and perform their duties conscientiously in pursuit of the proper ideals. Democracy gives a people faith in a civic order exhibiting beauty and design and the common man a chance to stand on his own. Political democracy, by abolishing rank, privilege, and caste, gives people a wider and more varied experience and deepens their consciousness of self.

Modern democrats generally acknowledge that the fact and the ideal of liberal democracy never completely agree and that the classic vocabulary of liberalism since the French and American Revolutions has been embarrassingly compromised by thought and events in the past two centuries. They are willing to acknowledge, too, the restlessness and dissatisfaction of modern men in a democratic system, while insisting nonetheless that "liberal democracy can be understood as the product of [modern] men of this sort and as one response to the problem of solving them . . . [and] an attempt to deal with such men in their own terms," as Charles Frankel puts it. And they will confess that the mass society that modern democracy promotes, and on which it relies, is a reality in every advanced industrial country today, threatening to reduce the once-proud words *liberty* and *freedom* to empty lies. Yet they remain convinced that there is no acceptable contemporary alternative to democracy. "Modernity," Frankel thinks, "implies a revolution in human consciousness. Democratic social arrangements reflect that consciousness and accept it; but they also provide instruments for guiding and controlling it. None of democracy's contemporary rivals possess [*sic*] these two qualities to the same extent."[1]

Defenders of advanced liberal democracy argue that a proper liberal state has a duty to help its citizens fulfill their individual lives, not by telling them what to do but by removing barriers from their path and building ladders by which they may ascend, in society and in their own self-esteem. The liberal state, they insist, has a further duty to help people "achieve control over their lives," a role that necessarily presumes a massive and highly intrusive government presence. A less ambitious, more classically liberal, aim is to see that as many people as possible are granted a chance to decide for themselves those issues on which their lives depend, insofar at least as that is feasible.[2] But, as Jouvenel says, Power means command, and it is impossible that everyone should command. The sovereignty of the people, as skeptics of democracy have always claimed, is a fiction, one that has become more misleading than ever in what a former official of the European Union calls "the new imperial age," when both the idea of sovereignty and the sovereign political body are beginning to lose sway in the world.[3]

More drastically, Jacques Ellul, writing in the 1960s, asserted that, once the state assumes control of every aspect of the lives of its citizens, politics becomes autonomous. "The difference," Ellul argued, "between democracy and totalitarianism is precisely in the area of means. If a government increases technology in society, steps up propaganda and public relations, mobilizes all resources for the purposes of production, resorts to a planned economy and social life, bureaucratizes all activities, reduces the law to a technique of social control, and socializes daily life, then it is a totalitarian government. At that level, concentration camps, arbitrary police methods, and torture are only secondary differences." Politics becomes independent of political values and ideals and expresses its absolute autonomy by its reliance on the principle of force to accomplish its autonomous aims.[4]

In the postwar era, roughly from 1945 until the collapse of the Soviet Union in 1991, most Western liberals and conservatives accepted liberal democracy as the best and most desirable form of government; democracy's most vocal challenger was the New Left, which claimed to want more and truer democracy, not less of it. More recently, a number of sophisticated theoretical and historical critiques of postrepublican and mass social democracy have been developed, most of them worked up from the premise that more democracy is actually less democracy. But at least one of them is based on the idea that democratic society, being derived from false moral and social principles, is inherently flawed in ways that were not so apparent in the early stages of democracy's history but have been magnified by mass democracy triumphant in the modern era.

Before the mid-nineteenth century in the United States and the late nineteenth and early twentieth centuries in Europe, suffrage throughout the Western countries was restricted by the "stake in society" principle. The idea behind this principle was that only those who had something to lose from political activity should be considered morally responsible enough to take part in it—or, as we say today, to be granted a "voice" in politics. In those days, politicians knew their classical political theory, for which it was axiomatic that to give the lower classes a voice in politics was actually to give them shouting rights to dispossess the higher ones. Ultimately, academic theory and popular politics compelled the political class to retreat from what it recognized to be both political common sense and a bulwark of civilization by giving in to the demands of the mob, which in Jacksonian America meant the vote and in Victorian England and Bismarck's Europe the vote plus the welfare state. Since that time, universal suffrage and the welfare state have prevailed throughout the Western world under the banner of liberal democratic capitalism, or simply "democracy."

One might be excused for supposing that people who demand a welfare state are people who feel themselves incapable of providing for their own welfare. If that is what they really fear, then perhaps it is unfair to blame them for casting a vote on behalf of setting some political-bureaucratic structure in place to do it for them. That, one could argue, suggests at least a minimal capacity for individual initiative and effort. But these are not the people who designed the welfare state, constructed it over a period of several generations, and have been running it ever since—who *are* the welfare state, in spirit and in fact. When we speak of the welfare class, we really mean to designate not the dependent clients of the state but the managerial elite that caters to and manages these dependents, after having, to a substantial degree, created them.

Conservatives from the beginning have accused liberal and socialist politicians of encouraging poor, and not-so-poor, people to sign up for benefits, go on the dole, and join the "culture of welfare." Yet, after generations of welfare, this has become a secondary concern. The crucial problem today is not, narrowly speaking, that the welfare state encourages indolence, lack of initiative, and the exploitation of the public purse. By assuming that a significant percentage of the *demos* is incompetent to look after itself, and that therefore neither the state nor society itself should require anything of it, the welfare state helps to form a dependent mind. If the proletariat did not exist, it seems, it would have been necessary to invent it. As it happened, invention was not required But expansion was, and so expansion has continued to proceed with no end in sight until, it appears, in the not so distant future the publics of the Western nations will have all become thoroughly proletarianized.

The great question for democracy is, If the proletarian is deemed incompetent to assume charge of his own life, how can he be expected to have a responsible voice in running the state? No politician, democratic or otherwise, honestly believes that he can be. And indeed, his assumed competence to understand questions of state, and his good judgment in these things, is not really the modern democrat's defense of the principle of universal suffrage; his private interest is. The presumed personal interest of the voter, not the good of society or of the nation, is the justification for consulting the will and advice of the incompetent or ignorant ward of the state at the polls. Even such a citizen as he, democrats assume, is capable of accurately perceiving his own best interest and has an inalienable right to vote it, no matter the consequences for the wider interest. But the first of these propositions is questionable, and the second is simply wrong. Most democratic politicians understand all this quite well. They know that the proletarian citizen is likely to vote responsibly on any matter of public importance only by accident, but they don't care—so long as he is competent to vote for them.[5]

Recently, democrats have asserted the desirability of democracy over other political systems on the grounds that it disperses its loci of power, forcing the "specialists in power" at the top of the governing hierarchy to share their influence with the leading members of subordinate hierarchies. Ultimately, however, democracy does not submit to rational justification, as the scholar Henry B. Mayo concluded; it is, like religion, something to be taken on faith.[6] Americans, for instance, are certain that monarchy and democratic principles are not compatible with each other, although the list of developed democracies today includes many monarchies, notably Great Britain.

Orestes Brownson, as we have seen, insisted that every political system contains an element of truth, since all such systems are created by the human intellect, and the human intellect, in turn, is a creation of God: there can be, he insisted, no best constitution for all people and for all times. Christianity, he noted, specifies no government or set of political institutions. "Fit your feet," was his advice. Political systems properly develop from societies, not the other way around. It is often argued that democracy and progress are one and the same thing, or at least are linked, and that it is obviously better, if humanity is to achieve something approaching perfection, that all should enjoy perfection together. But democracy, as Bagehot saw, is insufficiently self-critical to attain anything like perfection: short of catastrophe, he thought, a democracy will neither accept criticism of itself nor give up privileges that have ever been conceded to it. Nor is there agreement on the proposition that democracy guarantees efficiency in modern capitalist societies. In the end, democracy may be best understood as a means rather than an end—a means that, in a pinch, should be sacrificed to those conditions and amenities of life we call civilization.

6

The King's Second Body

✦   ✦   ✦

G. K. Chesterton, one of the most humane and kindhearted authors of the twentieth century, described himself as "a man who has not only a faith in democracy, but a great tenderness for revolution." In acknowledging that sympathy, Chesterton did not mean to avow an affinity for socialism (which, as a Catholic, he regarded as a heresy); rather, he expressed his disapproval of the landlordism and industrialism that for him were not an affirmation of property but its negation. He was convinced that "the poor are so obviously right."[1] It says a great deal about the distance between British democracy in 1925 and Western democracy in 2012 that Chesterton, who collaborated with his friend Hilaire Belloc in the social and political program they called Distributism, should have entertained so warm an enthusiasm for the popular democracy of his day, at least as he understood it. "He knows better now," Evelyn Waugh, a fellow Catholic but fierce Tory, might have said of Chesterton (as he said of another departed author). Even so, there is a touching innocence about Chesterton's testimonial on behalf of democracy and the democratic faith. Is it attributable perhaps to Chesterton's having lived in what was still, comparatively speaking, an age of democratic innocence (he died in 1936, two years before Munich), whereas those of us alive today "know better now"?

Certainly one can discover many arguments against democracy these days, although they are almost entirely obscured by the popular shouting in celebration of it. Among them is that democracy is inferior to republicanism, with which democracy has historically been confused. Another is that selfish individualism, not equality or fraternity, nor citizenship or compatriotism, is the real basis of democracy. A third contends that the managerial bureaucracy that supports modern democracy is suffocating democratic political life, while a fourth holds that mass democracy is a form of tyranny. And a fifth condemns the eagerness of democratic governments to acquiesce in the global diffusion of political and economic power, thus encouraging the disintegration of the nation-state that made modern democratic government and democratic society possible in the first place, and on which their survival depends.

Distinctions between republics and democracies are as old as Aristotle's *Politics*, and they singularly preoccupied the Founders of our own American republic as they worked to design it. In weighing the virtues of the republican form of government over the advantages of a democratic polity, one is compelled to take into account a number of considerations, the most important of which is *scale*. And since the United States of America in the twenty-first century differs above all from that of the eighteenth in size, extent, and population, scale is the obvious point at which to initiate a comparison between the government of the young United States and that of our own country—that is, between the former republic of the Founders and the modern empire.

Admirers of the American empire honor it as the world's sole superpower, the indispensable nation. Critics disparage it as Behemoth, a monster grown beyond all control, and self-control. Several years ago a Russian official predicted the imminent dissolution of the United States into several states, the southwestern of which he expected would either ally itself with Mexico or else return to the jurisdiction of Mexico City. Many Americans agreed with him, in particular those who had been warning against just such a scenario. One hundred fifty years ago, nearly half the country did secede, and was forcibly reattached to the other half by the bloodiest conflict in previous history. In 2009 the Republican governor of Texas, Rick Perry, commented vaguely in favor of state secession "in theory"; a year later he campaigned for reelection on an explicitly anti-Washington platform. California is too impoverished and chaotic to dare cut its lifeline to the District of Columbia, but one wonders whether the Union might be tempted in the future to expel the enormous state rather than go down with it.

Expanded across the North American continent and beyond to form a union of fifty states from one of thirteen stretched along the East Coast, the American nation has expanded globally as well: today, the federal government has more than seven hundred military bases spread out around the world and security agreements with twenty-five or thirty foreign governments. A population of about 25 million has swelled to 310 million—owing substantially to federal immigration policy—and a formerly homogeneous people drawn from the British Isles and northern Europe has been transformed into a multicultural and multiracial one derived from every country in the world and lacking an ethnic, racial, social, religious, and political identity. The direct results include a nation that is no longer a vast extended family, families that do not belong to communities, citizens who are strangers to one another, an increasingly centralized and authoritarian federal government, and an angry and incoherent political culture incapable of identifying crucial national issues and so of resolving them. This is not the America described in Tocqueville's book, nor is it the American Republic envisioned by James Madison—nor indeed is it a republic at all, as republics have been described by political theorists. It is true that more than a century has passed since America thought of itself in republican terms. Yet we forget that classic political theory holds that not republics alone but democracies also are properly societies

built to the small scale: city-states and compact, socially uncompli-
cated nations. What goes for the one form goes for the other as well.

The Greek city-states, in their hundreds, numbered about ten
thousand people each, or fewer. From them the classical concept of
republican society and government arose. The Aristotelian republic
depended on the citizenry's being not too numerous for its members
to enjoy a personal acquaintance with one another, a condition Aristotle believed necessary to encourage human excellence in government,
philosophy, and the arts. Plato estimated five thousand citizens—or
forty thousand denizens, counting their families, their servants, their
slaves, and foreigners among them—as the ideal population of a state
whose aim was to attain a high level of culture. Florence in the Renaissance produced its glorious civilization from a population of just forty
thousand people—ten thousand more than that of the largest city in
the United States in 1789. Rousseau took as the model for his republic
the city of Geneva, which in his day numbered twenty-five thousand
people. "So small is Rousseau's republic [as described in *The Social
Contract*] that he does not even allow representation but requires citizens to show up in person to conduct public business," the philosopher
Donald W. Livingston has noted.[2]

Yet proper scale alone is insufficient to the health of republics and
republicanism. Because the idea of a republic is a classical notion, it is
based on the classical understanding of what men are. That idea was a
fixed one, reflecting the classical philosophers' view of human nature
as unchanging and universal. This means republican government is
fundamentally a religious concept, something entirely alien to democracy in the modern epoch, which is a wholly secular form of government dependent on the sovereignty of the popular will as expressed
in elections, without reference to transcendental truth and based on a
belief in the sovereignty, even the divinity, of man. Modern democracies are morally relativist and inherently atheistic societies, devoid
of absolute principles and prepared to set the popular will (however
that may be determined) above even their supposed commitment to
pragmatism.[3] "One Nation under God" may be a pretty phrase, but it

is a lie nevertheless. More honest is "Liberty, Equality, Fraternity"—
though that slogan is hypocritical in its own way in its assertion of a
supposed brotherhood that shows itself, on examination, to be only
selfishness institutionalized.[4]

In any case, the republic that was the aim and ideal of the American Founders has been impossible, in the estimation of Donald Livingston, since as far back as the eighteenth century. America under
the Articles of Confederation was already too large a country to agree
with classical republican specifications, as Madison and Hamilton
understood. They sought a way around the problem by adapting David
Hume's scheme for "county republics," but in doing so they made a
serious judgment in error. "So Americans were on their own to conjure
with a republican political ideal that was entirely out of scale with the
size of the territory to be governed," Livingston argues. "Our political
history is largely the story of attempts to rectify this conundrum."[5]

American history is unlikely to have been other than what it is
anyhow, in the opinion of Livingston, who argues that all large republics are essentially absolute monarchies from the eighteenth century,
minus the monarch. Modern state sovereignty thus amounts to the
second of the "king's two bodies—the immortal body by which sovereignty has descended in the form of the new state corporations whose
founding began in the twelfth century. This royal second body succeeded in laying hold of the young republics of Europe; in time, it
conquered the United States, too. Hence, the actual power in every
modern democracy is the state and those who manage it; . . . the people are sovereign in roughly the way that the queen of England is
sovereign"—ritually, by way of elections. "As in the French Revolution, the person of the king became the nation-person. And, as the
state became the king's second body, so the central government of the
United States became the second body of the American people in the
aggregate."[6] Over the decades, this second body has grown more and
more powerful. This is how it came to be—Claude Polin thinks—that
the more democratic France became, the more tyrannical the French
state grew.[7] The tyranny of the king's second body has never been

resisted—or anyway successfully resisted—by the proudly democratic citizens of the modern democracies.

Polin, a former colleague of the political philosopher Raymond Aron, suggests an explanation for this failure. Of all the modern democracies, France and the United States are the most self-consciously democratic, the most looked up to by other democracies, and the most ideologically democratic democracies, in part because they are so widely regarded as the twin cradles of modern democratic society. But democracy in each country means, or implies, something different. In France, Polin thinks, it is selfishness; in the United States, freedom—a freedom established and maintained on a basis of what he calls "pessimistic individualism." For Americans, freedom is the right of every citizen to make himself, through intelligence and hard work, not the equal but *more* than the equal, materially and socially, of his fellow citizens. For the French, democracy is the absence of any discrepancy between each citizen's will and that of the sovereign, the "general will."[8] French republican democracy today, Polin says, is a society in which "everyone unites with everyone else, but obeys only himself and remains just as free as he was before." Under the Fifth Republic, "every citizen, to the last, is a king in his own right." And so, "Short of actually turning everyone into a king, the fight for ever more democracy in France has been a simple fight for ever more rights for the individual (which easily translates into a fight for more equality)."[9] For the French, democracy is institutionalized selfishness—as Rousseau understood when he wrote that "each citizen, while he deposits his vote, is thinking only of himself" (as suggested in the previous chapter, and as every democratic politician fully understands).

If modern democracy in France is the fulfillment of *The Social Contract*, democracy in America today confounds Tocqueville's expectations when he suggested that Americans' materialist values and ambitions would cause them to ignore their political duties altogether and leave to their politicians the task of creating a benevolent despotism. This has not happened—or rather, it has not happened in the way Tocqueville foresaw. Tocqueville described the United States as a commercial society largely unconcerned with national, as distinct from local, political issues. He never imagined the rise in America of an activist ideological minority, similar to the French revolutionary class, devoted exclusively to the radical destruction of existing social and political institutions and standing above the mass of the people, whose sole desire is to be left in peace to make more money and acquire more comforts for themselves and whose reluctant and sporadic political involvement is mainly a reaction against government's intrusions on free commercial activity.

"Is it necessary," Polin asks, "to point out how far we are from Tocqueville's benevolent despotism? Here are not industrious bees headed dutifully to work every day but people who are after the legitimacy of private property and who promote a system of redistribution that smacks of the exploitation they claim to fight—but an exploitation of the few by the many. . . . The welfare state is the natural child of a society whose supreme rule is every man for himself." It is a society that, like modern French society, is essentially selfish, based on relationships among citizens that are restricted to commercial exchange, by which each man hopes to get the better of the other.[10] Polin's words recall Orestes Brownson, who expected that a Lockean union would be one not of citizens but of confederates seeking to advance their interests at the expense of other people. They also recall Mencken, who noted that Americans, though they ought to be the happiest people in the world, are among the unhappiest, for the simple reason that they do not trust one another. Generalizing from his comparative considerations of French and American democracy, Polin concludes that democracy is the only form of government suited to the mentality of modern man. "The good to be satisfied in a democracy, not the common good but the private one, has two faces: vanity and greed, the two breasts upon which democracy feeds." Democracy does not tame and dampen the passion of self-love; instead, it makes a virtue of it.[11]

Claude Polin's critique of modern democracy invites two observations, both of which must be obvious. The first is that pessimistic individualism and codified selfishness are hardly compatible with the generosity of spirit ordinarily assumed to be necessary to the health and future of popular democracy. The second, as Polin himself points out, is that citizens in a democracy have an institutional interest in augmenting the power of the general will: the king's second body in which, theoretically, the sovereignty of the people resides, while in truth it is the sovereignty of the state that makes its home there.

7

The Business of Aristocracies

Democracy is the product of Western civilization. Western civilization is, arguably, necessary to the survival of democratic government and society. We must consider, therefore, the nature of the civilization of the West and whether civilization itself is the proper end of government, or if something else is.

A government congruent with Aristotelian principles would be a government whose aim was human excellence: the creation of the highest civilization that men are capable of attaining. On this classical aim, Christianity superimposed another: the establishment of government that conforms with Christian principles of governing, government for a Thomistic civilization. That was the presumed ideal, though certainly not always the result, of Western governments until the rationalist, or early democratic, age, when the ideal became the maximum personal liberty added to the greatest material good of the largest number of people. In modern times, governments have been judged on their success in reducing human degradation, subjection to authority, social inequality, and economic vulnerability.

Francis Fukuyama believes that the achievement of political and social liberty and economic affluence are the highest aim and responsibility of government. This is certainly the majoritarian view in Western societies, but the old idea died hard, and indeed it is not quite dead.

Orestes Brownson thought that the primary work of a republic is to further virtue and dedicate itself to truth, a proposition with which the Founders, whom Brownson respectfully described as "political atheists," would not have disagreed. Across the Atlantic, Matthew Arnold, in the late nineteenth century, held that "nations are not truly great solely because they are numerous, free, and active; but they are great when these numbers, this freedom, and this activity are employed in the service of an ideal higher than that of the ordinary man, taken by himself."[1] The difficulty for democracies, he added, lies in how to discover and maintain high ideals. One could argue that democracies do in fact have an ideal, and that is democracy itself. But if democracy is based on the notion of the divinity of man, then democracy is a human, not a transcendent, ideal. Either way, ideals, the nature of these ideals or their absence, are crucial to human societies, because these things make societies what they are and confirm their claim, if any, to civilization—or something else.

What is "civilization"?

For the civilized world today, civilization means, quite simply, liberal capitalist democracy. Historically, however, the conflation of these three things has been distinctly a minority view. *Merriam-Webster's Collegiate Dictionary* defines *civilization* as "1 a: a relatively high level of cultural and technological development; *specifically*: the stage of cultural development at which writing and the keeping of records is attained. . . . 3 a: refinement of thought, manners, or taste . . . b: a situation of urban comfort." Although it is not the lexicographer's job to make the point, civilization is also a moral duty of man.

Civilization is a relatively modern word, however ancient the concept might be. The term first appeared in France and England in the second half of the eighteenth century, when it was often used to indicate the opposite of rudeness; Dr. Johnson refused to admit the word into his *Dictionary*, though Adam Smith employed it subsequently. One notes of *Webster's* primary definition that it leaves unmentioned any political or economic element. The tertiary is clearly far removed, in meaning and in time, from the primary one; indeed, Clive Bell, in *Civilization: An Essay* (published in England in that cosmopolitan decade, the 1920s), stated explicitly that, whatever civilization may be, it has nothing to do with comfort, especially comfort of the sort provided by machines. (The princes of the Renaissance slept in cold stone castles devoid of indoor plumbing and appear to have been quite indifferent to their condition.) Nor does it imply that liberty and industrialism—which together, Matthew Arnold thought, cannot by themselves ensure "a high reason and a fine culture"—are requisites of the civilized state.[2] George Bernanos equated civilization with the nature of a people when he noted that "a civilization disappears with the kind of man, the type of humanity, that has issued from it."[3] C. S. Lewis, as a Christian, warned against the purely aesthetic view of civilization that Clive Bell embraced—he came close, in fact, to arguing that religion and civilization are incompatible—but certainly dedication to the intellect has been a principal component of every society in history deemed civilized. ("Here you shall pass among the fallen people, souls who have lost the good of intellect," Virgil tells Dante in the *Inferno*, canto 3.)

It is equally clear that, of the various elements hitherto thought necessary to civilization, democracy is not one of them; otherwise, we could not speak of civilizations in the millennia that occurred before the nineteenth century. If we estimate the ancient Attic population at five hundred thousand people, no more than about twenty thousand of them had the right to vote or had any political power whatsoever, although the citizens of Athens enjoyed complete political, and nearly complete economic, equality. The nineteenth-century French historian Ernest Renan thought a leisured class, allied with the ruling one, necessary to civil society (the term Johnson chose in preference to civilization), while Jacob Burckhardt noted in his *Renaissance* that a politically impotent people was capable of creating a various and vigorous culture. One could not, Bell argued, discredit a civilization simply by pointing out that it is based on slavery and injustice: "You must show that liberty and justice would produce something better."[4] Democracy and justice, he thought, were valuable only as a means to civilization and should not be considered as its end. "All civilizations of which we have heard have been either imposed by the will of a tyrant or maintained by an oligarchy. What is erroneously called 'the Athenian democracy' was an oligarchy depending for its means to civilization on slaves."[5] The question of what form of government is most favorable to civilization is, he declared, almost impossible to answer, yet one thing, for him, was certain. There never was in history a civilized democracy. If one single thing were essential to civilization, Bell declared, it was not this or that political system but simply human will—the will to be civilized, which, he suggested, might be nothing more than the drive toward refined and intellectualized pleasure.

According to the dictionary, civilization is a "development." It is the fruit of a lengthy social process and continues until that process has worked itself through, whereupon civilization and the process that created it collapse together and are succeeded by something else, which may or may not have its germ in the extinct civilization. Thus civilization is not a flash in the pan but a durable thing—more likely than not, quite durable indeed.

What gives it durability is tradition, and what causes its extinction is the loss of that tradition. During the life of a civilization, its tradition is received, upheld, cultivated, and transmitted to future generations by one or several associated agencies. In the absence of such agencies, the tradition is interrupted or rejected and the civilization collapses, in certain cases over centuries, in others with astonishing rapidity. Although the culture that is the core of any civilization arises from a religious cult (*cultus*), theology is not the tradition (*traditum*) but rather, as Josef Pieper called it, "the science of tradition."[6] Tradition preserves and passes on "what is genuinely worth preserving" in a culture, though, it is true, the sacred tradition forms the most important part of the whole. (Thus Christ's teaching, Pieper argued, was directly connected backward to the writings of the ancient philosophers, as Aquinas recognized.) Concerning the ancients, Pieper claimed: "Their dignity consists in the fact that they received from a divine source, a *phéme*, something spoken, and handed on what they had received in this way. This is the only reason why they are the 'ancients.'"[7] Tradition is not necessarily opposed to science (and therefore to "progress"), but it differs from it essentially in respect of its ontological nature. It is the basis of all human unity and also of human freedom and independence, which it champions against an inflexible "conservatism" that opposes all change reflexively, including whatever change concerns mere human custom and fabrication. "The only reason," Gerhard Krüger has said, "we are still alive is our inconsistency in not having actually silenced all tradition."[8]

Who, or what, are these agencies responsible for the reception and transmission of tradition? They have typically been a priestly or intellectual clerisy joined by a social class, the aristocracy; very often there has been considerable overlap between the two ("the army, the navy, the church, and the state," as W. S. Gilbert wrote). It is quite true that both classes have often wished to preserve too much of the purely human tradition; still, they have acted more or less conscientiously to transmit the sacred vessel, of which they are both representation and symbol.

Democracy, which is rooted in the notion of the sovereign people and recognizes no authority above or beyond that sovereignty, is inherently antitraditional. In medieval times, authority and tradition were synonymous, but tradition, by its nature, does not derive its authority by vote of the present generation, or of any generation at all. Democracies, in theory at least, are meritocratic societies, in which heritage is not supposed to entail social, or any other, advantage. Yet Albert Camus believed that, all protestations to the contrary, the twentieth century was a century in search of an aristocracy, which he considered a vital need of man's nature. "This world wiggles quite a bit," he jotted in his notebook, "because, like a cut worm, it has lost its head. It searches for its aristocrats."[9] T. S. Eliot, the most critically revered poet of the "democratic century," described himself as "classicist in literature, royalist in politics, and Anglo-Catholic in religion." And Nietzsche, the prophet of the Übermenschen, considered the tradition of which aristocracy is a part to represent one of those instincts of the will that the modern intellect strove to destroy but that "laughing lions" to come would restore to the world.

Tradition and culture apart, classical political theory has always recognized the role aristocracies have played in opposing the tyrannical tendencies of despots. Montesquieu argued that the aristocracies of Europe prevented the rise of despotisms in the oriental style, whereas in our own time Bertrand de Jouvenel believed that aristocrats, owing to loyalties to family and class, and influenced by predispositions molded by education and religion, could not easily be persuaded to yield their property and their liberty to the state. "Resistance . . . is the business of aristocracies," Jouvenel said.[10] Although at the time of the French Revolution and the Bourbon Restoration there was a popular perception that the king had acted as an ally of the people against the nobility, it was truer to say, as Tocqueville (and later Camus) recognized, that the monarchy created the centralized state that the revolutionists appropriated to terrorize and subdue the French nation. Seen in context, the social inequalities that aristocracy entailed were a fair exchange for the political liberty that landed aristocrats exacted from the monarch and jealously guarded—on their own behalf, of course, but also on behalf of the kingdom as a whole. This is why Sir Henry Maine was convinced that "history is a sound aristocrat." The progress of the human race, he believed, was measured by the rise and fall of aristocracies.[11]

We have already referred to Tocqueville's instinctive distaste for the bourgeoisie. By the middle of the nineteenth century the upper ranks of the industrial bourgeoisie, the plutocracy, was taking form as a class and pressing the landed aristocracy hard. The rise of the pluto-crat invited comparison with the aristocrat—usually to the benefit of the latter, whose humane and leisurely qualities, when contrasted with the hard-driving barbarism and ignorance of the new men, seemed not just admirable but socially and politically valuable besides.

No writer has more ably, sensibly, and humanely defended the aristocratic principle than Walter Bagehot did in that remarkable book *The English Constitution*. The Victorian age offers few examples of first-rate expository English prose, and Bagehot's work was, in that sense, an overlooked model for his time. With elegant simplic-ity, Bagehot described nobility as "the symbol of mind" among whose various functions is to act on the imagination of the common people, a view with which Matthew Arnold concurred.[12] "All but a few cynics," Bagehot observed, "like to see a pretty novel touching for a moment the dry scenes of the grave world."[13]

Bagehot appreciated the English monarchy preeminently for what he called its mystery. ("The mystic reverence, the religious allegiance, which are essential to a true monarchy, are imaginative sentiments that no legislature can manufacture in any people.")[14] Partly for this reason, he thought that mystery infused the strength of religion into a government that the monarchical principle already made intelligible. Moreover, having a family on the throne helped to make the English system comprehensible to the people by reducing the pride of sover-eignty to the popular level and by placing the crown at the head of English morality. Lastly, he argued, constitutional royalty serves as a disguise, by "enabling our real rulers to change without heedless people knowing it."[15]

Perceptive as Bagehot was in respect of the monarchy, he was keener still in his appreciation of the role the English aristocracy played as a class. The order of nobility, he thought, preserved English society from a succession of idolatries: that of "the rule of wealth, the religion of gold"; the worship of office; and the conflation of political power with social position. (The queen, not her majesty's prime minister, stands at the head of British society.) So long as the aristocracy endured, there was in England something of higher value than money and the "conspicuous life," and that something was placed beyond the reach of vulgar ambition, of "clever base people" and "stupid base people" alike. "In revering wealth we reverence not a man, but an appendix of a man; in reverencing inherited nobility, we reverence the probable possession of a great faculty—the faculty of bringing out what is within one."[16] The aristocracy, Bagehot thought, should stand above the plutocracy, though it ought not thoughtlessly to reject the plutocrats' admiring advances. The industrial rich lacked manners, which Bagehot supposed to be half hereditary and which he described as being among the five arts: the style of society, the equivalent in daily intercourse of fine literary expression. In short, English aristocracy, for Bagehot, was the fixed and irreplaceable seat of English civilization, on which the English polity, along with the rest of English tradition, depended for its survival.

Advocates of the aristocratical system, or those (Tocqueville included) in sympathy with it, whether in principle or ideal, have usually based their case on what might today be called the quest for excellence, what Matthew Arnold called the "grand style." All human accomplishment, they argue, was historically the work of aristocratic societies. But Tocqueville believed the argument to be moot, since modern people no longer tolerated monarchical governments and aristocratical societies. Arnold reluctantly agreed, and so far history has proved both men right. Arnold believed that, while a governing class perhaps could not lead the mass to the highest degree of material welfare, it could set examples of quality (as both the Roman and the English aristocracies had done) without which human well-being at the highest level is impossible. The chief fault of aristocracies, in his estimation, was their inability to apprehend the instinct of the mass toward what he called "expansion and a fuller life," a failure Arnold attributed to the historical incapacity aristocracies have shown for ideas. But beyond that particular failure lay the force of democratic destiny itself. "The time has arrived . . . when it is becoming impossible for the aristocracy of England to conduct and wield the English nation any longer. . . . This change has been brought about by natural and inevitable causes, and neither the great nor the multitude are to be blamed for it."[17] Although in sympathy with the democratic tide, Arnold wondered what agency or influence the nation could rely on to replace the aristocracy, which had heretofore provided the country's motivating ideal and in whose absence England ran the risk of courting "the dangers of America," a country ruled by common citizens "with no adequate ideal to elevate or guide the multitude" from which these plebeian rulers had been drawn.[18]

Although the aristocratic classes have usually proved more or less apt at preserving tradition and maintaining ideals, neither of these activities is necessarily associated with serious intellectual or artistic accomplishment, and indeed aristocrats have not ordinarily been associated with such mental achievement. The English historian David Cannadine, a contemporary chronicler of the decline and fall of the British aristocracy, candidly remarks that his subjects were essentially philistines, an estimation Bagehot appears to have shared in suggesting that "a good government is well worth a great deal of social dullness." (Bagehot ascribed the "dignified torpor" of English society to the precedence the oldest classes take over the cleverest ones.)[19]

An aristocracy, by definition, is not a meritocracy, and by the middle of the nineteenth century, at least, the second was rapidly overtaking the first. Sir Henry Maine called this "intellectual democracy," and he did not like it. "An ascetic society of men of science," he thought, absolutely certain of themselves and their conclusions, and holding the power with which science had provided them in their hands, could hardly be a beneficent one. Yet he perceived that the modern coupling of the democratic and scientific movements made the rise of intellectual aristocracies probable. Maine guessed rightly. A century later, the American social critic Christopher Lasch deplored the aristocracy of talent that had arisen during the interval. It displays, he asserted, all of the vices of a hereditary aristocracy and none of its virtues; it is a class that is loaded with privileges without bearing the corresponding responsibilities of privilege, no matter its reflexively expressed compassion for the "under-privileged."[20] Moreover, an aristocracy of talent, unlike a hereditary one, is prone—one might even say doomed—to divorce intellectual activity from all other social activity and the wider human experience, and to make belief in unaided reason an article of faith.

Democracy, as a child of Western tradition, relies on that tradition for its future. But, deprived of a genuine aristocracy, it lacks an efficient means of transmitting the heritage that is its lifeblood. In place of aristocracy, it has what Milovan Đjilas called the New Class (the intellectuals, academics, communicators, "experts," technocrats, and bureaucrats) on the one hand and the plutocracy on the other: meritocracy's two faces. (It is true that the meritocracy seems more and more a closed and self-perpetuating system, a development we shall consider later.)

A meritocracy, by its nature and to the extent that it really *is* run on meritocratic principle, is inherently an agitated, uncertain, and unstable society whose members are constantly being propelled upward like rockets into the elite ranks, from which they are equally liable to be hurled down like spent boosters. Individuals may be made and unmade in the course of a lifetime; families, over the span of a generation or two. In spite of complaints of undeserved "privilege" that supposedly impedes social mobility at the top, the surprising fact is how little the power of what we call "class" today protects against the vicissitudes of economic fortune and of social position, and the wages of personal irresponsibility.

An example—there is no better one—is the fate of the WASP patriciate that ruled the United States as late as the 1950s and has been in precipitous decline ever since, owing in part to the aspiration of a substantial portion of its mysteriously guilt-ridden children to déclassé status but also to a weakening of character, confidence, and conviction (which amounts, really, to the same thing). The displacement of the WASP establishment has not been accompanied by the rise of an equivalent upper class in America; most likely, it never will be. Whatever one's opinion of the old WASP aristocracy—its culture, values, and ideas—it succeeded for three and a half centuries in preserving and transmitting the tradition that formed it, while exercising an ethic of civic responsibility and noblesse oblige in a society lacking a titled nobility. The untitled American aristocracy was an establishment of birth, religion, learning, and (often but not necessarily) inherited wealth, all of which endowed it with a longevity and continuity that are impossible for a meritocracy.

Meritocracies despise background and breeding, however much individual meritocrats may envy people who have these things and seek to associate with them. Beyond that, their education and their means of livelihood, the conditions of their employment, and their own peculiar form of social life ensure that they have neither roots nor loyalties, neither a past nor a future to which to look backward or forward. What they are today bears no resemblance to what they were yesterday, nor is it a guarantee of what they will be tomorrow or what their children and grandchildren after them will be. They cannot, in Francis Bacon's phrase, be a "root of gentlemen." In these circumstances, there is no possibility of cultural continuity, of the transmission of the tradition on which societies rely for their present strength and future survival. T. S. Eliot (writing at the beginning of the second global conflict in twenty years to rescue democracy from its enemies) distinguished between modern elites and formal aristocracies, the second of which alone he thought possess the capacity to transmit traditional culture: "No true democracy can maintain itself unless it contains . . . different levels of culture." "It may be argued," he continued, "that complete equality means universal irresponsibility; and in such a society as I envisage, each individual would inherit greater or lesser responsibility toward the commonwealth, according to the position in society which he inherited—each class would have somewhat different responsibilities. A democracy in which everybody had an equal responsibility in everything would be oppressive for the conscientious and licentious for the rest."[21]

In a democracy, the upper class is neither an untitled aristocracy (the socially superior but politically equal class that Orestes Brownson looked for in America) nor a true establishment (which by definition is secure in its position) but what meritocrats call an elite. An elite is an upper class that holds, for so long as it lasts, the political and economic power it has won for itself but remains, socially speaking, too close to its origins to differ very much from the mass of the people. Unlike an aristocracy or an establishment, a meritocracy enjoys power and wealth without the corresponding responsibilities that aristocracy and membership in an establishment entail. Jouvenel wrote of the capitalist aristocracy: "An aristocracy indeed! But without the honour that belongs to aristocracy and directs its actions in well-ordered channels; one which was careful to divorce, from the command, which it exercised, the responsibility, which it rejected, and the risks, which it palmed off on the shareholders."[22]

In a time when the United States is widely supposed to have entered another populist phase of its history, the liberal-managerial elite has been widely criticized as an ill-founded and decadent establishment. In fact, the great weakness of our present elite (like that of other Western countries) is its inability to think like a true establishment, a de facto aristocracy. Establishments by nature are conservative; elites, on the other hand, are often eager to debase or destroy everything an establishment, aristocratical or not, would attempt to preserve, beginning with the general welfare of the people and the future of the nation that has been entrusted to it. According to the Misfit in Flannery O'Connor's story "A Good Man Is Hard to Find," Christ had "thrown everything off balance" by His act of raising the dead. As the Misfit thought Christ had done, so the antiestablishment has thrown the nations of the West off balance, very possibly with consequences fatal to most of them. Western political theory is simply unable to accommodate the fact of an elite that is rootless, resentful of history, and revolutionary rather than grounded, traditionally minded, and conservative. The ages-old theory of mixed government is fundamentally incompatible with a thing so unnatural and previously unheard of.

In spite of its great and many virtues, and irrespective of the critical role that aristocracies have played in the past in maintaining social and political integrity, aristocracy as an institution is impossible in modern capitalist-industrialist societies, as Eliot conceded. Aristocracy is associated with a landholding system, and every true aristocrat is a landholder whose wealth is founded on great estates. Land, unlike stocks, bonds, and cash, is a relatively stable form of wealth, and rural societies are essentially conservatively minded ones. "Broad acres," as the British still say, are, in the most literal sense, a physical portion of a geographically defined country—"the land of Great Britain," for example.

Before universal suffrage, the crucial consideration in extending the franchise was (as noted previously) whether the prospective voter had, or had not, "a stake in society," meaning wealth sufficient to expect that he would vote both responsibly—keeping the best interests and the future of his country in mind—and honestly, not employing his vote as a highwayman holds a knife to the throats of citizens wealthier than himself. There can be no stake greater than ownership of a physical part of the commonwealth—meaning soil, and not the temporary industrial excrescences erected on the soil. Men who own land may be assumed to love their country and to hold a vested interest in its proper culture, its social and political integrity, and its long-term survival. By contrast, the man whose wealth is in international finance, or in international trade and manufacturing, often calls no country home and has no special material interest in its future. As a head of the National Cash Register Company has commented pointedly, his business "happens" to be based in the United States. That is what the global economy is about, and the global economy is largely the creation of international meritocracies. Unlike the old WASP establishment, which saw America as its own creation and reflection, and itself as the creation of America, the new elite feels no attachment to the United States beyond what a resident of Las Vegas feels for the illusory, impermanent city that makes riches, freedom, and endless enjoyment available to him. In the same way, when the old aristocracy becomes removed, or removes itself, from the land and converts its holdings into more abstracted forms of wealth, it too becomes internationalized, and its interests, its loyalties, and its checkbook follow suit.

The impossibility of aristocracy in the modern world is, for many reasons, unfortunate. As Maine observed, great estates are descended from a form of sovereignty, which "implies more administrative power and kindlier relations with other classes having subordinate interests than almost any other kind of superiority founded on wealth."[23] And it is easy to overlook, from our present vantage point, that a hierarchical society ruled by a constitutional monarchy, as Britain was well into the nineteenth century, is a limited, but still legitimate, type of democratic government; it is easy to forget also that *liberty* and *democracy* are not interchangeable terms, as almost the whole of the history of a free British people proves. But the advanced countries of the world, former aristocratic societies based on nobility with a monarch at their head, have moved far beyond aristocratic agrarianism: land values in modern societies are either speculative or tied to industrial farming—as far removed from the former great estates and broad acres as one can imagine.

If aristocracy can exist only within the context of the old system, then aristocracy is dead forever in the developed world—unless, somehow, modern democracy should prove itself capable of developing, during the next century or two, a postindustrial form of aristocracy from the crude materials provided by the plutocratic meritocracy that presently rules it. Is such a thing possible? It may be mass democracy's only hope as a type of civilization. The odds are long against it. The Western nations have worked for two centuries to rid themselves of aristocracy, successfully but with regrettable results. Although David Cannadine does not draw conclusions, it is a fact that the decline and fall of the British aristocracy coincided exactly with the decline and fall of Great Britain itself, both as a world power and as a civilization. The two phenomena are directly related. But if the re-creation of aristocracy is not possible, or if it simply should not occur, that form of society we call democratic will most likely be transformed, almost insensibly, into something quite different: a sociopolitical construct that has been taking shape among us for generations, though it remains nameless.

8

Christianity: The Vital Spot

Religion is culture (*cultus*), and high culture is what is meant by "civilization."

The medieval monarch's resistance to Rome, and the later rebellion of the towns against the kings of Europe, was a revolt against secular authority that had implications for religious authority as well. Much later, Henry VIII's rejection of papal authority in England illustrates how the authority of both church and state had come to be resented as simple Authority, while the secular consequences of Martin Luther's Reformation on the Continent demonstrates the direct connection between liberal religious and political reform.

Seventeenth-century liberalism scarcely concealed its rationalist bias, and liberalism in the eighteenth century flaunted its anti-Christian and antimonarchical prejudice. The depth and intensity to which that prejudice was susceptible was first revealed during the French Revolution, when the Left as we know it was born in the French General Assembly. Liberalism and the atheistic Left in those days were not the same thing (though there is a case to be made that they represent points along the same continuum). The aristocratic liberals were not the same thing as the Jacobins, and the American Founding Fathers (whom Orestes Brownson called "political atheists") were not irreligious men, though many of them were not Christians, either. While some Enlightenment liberals, most of them French, wished to destroy the existing social order and European civilization along with it, most, especially in Great Britain, did not. The Left, on the other hand, was dedicated almost from the first to destruction, from the church and the monarchy on down. And from its very beginning, and with deadly instinct for the vital spot, it identified institutional Christianity as the most vulnerable aspect of the existing social, political, and moral structure—the element of society that was easiest to present to the mass of the people as a form of intrusive authority, and against which potential adherents could most easily be raised. In the long historical run, that instinct has proved sound. What Robespierre began, Antonio Gramsci in the 1920s and his successors continued with their "long march through the institutions" that has succeeded, or nearly, in accomplishing what the international revolution of the proletariat failed to do.

When one considers all in the Western world that has been under siege during the past century, one notices that the denominator common to those things is their connection to, affinity for, or compatibility with Christianity. The Left today places Western culture, rationality, the rule of constitutional law, free markets, the white race, the human male, sexual morality, the family, "patriarchy," intermediate social institutions, moral restraint, and religious authority at the top of its list of idols for destruction. Yet these are finally secondary targets, selected for their (often unique) compatibility with Christianity or else as direct products of that religion. The story is reminiscent of *The ABC Murders*, a novel by Agatha Christie in which the murderer kills off a series of victims, chosen alphabetically by name and town of domicile but otherwise at random, in order to conceal the one murder for which he had a motive. The reason for this is as simple as it is obvious. The Left hates Christianity and its satellite institutions because they represent metaphysical reality, which leftists have always despised, denied, and labored tirelessly to overthrow, for the purpose of supplanting it with a synthetic version of their own construction.

Democracy is a creation of the Christian West that conceived and nurtured it. Democracy depends on, if not Christianity itself, then at least a moral and philosophic bent of Christian origin or affinity. Thus the Left has been changeless in one respect: it is by its nature immovably antidemocratic, however much it has played with its tortured and dishonest definitions of the word *democracy*. By succumbing to the Left in the guise of "advanced" liberalism, modern democracies have surrendered to a pseudopolitical movement that attacks more or less forthrightly both democracy's root and the soil in which the tree grows. And they do this in the name of "democracy"—a false religion whose acolytes and adepts cultivate a sense of moral self-righteousness and intellectual pride unmatched by the false piety of the most hypocritical churchgoers.

One wonders how the Left since World War II could have had such remarkable success in the West—the United States especially, where the majority of people do not consider themselves socialists—to the point that the dominant culture of western Europe and America is now strongly ideological, owing to the temptations of the entitlement state; the softening effects of relativism and the pragmatic incentives of positivism; radical individualism; corruptive mass democracy; and an unwillingness to stand against the idols and shibboleths of the dominant class—the desire for respectability, in short. Yet beneath these things are the casual, almost careless revolt against Christianity gently incited by mass affluence and ease, and the sloth, indiscipline, indifference, and—finally—unbelief in the faith that for nearly two thousand years gave the peoples of the West their identity and their will to survive and prevail, and through them their historical success. Modern democrats have closed their ears against the saying of Pope Leo XIII: "*Clamat enim quodammodo omnis historia, Deus esse*" ("In a way all history cries out that God is"). "The idea most useful to tyrants is that of God," Stendhal wrote in *The Red and the Black*. That may or may not have been true in the early nineteenth century. It has certainly *not* been so of tyrants in the twentieth, but rather the opposite.) But the secularization of modern nations, whether coerced or encouraged, may now be retaliating on their rulers. Pierre Manent suggests that the Christian nations, having absorbed the Church to the point of transforming the nation itself into a church and making democracy a form of communion, are presently suffering secularization themselves by the progressive perception of a loss of national legitimacy.[1]

David Hume despised what he called "the philosophic age": the age of false philosophy—destructive and deconstructive philosophies invented by "false philosophers" burdened by a false philosophic consciousness; the first ideological thinkers in the history of the world.[2] Jacques Ellul thought the endless confusion between political affairs and social ones to have been something very new indeed under the sun.

Democracy being a false religion, it is therefore the natural and inevitable enemy of true religion and a friend to the various other false or substitute religions, many also of a political nature, as well. Among these is advanced liberalism, modern democracy's alter ego. Another is ideology, which for the intellectuals of the 1920s through the 1960s was Marxism; it has been subsequently replaced on the Left by the phenomenon called multiculturalism, which has infected the cultural mainstream of the West over the last generation or so to the extent that it has become a form of popular culture—almost popular culture itself. The political Right, too, is compromised by ideological thinking, most notably in the United States, where the Republican Party represents a fusion of small-government-in-theory-and-big-government-in-practice with an aggressive nationalism that is contradicted, theoretically and in fact, by its commitment to global democratism. Kenneth Minogue has observed that, unlike Marx, multiculturalists are not necessarily antagonistic to religions per se, many of which they

are prepared, even eager, to respect as integral and authentic aspects
of non-Western cultures. They are united, however, in their hatred
of Christianity, which "remained the central enemy of ideology, basically because it affirmed a spiritual world that all ideologists deny."[3]
What is this thing called ideology? In Minogue's formula, it is "any
doctrine which presents the hidden and saving truth about the evils of
the world in the form of social analysis."[4] (A wag might say simply that
ideology is an idea that has taken leave of common sense.)

The problem with ideological democracy is that democracy is a
form of politics, and politics can never be wholly separated from religion. But ideology is a nonpolitical construct; rather, it is an antipolitical one. Ideology, Minogue argues, can only parody politics and
the political life. The reason for this is paradoxical. Ideologues believe
that every human relationship is based on some form of domination
or another. Therefore, every human relationship is political. Now, if
everything is politics, then nothing is politics. For ideologues, utopia
is the end of politics. Yet, even in a pre-utopian age, for the ideologue
politics is a matter of universal historical process, not of multiple individual human actions. Moreover, in this process (unlike the Marxist dialectic) there is no "specific" political conflict, only "ubiquitous"
political conflict exists. Thus an ideological party and a true political
party would be as politically effective as the Dalai Lama and Boss
Tweed locked together in a smoke-filled room to complete a deal. The
politician's job is to persuade and lead; the ideologue's, to convert. In
ideological "politics," political activity must be absent. Politics pre-
supposes the availability of free men, and the free consciousness that
free men possess. But, in an ideological utopia, individual free consciousness would be impossible, since one man would live and think
exactly like every other man. This is unsurprising, the aim of ideology
being a world without conflict and therefore without politics, which is
essentially conflictual. Ideologues have no interest in governing unre-
generate society: they wish to transform it. The fact that the proudly
avowed intent of the great majority of Western democratic politicians,
whether they call themselves liberal or "conservative," is to do exactly

that (they call it promoting "change") is a sign of the extent to which ideologues have already succeeded in their quest to submerge politics in ideology. This is why the modern era is the first in history to be in love with constant, endless change.

Well before the collapse of the Soviet Union in 1991, the ultimate futility of revolutionary Marxism was apparent to most revolutionary Marxists, though by no means always to democratic-capitalist politicians in the West. As early as the 1960s, Jacques Ellul discerned a "vacuity of current ideology" that did not, he thought, imply the disappearance of radical belief but simply of any real revolutionary power capable of radical political and social transformation. Two decades later, Marxism reinvented itself as "multiculturalism," in which form it has managed—by transferring its efforts from the economic to the cultural sphere (as Gramsci and the Frankfurt School had advocated from the 1930s onward), and in about a generation and a half—to inflict more damage on Western society than 150 years of Marxist revolution had accomplished.

From the beginning, Marxists prided themselves on the coldly scientific nature of their dialectic and the amoral values that undergirded it. Orthodox Marxists were neither intellectual skeptics nor moralists. The post-Marxist ideologues, on the other hand, are both skeptics and *ethicists*—ethics being understood as a code of social, as distinct from personal, conduct. The transition was accomplished quite naturally and with perfect ease; as Minogue writes, "the term 'ideology' always referred not only to an instance of a type of revolutionary doctrine, but also to a collection of interchangeable devices whose persuasive point was to achieve power in order to transform society."[5]

Unlike Marxism, however, this new type of doctrine, naturally lacking in formal political content, has been compelled to create the illusion of content in order successfully to compete with liberalism, socialism, and conservatism. Hence multiculturalism. Hence, too, a radical skepticism that denies the existence of metaphysical truth and descends into nihilism in its rejection of Western ("white male") logic and science, art, learning—and Christianity. Charles Péguy observed that everything begins in mysticism and ends in magic. Ideology has succeeded in transforming the historical concept of political democracy into a mystical vision in which "democracy" intrudes itself into every aspect of human existence. Behind this vision Minogue perceives riddling, incantations, witchcraft, and the invocation of curses by the power of the magus at work. Barack Obama, with his pseudo-intellectualism and suprapolitical vision—his professed intent to bring a version of "change" far more transformative than what the Clintons had talked about, and social healing to the United States and to the world—is really America's first ideological president, in a sense that even his most partisan predecessors were not.

Kenneth Minogue views the multiculturalist ideology as the expression of Western self-hatred in its most acute form. Having failed to destroy the civilization of the West by armed revolution and Soviet arms, Marxism behind the mask of multiculturalism seeks, "like Samson among the Philistines, [to] pull down that whole edifice of science and technology that the hated modern West used to destroy [the former communist states]."[6] Civilization and ideology are mutually exclusive things. So are ideological thinking and historical democracy, yet what remains of Western democracy is widely infected by the ideology that hides behind its pleasantly inclusive, but deceptively benign and anodyne, name. *? Palestinians*

Liberals insist that their program has traditionally been dedicated to realizing and ensuring the natural rights of mankind. In point of fact, it has rather served as the means by which the upper strata of society, including the intellectual class, has sought to escape the authority of religion while establishing itself as a secular church to which the lower orders are made subservient. Liberalism is inherently atheistic. So is its creation and alter ego, modern democracy, which for democrats is society's supreme moral arbiter, democratic politics being for them the foundation of all human values.[7] It follows that democracy is naturally and fundamentally antagonistic toward religion, save in such instances where religion forms the basis of a religiously homogeneous society in which the religious identity of the citizens may be taken for granted.

The United States, like other democratic nations, proudly guarantees freedom of religion, along with other so-called entitlements. But a society that regards freedom of religion, like the freedom to bear arms or freedom of speech, as an entitlement is not democratic at all. "Religious freedom is something citizens bring *to* a democracy," the rabbi and Jewish theologian David Novak argues. "It is not only their claim upon democratic society; it is their gift *for* it as well."[8] Religious freedom in this view is one of those natural rights of man that representative democracy is expected to recognize and safeguard. But this is a proposition that modern ideological democracy is not prepared to acknowledge, and is increasingly unwilling to tolerate. The new democratic state is its own god, and that god is a jealous god. As Novak says, "Only a society making divine claims on its citizens can *grant* them freedom of religion instead of *recognizing* the freedom of religion which is theirs, as Scripture puts it, 'from another place.'"[9]

Because religious observance is the most public act of which a human being is capable, and since it is at the same time a communal one, the concept of the privatization of religion is manifestly undemocratic in theory and in practice. The modern democratic state insists that ideas drawn from religious belief must never be admitted in moral debates, in particular those controversies bearing on political and legal issues. Further, it resists the moral claims made by all religious traditions to govern and enforce moral standards on its members without interference by the secular authorities. The state is fortified in its persecutory attempts by secularists who, having chosen to live as autonomous individuals, regard their own rights as entitlements, comparable to the religious freedom "granted" by the state to believers.[10] Consequently, the secular ideological state has been emboldened to extend the political attack on behalf of rational morality to an assault on religious freedom, as the Canadian province of Ontario has recently done in its attempt to deny to Catholic schools the right to operate according to Catholic doctrine.[11]   eh ?

What the political philosopher J. Budziszewski has called "the illiberal liberal religion" is also the religion of ideological democracy. Orestes Brownson anticipated that Catholicism, being rooted in the same natural law recognized by the "atheistic" Founders, would in time rescue the United States from fissiparous Protestantism and its contradictions. "The Church of the Future . . . already exists," he declared.[12] But Catholicism in the United States, rather than Catholicizing America, became Americanized by it instead. (A direct result of this process was the Second Vatican Council of 1962–65, which we shall consider presently.)

In Budziszewski's estimation, the illiberal liberal religion steadily approaches the conviction that "the great moral evil is moral order, and the great moral good, moral chaos."[13] It advances by deceit, giving new meanings to old words like "liberty" and claiming for itself a tolerance that is not only hypocritical but logically impossible. Unsurprisingly, its theoretical neutrality, or toleration, does not extend in practice to Christianity, while its hypocrisy is blatant to those with ears to hear and eyes to see. (Liberals appealed to religious principles in respect of the civil rights campaign in the 1950s and 1960s, yet they deplore them in application to the anti-abortion movement.) "Far from being essentially tolerant, liberalism is essentially estranged from the proper grounds of judgment as to what must be tolerated and what must not. . . . Neutralism is *essentially* at odds with the goods of transparency, truth, and human dignity," Budziszewski observes.[14] Even in neutrality one must choose, but liberalism claims itself incapable of such discriminatory action—while making heavily biased choices based on ideological preference rather than objective moral grounds. As a result, religious and antireligious people alike are brought round to accept and exhibit supposedly tolerant—meaning "nonjudgmental"—attitudes.

The Church of Rome, commonly pilloried as a bastion of antidemocratic reaction, has in fact been strongly influenced, and greatly altered by, liberalism (beginning with Vatican I in 1869–70) and a form of ideological democracy adopted during Vatican II in the middle 1960s. The late French political scholar Emile Perreau-Saussine has made the most sympathetic case for the church's century-long journey from monarchism to democracy in a recent brilliant, posthumously published book, where he argues that the church, after two devastating world wars and the rule of two brutal totalitarian regimes, concluded that the modern world offers two political options only—totalitarianism and liberal democracy—and so made its peace, inevitably, with the second of them.[15] A decade earlier, another scholar, Robert P. Kraynak, had suggested a rather different explanation for the liberalization of the Vatican, taking an approach opposite to Francis Fukuyama's by viewing the causal relationship between metaphysics and politics from the perspective of the former subject rather than the latter one.[16]

Kraynak claims that Christian theology has passed during the last two thousand years from the Platonic period of the early church fathers, through the Aristotelian scholasticism of the Middle Ages, and into its Kantian era. The first of these periods was shaped by Augustine's formulation of the Two Cities, the City of Man and the City of God; the second by the Scholastics' concept of the hierarchical chain of being; and the third by Immanuel Kant's philosophy of freedom, according to which the human spirit has been impelled throughout history to assert its own dignity and autonomy. In Kraynak's judgment, Kant's influence—more than that of the conciliar movement in the Middle Ages, the Protestant Reformation, the Enlightenment, and various other forces historians have suggested—is responsible for Christianity's acceptance of the doctrines of human dignity and natural rights that infuse modern liberal institutions. Traditional Christian doctrine teaches that human dignity derives from man's having been made in the *imago dei*. An immortal creature who forfeited his immortality by the Fall, he can nevertheless, through Christ's redemptive self-sacrifice, be reunited with God and received into eternal life. "Kantian Christianity," on the other hand, attributes man's dignity to his unique, autonomous personhood, whose nature (therefore his natural right) is to achieve personal fulfillment and even self-transcendence. The Catholic Church was the last of the Christian churches to embrace this dangerous misconception of man and of his relationship to his God and to his fellow men.

The Second Vatican Council and the postconciliar church since 1965 result directly from this error. Three generations before, the church had embarked on a program of *aggiornamento* that reconciled it in the course of the twentieth century with democratic government and democratic society, which it had previously resisted. Indeed, *aggiornamento* ended in wholehearted conversion. Since the pontificate of John XXIII, the Catholic Church has accepted as axiomatic the proposition that not only is liberal democracy compatible with church doctrine but its inspired teachings also imply democratic liberalism as the sole legitimate form of government, whose legitimacy derives from its grounding in the secular doctrine of human rights. The new spirit of the church imposes itself daily in the pages of the Vatican's newspaper, *L'Osservatore Romano*, which emphasizes the modern church's commitment to equal rights, human rights, minority rights, women's rights, human development, economic rights, social justice, and most of the rest of the liberal rights agenda. The exceptions are homosexual rights and reproductive rights, which the Vatican, of course, continues to deny.

By acquiescing in the Kantian basis of modern liberal democracy, Christianity has embraced the liberal democratic commitment to the radical individuality of democratic man, conceived as an autonomous individual whose unassailable dignity is a function of his autonomy and his will to self-realization (the fulfillment of his "dreams," as American politicians say), irrespective of any other individual, provided only that, in this business of realizing himself, he "does no harm" to anyone else. Obviously, this view of human beings is diametrically opposed to that of traditional Christianity, which attributes human dignity to the divine spark each person carries within himself and to his place in the hierarchical chain of being. Such a creature has no need of "rights" or of "freedom," though certain liberties, recognized over the centuries by both the church and the state, are certainly appropriate to his nature. But these liberties are hardly contingent on liberal democracy, which they precede by millennia.[17]

Samuel Huntington noted that what he called the "third wave" of democratization that began in the 1970s and lasted through the 1980s was overwhelmingly a Catholic wave, occurring largely in Catholic countries and breaking precedent with past history, in which democracy had been associated with Protestant nations and authoritarianism with Catholic ones. In this period, six South American and three Central American countries democratized themselves, followed by the Philippines, Chili, Poland, and Hungary. Quite correctly, Huntington attributed the Church's unprecedented role as a force for democracy to changes within the Church itself—liberation theology, the so-called Option for the Poor, anti-"fascism," the "social justice" movement, and grassroots mobilization—that issued, together with the Novus Ordo Mass, from the Great Conclave of 1962–65. "With the accession of John Paul II, the pope and the Vatican moved central stage in the Church's struggle against authoritarianism" and on behalf of "human rights," Huntington noted. On a trip to Chile in 1987, John Paul II took a rhetorical shot at General Pinochet when he told a crowd of the faithful: "I am not the evangelizer of democracy; I am the evangelizer of the Gospel. To the Gospel message, of course, belong all the problems of human rights; and, if democracy means human rights, it also belongs to the message of the Church."[18]

This is not the place to consider the liberalizing, the democratizing, and the ultimately demoralizing effects of Vatican II on the Roman Catholic Church, none of them beneficial and some of them catastrophic. (Had it not been for the Second Vatican Council, the priestly pedophile crisis might have been avoided, though pedophilic crimes perpetrated by Catholic religious figures certainly predate the 1960s.) Nor are we concerned here with the quality and completeness of the democracies encouraged by the pope. Relevant to our purpose is Pope John Paul II's assertion in his first encyclical, published in March 1979, that the church is "the guardian" of freedom, "which is the condition and basis for the human person's true dignity." If by "freedom" the pope meant "democracy," he was saying that only a tiny minority of human beings—including Catholics—anywhere have enjoyed true dignity at any time in history before the past two centuries, and relatively few since then.

The classical and Christian view of human nature is that man's nature is fixed and that men are part of a whole, linked to the created world, their fellow men, and the cosmos; they are creatures with an appointed role, whether large or small, that they are expected to perform conscientiously. A condition of successful performance is their understanding of themselves as "beings linked together by their common ability to believe it was a grace to be linked to the rest of the world and to one another," as Claude Polin has written. And man's social nature is an aspect and expression of his religious nature. Religion, the basis of culture (*cultus*), is communion, and communion is the basis of society; this is why classical political philosophy taught that the only authentic type of society is republican society. "There is no real bond between men unless it partakes somehow of that quintessential one, woven by religious commitment, the only one which, not being man-made, cannot be unmade by men. In other words, a republic is by nature a city which cannot attain its own perfection unless its citizens are inclined to religion."

But the Western world has banished classical political philosophy from its intellectual precincts, and modern—democratic—man regards himself as a fully autonomous being, endowed with no fixed nature that he may not alter to suit himself and no fixed role to play in the world. He is, instead, a world unto himself. Consequently, Polin says, "Perfect democracy being the perfect embodiment of the cardinal sin for a man to love himself above and beyond anything else, can there be any other religion in a democratic system than that of the system itself? This is why a democracy cannot be but an entirely artificial society . . . a revocable society"—a momentary society of convenience and therefore a tragic one.[19]

Not democracy alone but God the Creator is ultimately dependent on a majority vote of one.

9

Speechless Democracy

✦   ✦   ✦

Before Marx, the human threat to civilization was called "the mob." Until about the time of the Great War, it was "the masses"; after the war, it became the "mass man." Nietzsche, at the end of the nineteenth century, spoke of the mob but also of "the last man," whom he likened to a jumping flea: "The time of the most despicable man is coming, he that is no longer able to despise himself."

A generation later, Ortega y Gasset, a political liberal and antimonarchist who sat in the constituent assembly of the Spanish Second Republic in 1931–32, wrote a small but potent volume called *The Revolt of the Masses* deploring what Evelyn Waugh called "the century of the common man," whose lately acquired social, cultural, and political dominance Ortega viewed as a disaster for civilization. Democracy had become hyperdemocracy. The mass man is the product of a new world made possible by democracy, scientific experiment, and industrialism, abandoned to his own devices by the century that created him. The mass man is he who feels himself to be exactly like everybody else and takes pride in the fact; thinking he is perfect, the mass man has no aspirations and makes no demands on himself, while demanding everything.

The modern world itself is civilized, but it is inhabited by barbarians who are unable to keep pace with civilization and comprehend its challenges: "the spoiled child[ren] of human history" who mistake the civilizing impulse for a force of nature that need not be summoned or harnessed. The rule of the mass man threatens the future of European civilization, and it has already deprived Europe of the historical sense of destiny on which its survival depends. By "mass man," Ortega had in mind something beyond the modern proletarian: for him, the category included the specialized man of science, the barbarian updated for the modern world in which he plays a dominant role. "Man's fate," Nietzsche had said, "knows no harsher misfortune than when those who have power on earth are not also the first men." At the end of the twentieth century, Christopher Lasch wondered whether the principal enemy of the Western civilizing tradition really was the masses, or whether it might not be the ruling elite itself.

Western societies pride themselves on having largely erased class distinctions, and in a very real way they have done so. The Western publics are nearly identical with one another and, skin color excepted, largely homogeneous. They are what the classless society looks like, what socialism looks like, what mass society looks like. In the short run, that is a good thing for liberalism, but it is disastrous for democracy. The mass man is simply not the stuff from which a good democratic citizen—a person of sufficient character and independence who knows enough and thinks enough to play his proper part in the untiring effort to support and maintain democratic institutions—is made. The mass man is fit for nothing but socialism; insofar as we are all socialists now, we are all mass men as well. At any rate, what good is freedom when minds—by their own volition and consent—are unexercised and therefore unfree?

Pitirim Sorokin distinguished between three fundamental types of civilization: the ideational, the idealistic, and the sensate, which he described as a mixture of the first two. The last of these corresponds with our own; one might say, following Sorokin's typology, that democracy amounts to the freedom every social class now enjoys to be unabashedly—indeed, defiantly—sensate.

Sorokin defined ideational culture as "a unified system of culture based on the principle of a hyper-sensory and super-rational God as the only true reality and value." This was Western medieval culture. Idealistic culture assumed that reality is partly sensory and partly supersensory—examples include Greek culture in the fifth to fourth centuries B.C. and European culture in the thirteenth and fourteenth centuries—while sensate culture, beginning in the West in the sixteenth century, supposes a sensate basis for authentic reality and value. The "positive fruit" produced by sensate culture is its astounding progress in the natural sciences and in technique; the "poisonous" one, a blinkered view of reality and value.[1]

According to Sorokin, the sensate culture is presently in crisis ("the crisis of our age"), collapsing toward a second ideational culture, or perhaps another idealistic one. Sorokin took a philosophical view of the matter: he believed that the future of the West depends on its ability to make the transition from the one culture to another by abandoning the dead husk of the sensate epoch to create a new shell for the "creative tomorrow." In this crisis, government is helpless; hence the question of which forms of government are preferable is irrelevant to the new age. As the culture disintegrates, the varied components of the form disintegrate with it and the whole descends toward barbarism as it falls away from the glories of sensate culture at its height, and the deterioration of sensate systems, meanings, and values proceeds apace. The sciences, the fine arts, literature, history, and philosophy will succumb to professionalization, standardization, commercialization, trivialization, and even unionization, as genuine standards are replaced by counterfeit ones and culture at every level is progressively vulgarized. Meanwhile, the sensate components war with one another other to determine which of them is "more sensate than thou" as the sensate *isms*—humanitarianism, utilitarianism, scientism, materialism—clash together. Concurrently, the hedonistic and cynical elements of society diverge from the mystics and the ascetics—the vanguard of the coming ideational culture—while mental and moral atomism assert themselves in conditions of growing anarchy. Sorokin's assurance that the crisis need not end in the physical destruction of the West and Western peoples appears unfounded from the vantage point of the present age, as the Western populations are swamped by widespread immigration from the Third World. And one is tempted, seventy years later, to speculate on how far modern ideological thought fits with Sorokin's expectation of a coming ideational age. A more sobering thought is that the age we live in might represent his predicted ideational one in perverted form.

At any rate, the decadent age Sorokin described three-quarters of a century ago is recognizably the project of mass culture and the mass media: a hybrid of the positive fruit produced by sensate culture and the poisonous one.

Antidemocrats, and democratic critics who believe that a democratic culture should, and can, produce something better, have deplored popular culture (not to be confused with folk culture) since at least the eighteenth century, and mass culture for the past century and a half. Thus popular culture has long been a dead horse to beat, even if the rotting carcass goes increasingly unnoted in a world in which the old guard is dying and the field has been nearly overrun by the new model armies of modern culture.

The mandarins complain that popular, or mass, culture is an artificial commercial creation, not a spontaneous and human one. Although folk culture naturally embodies a lowest common denominator, the creators of popular mass culture deliberately search out that denominator and pander to it wherever they find it. Mass culture gives the masses not what they want, necessarily, but rather what they can be persuaded they want, or what they are willing to accept for lack of something better, or because what they are offered requires no effort for understanding or enjoyment. To persuade them to accept it, the purveyors of mass culture exploit the natural human tendency toward mental laziness and passive receptivity and the natural disinclination to critical consideration and imaginative response, while discouraging the human impulse to create and invent for oneself. The British author A. N. Wilson has noted that, in the late 1950s and the early 1960s, the arrival of rock music, commercially recorded and technologically reproduced in public places as well as private homes around the world, banished scores of generations' worth of traditional folk music from the minds of listeners—music that anyone who cared to could sing himself and to which, were he so inclined, he could contribute compositions of his own. (Wilson remarks that rock fans can and do learn the lyrics to the songs they hear, but it is hard to sing along with Mick Jagger, whose music, unlike the old Irish ballads, does not lend itself to ad hoc performances—in a pub, say, or at a picnic.)

Mass culture encourages easy sentimentality over deep feeling, superficial connection over recognition. It is only entertainment—but unwholesome entertainment, corrupted by the fundamental dishonesty and manipulative intent of its creators and shopworn even before it leaves the studio or the printing press. (Consider the difference between mass-media fantasy, based on fantasy itself, and the fantasies of C. S. Lewis and J. R. R. Tolkien, which are grounded in human experience and in history.) Tocqueville feared the conformity that democracy encourages. He had in mind the mental conformity exhibited by democratic publics, not the imaginative kind engineered by rich cynics who regard democratic publics as a highly exploitable mass public. (John Lukacs says somewhere that the tendency of the elite classes to overestimate those beneath them has been replaced by the possibly even worse inclination to underestimate them.)

The mass media transformed popular culture into mass culture. In doing so, they took the latent, unstressed political element that has always existed in popular culture and drew it out as the dominant element, while taking care that it should be a nearly subliminal one. In this way, the media harnessed mass art and mass politics together as commercial-ideological commodities promoting political indoctrination on the one hand and consumerism on the other. (Government wants mass undifferentiated man because he is easier to govern; corporate capitalism, because he is easier to sell to.) This is why mass culture and mass democratic politics are the equal of each other in their nearly total unreality, their ephemerality, and their ultimate and profound *meaninglessness*.

Federalist No. 1 proposed that American political order could be established only "through reflection and choice." A century and a half later, Jacques Ellul worried that, absent a continuous perception of reality based on something more than mere "information," liberty is impossible. But the integration of liberty with continuity can be achieved only by reflection, which requires in turn an attained distance from the omnipresent "news" and the "facts" that comprise it in the never-ending video stream of democratic social and political life today.

Walter Bagehot, a firm believer in the superiority of the parliamentary system of government over the presidential one, believed that the British Parliament's most important function was its educative role, which it fulfilled through regular debate. Unlike congressional speeches, which are mainly pro forma and which no one expects to carry influence with an already determined chief executive and his administration, parliamentary exchanges over the Dispatch Box (Bagehot argued) have frequently helped to shape or reshape policy and in so doing to educate an entire nation. Christopher Lasch made a related point when he complained, "Since the public no longer participates in debates on national issues, it has no reason to inform itself about civic affairs. It is the decay of public debate, not the school system (bad as it is), that makes the public ill informed, notwithstanding the wonders of the age of information. When debate becomes a lost art, information, even though it may be readily available, makes no impression. What democracy requires is vigorous public debate, not information."[2]

Tocqueville, like every European visitor to the United States in his day, was impressed by the extent to which the Americans immersed themselves in the politics of their towns, their states, and their nation and by the freedom and unselfconsciousness of their public debates. One could not encounter an American, Tocqueville noted, without risk of being promptly buttonholed and held hostage to an interminable political oration. In the twenty-first century, by contrast, Americans tend to avoid the subject of politics in social situations. Instead, their political conversations occur almost in hiding, among family and like-minded associates, or else are one-way—nightly, in the privacy of their dens before the television set, as rabidly partisan commentators reinforce their own opinions: remote and unanswerable presences, but reassuring ones. It is all rather like watching pornography. And it is an example of the power of ideology, joined with that of the mass media.

Lasch observed that the American establishment's preference for providing the public with information rather than encouraging it to public debate dates at least from the influence of Horace Mann, who as a public educator wished to avoid at all cost what he considered to be the dangers and unpleasantness of public disagreement on political and religious matters—an avoidance, Lasch thought, that has served as the guiding principle of American education since the 1840s. In England, J. S. Mill suggested that the public press could act as a substitute for the Athens Assembly. Nearly a century later Walter Lippmann argued that, owing in part to the disappearance of self-contained communities and the impossibility of an "omnicompetent citizen," the job of the press should be to distribute information while discouraging argument among what he called "a phantom public." It had not been so, Lasch added, from the 1830s to the turn of the century: a period of extremely outspoken and combative journalism that coincided with the highest degree of public participation in politics through parades, rallies, and oratorical debates, and produced turnouts of around 80 percent for presidential elections. "Unless information is generated by sustained public debate," Lasch concluded, "most of it will be irrelevant at best, misleading and manipulative at worst."[3]

+ + +

The law of diminishing returns weighs heavily on the progress of technique, including the technique that makes mass communication possible. Technique answers to human material wants, yet, pressed beyond certain limits, technique, which is a product of our nature, denies, defeats, and corrupts that nature. Thirty years ago Edward Abbey, the nature essayist and novelist, answered the argument that technocratic development cannot be selective by countering that, if the human race is to survive the products of its own ingenuity, it cannot be anything *but* selective.

The mass media have made the news a ubiquitous, indeed inescapable, fixture of Western culture, a condition of modern life some critics have found not only unpleasant but also dangerous. "I will posit it as a sort of principle," said Jacques Ellul, "that the predominance of news produces a fundamental political incapacity in the individual, be he a leader or just a citizen." (Ellul described the man obsessed by the news as a man without a historical memory.)[4] As for the content of the news, that has been largely transformed into a sequence of "symbolic pictures" (as Lasch called them) or perceptions, carefully staged by the media producers and wholly ephemeral. "The ultimate stage of democracy by media will be reached when political debate no longer has any influence on actual decisions but on the collective perception that a people has on itself," Lasch argued.[5] That stage would represent the triumph of ideology in politics—for example, in the American national elections of 2008, when the first truly ideological candidate was elected president of the United States.

The Internet particularly has been welcomed as a forum, unlimited in every sense of the word, for democratic debate and as an unprecedented means of political organization, communication, formation of popular opinion, agitation, and the exercise of popular pressure on individual politicians and political institutions alike. Enthusiasts of the technoculture have even claimed that the Internet and other media lay to rest the classic republican fear that a society too extensive to allow for its citizens to enjoy a personal acquaintance with one another is a society too large to facilitate deliberative discussion. The Internet and the so-called social media represent themselves as a democratic community addressing, informing, and enabling the wider democratic public to act by providing it with information and a means of public access. In fact, there are reasons to doubt that this is so.

One of them is that the conception of the Web as a public sphere does not hold up. The soul of the Web, according to Jodi Dean, a media researcher, is publicity, and publicity is the engine of the communications industry, which ranks perhaps as the wealthiest capitalist enterprise in the world.[6] (Silvio Berlusconi, the Italian media mogul, not only is the richest man in Italy but for years was his country's prime minister as well.) No one who follows politics as a scholar, a journalist, a politically engaged citizen, or even a reader of the news will be surprised, as the recipient of scores or hundreds of forwarded political e-mail stories daily, by the assertion that technique discourages political action in favor of simply keeping abreast of arcane, and often totally unverified, political tidbits and rumors. In fact, the information industry has cleverly managed to retard the maturation of the Web as a political vehicle by presenting it as almost inherently democratic and by establishing the notion that the public is actually a creature of the market. Hence, Dean says, "Instead of public deliberation, we have private acts of consumption."[7] The reduction of politics to the level of just another available commodity is an obvious commercial strategy.

(The same thing was accomplished generations ago with another fundamental human activity, sex.)

Meanwhile, huge structural changes in the political system are occurring beyond the awareness of the public—which, despite its voracious need to "know," may be perfectly content to let its leaders make the broader decisions for it.[8] When Jürgen Habermas said that the digitalization of communications does not enable the public sphere but is itself the public sphere, he was placing a tiny but supremely powerful portion of the public outside that sphere. Dean concludes that the sole means of escape from communicative capitalism's "endless reflexive circles of discussion" is through old-fashioned political action. The ideal of a unified public, from which, she says, we derived our ideal of democracy itself, is nothing more than a cybernetic fantasy.[9]

The Web's fundamental weakness as a political vehicle is its total absence of authority, some sort of authoritative reference point—indeed, of any reference point at all. By comparison with the mass media's carefully controlled, homogenized, disinfected, and professedly neutral content, the Web appears to offer an inexhaustible well of raw, unregulated, authentic human opinion. Certainly the Web, unlike the official media, is a bedlam of unfiltered exchange, but here the lack of constraint produces the same result as overconstraint: uncertainty tending toward suspicion. The unpopular truth is that every writer needs a trustworthy editor, an editor who is also a human being and a unique person, not a corporate censor or automaton. Ultimately, unrestrained populist or revolutionary babble is no more reliable than the corporate monotone that pretends to inform us about the shape and content of the modern world we inhabit.

Inflation, which is inherent to democracy, is not restricted to money and finance. Too much of anything reduces the value of that thing, and with it of others. Bad money drives out good. Bad money means cheap money—money in too great quantity. The classical-liberal maxim is that, in the marketplace of ideas, good ideas will prevail in the end over bad ones. But liberals have never claimed that inflation of the supply of ideas could operate to the same effect as inflation in the money supply does. Indeed, the contrary: liberalism has always encouraged what it calls the free exchange of ideas as an unqualified good, on the assumption that the more widespread the exchange and the more numerous the circulating ideas, irrespective of their worth, the better. Thus liberalism's historically unqualified support of the popular press, from the eighteenth century to the present time.

The popular press has been inseparable from what we call self-government, but it is far from being a demonstrable fact that it has helped self-government, or indeed government of any kind at all. Having begun life as a partisan sheet, the press has remained intellectually unreliable ever since. With the advent of the British tabloid and the Hearst papers in the United States around the turn of the twentieth century, journalism added to these qualities its lurid and sensationalist ones. Following the Great War, journalism—a trade, as Mencken argued, wonderfully suited to third-class minds—further degraded itself by embracing the conviction that, as Walter Lippmann observed in 1920, its mission was not to report but to instruct. The presentation of facts simply as facts, editors and writers reasoned, cannot accomplish the exalted goal of saving civilization. To do that, facts needed to be presented according to those rhetorical patterns of thought we call opinions, patterns pointed in some particular direction with the intention of convincing an imagined jury. And who is that jury? "Everybody," Lippmann explained, "who creates public sentiment—chattering gossips, unscrupulous liars, feeble-minded people, prostitute minds, corrupting agents. To this jury any testimony is submitted, is submitted in any form, by any anonymous person, with no test of credibility, and no penalty for perjury."[10] So much for the virtues of the press. What would Walter Lippmann have to say about the Web he never lived to see?

My guess is that he would have had nothing further to add to that indictment—except, perhaps, one thing. The Web has taken the old popular journalism and transformed it into participatory journalism, which was the next logical step forward in the progress of communicative democracy. The most obvious characteristic of online journalism is that it places writer and reader, producer and consumer, on an equal footing. The reader assumes he knows as much about the subject addressed as the writer does and is therefore equally entitled to assert his own opinion on that subject, whether it agrees with the author's or not. The COMMENT button is the absolute guarantor of that equality. Posting a rejoinder to an online article is hardly comparable to sending a letter to a newspaper editor, which may or may not be printed, according to editorial discretion. Moreover, the process of comment and countercomment narrows the distance between the two parties in a way that the seemingly endless chains of punch-counterpunch correspondence the old *Times* of London once was famous for never could. The fact that additional comments can be posted to the same article creates a situation in which many people are "speaking" at once, thus confusing the issue, as during a debate on a televised political talk show. In the ensuing chaos the "facts" at issue, assuming any were offered in the first place, are buried beneath that pile-on of narcissistic opinion and raw, conflicting emotion that Internet writing exalts over everything else, authority especially.[11]

In the world of the mass media, including the Web, journalism and politics meet and meld on equal yet indistinguishable terms, in company with commercial advertising and public relations. In the media, as in modern society as a whole, these things merge as an inseparable whole, a vast conglomerate of associated interests and mutual or supporting aims that can hardly be disentangled. In these circumstances, democratic politics, and even politics itself, become unworkable—impossible—as the media manipulate reality, obscuring vital connections and ignoring means and motives, while deciding for themselves what is significant and what is not, what people should know and what people ought not know. A republic, which Orestes Brownson defined as a government founded on a polity, depends entirely on its citizens' connection with reality—a thing the mass media in every nation are doing their best to replace with a huge, amorphous social, political, and existential myth they could not begin either to fathom or to explain to themselves.

Still, the media, the Internet especially, are supposed to present us with information—"facts"—not myth. But it is not so. (Let us set aside, even while taking note of it, the insight that the word *information* is an inaccurate one. "It is not information," John Lukacs corrects. "Its proper description is *the imaging of matter*.")[12] "A fact," Jacques Ellul said, "that does not command attention and does not become a political fact ceases to exist even as a fact, whatever its importance may be."[13] But the Internet is credited with giving the public access to all the facts. Can we not infer from this that the facts thus established are political ones? Ellul would have denied it. The notion that they are indeed such (he would have countered) is merely a dream on the part of people wishing to be convinced that the mass media and democracy can be successfully integrated. "Only propaganda can make a fact a political one."[14]

The "fictitious universe," as Ellul called it—the media's myth—is itself a piece of propaganda. But it is propaganda that enthralls both the perpetrators and their victims, the rulers and the ruled alike, compelling modern politicians themselves to operate within this universe. In the mediated world, the nature of political acts is altered by "the verbal translation of facts operating in a universe of images."[15] All political problems, in this view, take form in the fictional universe of political "facts," and all of them are, therefore, the creations of propaganda. They are not, objectively speaking, problems at all, yet the public demands that they be "solved." A result of the confusion is, according to Ellul, a "double paralysis": government is weighed down by incoherent public opinion, and the public cannot express a collective mind that propaganda has formed for it. Another result is the inability of the public and the government to identify real problems, and the government's loss of power in respect of almost anything.[16]

The mass media are not the result of a malign plot; they are a technological excrescence that was not designed overall but was created incrementally in accordance with technological and financial, rather than human and social, logic. There is the problem. Mass communications are destructive because they claim to communicate without really doing so. The reason they cannot communicate is that human communication by an impersonal message multiplied scores of millions of times is a human impossibility. To address everyone at once is to address nobody at all. Christ Himself appears to have limited His audiences to five thousand people, while saving His choicest teachings for private discussions with the Twelve. And the thing works both ways. As a broadcasting company cannot address the masses in any significant way, so the masses, taken as individuals or collectively, can take nothing of significance from the central impersonal source— except, of course, "information" and political "facts." On the receiving end of the airwaves or the fiber-optic transmission line, there is the illusion of having been addressed, the illusion of comprehension; on the sending side, the dumb silence of the voluntarily mute, the sound of a silence that is not golden.

It is frequently claimed on behalf of the mass media that at the very least they create community, from the local to the global level. Again, nothing could be further from the truth, as the history of the world in recent decades has confirmed over and again. To know the Other is to distrust and even to despise him. The reason is obvious. As Pierre Manent knows, "It is not speech that produces the community, but the community that produces and maintains speech."[17]

10

Democracy and Modern Man

Among the gravest threats to the Western democratic nations is the transformation—and in some countries, such as the United States, almost the replacement—of the original populations. Tocqueville recognized that a people's character is more important than the nature and structure of its institutions. During the past hundred years or so, the character of the established democratic peoples has been greatly altered by two major forces. The first is profound demographic change, an ethnic and racial alteration of the Western democratic publics. The second is the modern era—a product of advanced democratic theory, positivism, and scientific materialism that has been reshaping the classical understanding of man, nature, and the universe that made democratic government first a possibility and later a reality, but that has since become so altered by the extension, exaggeration, and deformation of its original principles that it threatens to stifle and destroy the achievement that had once seemed its most glorious contribution to humanity.

"Providence," John Jay wrote in *Federalist* No. 2, "has been pleased to give us this one connected country to one united people—a people descended from the same ancestors, speaking the same language, professing the same religion, attached to the same principles of government, very similar in manners and customs."The contemporary American debate concerning the benefits and liabilities of immigration dates from colonial times and was acknowledged by the Founders, who made their individual contributions to it. While quoting these men on the subject has lately become a sort of intellectual parlor game in which both sides can score points, modern restrictionists enjoy a distinct advantage. Washington, Jefferson, and John Adams believed that immigration could have only deleterious consequences for the young United States, while Hamilton warned that "the safety of a republic depends upon the energy of a common national sentiment; on a uniformity of principles and habits; and on that love of country which will almost invariably be found to be closely connected with birth, education, and family. . . . The influx of foreigners must . . . tend to produce a heterogeneous compound."[1]

Against their wishes and advice, the heterogeneous compound proved to be the American future. The arrival of millions of starving Irish peasants during the potato famine of 1845–1850 and then, after the War between the States, successive waves of immigrants from central, eastern, and southern Europe—encouraged by American industrialists demanding vast supplies of cheap labor—transformed a demographically and culturally unified society into its opposite. The influx ceased with the First World War, but immigration resumed in the 1930s after the Nazis came to power in Germany. Since the passage of the Immigration Act of 1965, the flow of immigrants to America from the Third World (Mexico especially) has been literally uncontrolled.

An estimated twelve to twenty million immigrants, the large majority of them Mexican, are resident in the United States today, and the Spanish-language network Univision is expected to become the nation's largest broadcast network in the near future. Spanish is the alternative national language in all fifty states and recognized as such, whether officially or not, by government at the federal, state, and local levels and by commercial advertisers of every sort. Similarly,

Mexican culture, promoted not only by minority radio and television stations but also by the "mainstream" media, the public educational system, academia, and the advertising industry, has become the informal alternative national culture of the United States. Although the spirit of *reconquista* is limited to a minority of the Mexican immigrant community, mainly in California and Texas, the Mexican government covertly but strongly encourages it. That government need not consider—for now—whether the possible eventual secession of the states of the American Southwest and their reattachment to the Republic of Mexico would benefit its interests. Even so, the Mexican immigrants, save for their numbers, would be an almost inconsiderable presence in the United States, in whose greatest cities more than a hundred different languages are spoken across a spectrum of thousands of various immigrant neighborhoods.

After World War II, the sending countries of the Old World joined the receiving ones of the New. In 1968, J. Enoch Powell, a British classical scholar and former secretary of state for health in the government of Harold Macmillan, delivered a speech in which he quoted from the *Aeneid*: "I see wars, horrid wars, and the Tiber foaming with much blood." Powell continued: "Those whom the gods wish to destroy, they first make mad. We must be mad, literally mad, as a nation to be permitting the annual inflow of some 50,000 dependents, who are for the most part the future growth of the immigrant-dependent population. It is like watching a nation busily engaged in heaping its own funeral pyre." The speech hit home with the public (Powell received 100,000 letters, 800 of which disapproved of his remarks), but Prime Minister Edward Heath sacked him from his shadow cabinet anyway. Forty years later the United Kingdom, with a population of sixty-two million, is home to more than seven million foreign-born people.[2] Enoch Powell had urged "the discussion of future grave but, with effort now, avoidable evils [which] is the most unpopular and at the same time the most necessary occupation for the politician." He added, "Those who knowingly shirk it, deserve, and not infrequently receive, the curses of those who come after."[3]

Today it is an open secret in Britain that during their tenures in office, Prime Ministers Tony Blair and Gordon Brown deliberately—in brazenly undemocratic disregard of their constituencies' wishes—flooded the British Isles with Third World immigrants, the majority from Britain's former colonies. The Prince of Wales himself has remarked, "Let me say how much pleasure the whole idea of diversity gives me. All the people from diverse backgrounds, black, brown, yellow and the like, represent an amazing and very jolly cross section of the different communities that make up Britain. In my view, this should be a source of pride, not envy or resentment. I fully understand the problems and the difficulties experienced by immigrant communities in Great Britain. What we need, I think, is a level of civilized tolerance in a multiracial society."[4]

Unimpressed by Prince Charles's vision of jollity in diversity, the English scholar Christie Davies, a man well traveled in the Muslim world, predicts that "the logic both of democracy and of aggression" ensures that a future Muslim takeover of Britain is virtually assured, owing to the high birthrate among Muslims that manifests "the great source of Muslim strength"—keeping women down. The Muslim conquest, should it happen, will not have been a planned event; rather, it will be "the spontaneous consequence of uncontrolled immigration, demographic collapse, and cultural decline. Gradually, Britain will become part of the Muslim world, with all its innate backwardness, leaving the modern world to be divided between the fiercely Christian Americans and the secular Confucian Chinese."[5]

Several years after Powell's speech, the French novelist Jean Raspail published *The Camp of the Saints*, a novel that owed much of its force to its being at once a futuristic and a realistic story about hundreds of thousands of impoverished refugees from Calcutta who invade southern France; the French media, government, churches, and academics instantly welcome the refugees. Raspail's personal response to this fictional scenario is unequivocal. Nevertheless, he states the moral dilemma in dispassionate terms: if we accept these subcontinental hordes, they will destroy us; should we turn them away, we shall destroy them. The book was an immediate bestseller and caused great controversy in France. Today the French, after earnestly debating whether the public display of the head scarf and the burka are compatible with the ideals of an explicitly secular republic, have banned the full veil in public places, and the number of Muslims in France has climbed to five to six million people (or perhaps higher). Even if the low-end estimate is correct, France has the largest Muslim population of any country in Europe, both in real terms and by percentage.[6] (The high percentage is explained partly by the French government's willingness to tolerate polygamy among an estimated twenty thousand families in France, each of which is thought to include more than two dozen sons.) The government's policy of *regroupement familial* has permitted immigrant families to live an existence separate from the French, a world unto themselves within the close and exclusive confines of their native cultures.

Southward across the Alps, the Italian judiciary labors to undermine the anti-immigrant legislation that the center-right coalition passed. The Supreme Court of Cassation has ruled that a recidivist illegal immigrant, once apprehended, may not be arrested but instead must be escorted to the Italian border and expelled. Below the Pyrenees, Spain for the past twenty years has pursued a policy of virtually open borders, welcoming immigrants from eastern Europe, North Africa, South America, and elsewhere. Presently these amount to better than three million people: 11 percent of the "Spanish" population of forty-four million is now foreign born, approaching the United States's 12.9 percent. Immigrants, many of them Turkish, restless, and often aggressive in their social and religious demands on the state and society as a whole, account for nearly 9 percent of the total population of Germany. In the Netherlands, 6 percent of the population consists of Muslim immigrants; Rotterdam, Amsterdam, The Hague, and Utrecht have Muslim majorities, or close to it.[7] We are concerned here not with the multiple effects of non-Western immigration on the myriad aspects and corners of Western culture but solely with its implications for Western democratic institutions. (For the rest, Christopher

Caldwell provides a survey in his admirably comprehensive book, *Reflections on the Revolution in Europe.*)[8]

So far, the United States has been the target of a series of specific attacks by Muslim terrorists. Europe is the object of a far wider aggression signaled by direct threats and boasts by Muslim immigrant mullahs and popular leaders tracing back at least to the mid-1970s. That is when the project "Eurabia" was launched by the eponymous magazine, published in Paris in the French language and supported by a variety of institutions connected with Middle Eastern interests, on the one hand, and, on the other, by an arm of the European Economic Community. The late Italian journalist Oriana Fallaci described Eurabia as part of "the biggest conspiracy that modern history has created."[9] The original goal of this conspiracy, Fallaci asserted, was to compel Europe to import Arab immigrants along with Arab oil, to promote the superiority of Arab culture and religion over the religion and culture of the West, and to diffuse the Arab language and the teachings of Muhammad throughout Europe. This was around the time when, in 1974, President Houari Boumediene of Algeria warned the UN General Assembly, "One day millions of men will leave the southern hemisphere of this planet to burst into the northern one. But not as friends. Because they will burst in to conquer, and they will conquer by populating it with their children. Victory will come to us from the wombs of our women."[10] In 1997 a London mullah was reported to have said that because Muslims could not conquer the Europeans with tanks and troops, they would have to overcome them by force of numbers instead.

These threats, apparently reflecting the sentiments of some hundreds of thousands of Muslim immigrants in Europe, are not posturing; they have been made in all seriousness. Whatever the modern West makes of the proposition, the truth is that every society ultimately derives its strength, purpose, and resolve from religion. This includes false religions. But liberalism, the false religion of the West, neither believes in nor practices resistance to those who threaten its religion at home, however much it is given to waging offensive war at arm's length. The historic religion of the West, which did inspire resistance and gave it theological justification, is nearly dead in western Europe. Across the Continent, the first (and last) impulse of Western "leaders" in every sphere of society is to placate, to excuse, to ignore—and so tacitly to encourage—the ostensibly peaceful invasion by a culture that is the avowed enemy of Christianity and of the free, liberal, and democratic societies that Christianity made possible.

Among its many effects, immigration, and the resulting displacement of Western culture by Muslim culture, "exacts a steep price in freedom," as Christopher Caldwell notes. "The multiculturalism that has been Europe's main way of managing mass immigration requires the sacrifice of liberties that natives once thought of as rights."[11] For example, if government is to intrude on Muslim families to ensure that women are not repressed by their husbands, then it feels encouraged—even required—to interfere in relationships within non-Muslim families as well, since to do otherwise would amount to discrimination. In this way, the right of freedom of religion is compromised by newly recognized "cultural" rights to such an extent that it is no longer really a right at all.[12] Similarly, Britain, historically the land of free speech and freedom of the press, has made criticism of immigration and immigrants a crime of "hate speech." When a newspaper in Denmark printed an unflattering cartoon representing Muhammad wearing a bomb in his turban, European governments responded pusillanimously to Muslim threats and demands for apology. In France, Interior Minister Nicolas Sarkozy later retracted his harsh condemnation of the Muslim riots in the *banlieues*, and the government made concessions to the adolescent rioters. Even the Vatican, despite its concern for the future of Christianity in Europe, resorts to ropey lengths of platitudinous verbiage concerning "human rights," "the dignity of man," the rights of migrants," "human development," and the biblical injunction to "welcome the stranger." The historic Church of Rome was made of stronger stuff. Had it not been, the civilization of the West could not have been created in the first place. But if the West will not defend what is, or used to be, its faith, it will not defend the liberal principles and democratic institutions that, before advanced liberalism corrupted them, stood as pillars of modern Western society.

"Thanks to your democratic laws we will invade you," a Muslim delegate told an official meeting of Islamic-Christian "dialogue" in 1999, and "thanks to our religious laws, we will dominate you."[13] As James Burnham suggested a half century ago, there must be something fundamentally wrong with a political philosophy (liberalism) that can survive in application only by violating its own principles.[14]

Europe is impotent in the face of Muslim immigration—the greatest threat faced by the European democracies, and indeed by the European democratic principle itself. The Muslim invasion of Europe is the result of three phenomena: the market liberalism that brought the first wave of African and Asian "guest workers" to the Continent in the 1950s and '60s; the aggressive theocracy espoused by those workers and by successive waves of Muslim immigrants; and the ideological bent of European politicians and bureaucrats following World War II. ("We live in a borderless world," in the opinion of one European cabinet minister, "in which our new mission is defending the border not of our countries but of civility and human rights.")[15]

As for the native populations of Europe, which have always been, and remain today, opposed to the immigrants' presence among them, they were never consulted on the matter. "If Europe is getting more immigrants than its voters want, this is a good sign that its democracy is malfunctioning," Caldwell argues.[16] (He adds that "this is not the essence of liberalism, but it is the essence of democracy.")[17] Eager to present Europe's immigration issue as a racial one, analogous to the historical black problem in the United States, European governments have chosen to ignore the fact that, unlike American blacks of the pre–civil rights era, Muslim immigrants do not want what the native European publics want. They are demanding not integration with the natives on equal terms but acceptance by them on terms favorable to, and dictated by, Islam. When a weak and uncertain majority culture—like that of Europe—lacking confidence in itself and in its past is challenged by an assured, self-confident, and aggressive minority—such as Islam—the consequent conflicts are likely to be settled in favor of the minority. Demoralized by its loss of religious faith, by its collective guilt about Continental history in the first half of the twentieth century and about its colonial past, and by its conversion en masse to the secular religion of multiculturalism, Europe has disarmed itself in the face of cultural and demographic invasion—the opening phase of Samuel Huntington's clash of civilizations, the intraplanetary equivalent of H. G. Wells's *War of the Worlds*. Suppose, half a century from now, a newly formed Muslim plurality (or even, here and there, majority) of the European republics were, by democratic decision, to declare their new homelands Islamic republics, ruled by Islamic politicians and subject to Sharia. Such an event would not amount to a liberal revolution, but it would assuredly be a democratic one—followed by the construction of a Muslim Europe that would be neither liberal nor democratic.

"What we call the 'spirit' of politics," said Walter Bagehot, "is more surely changed by a change of generation in the men than by any other change whatever."[18] The men and women of the modern democratic West are almost unrecognizably altered—morally, religiously, intellectually, and culturally—from what they were in the time of the American Revolution, the French Revolution, the unification of Italy, and the consolidation of the Germanies under Prussia. Human nature is a given; it never changes. Human character does not greatly change over the generations either, yet it is malleable, and such changes as occur in respect of it are caused by changed ways of thinking.[19] Western thought has revolutionized itself since the beginning of the modern democratic experiment two centuries ago, and it has done so in ways that are not in agreement with democratic theory and practice. The loss of traditional religious faith as the basis of Western philosophy

and science has radically undermined both the intellectual foundations of democratic government and its operation. The sociologist
Richard Rorty understands modern democratic man as "a new sort
of individual . . . [who] will take nothing as authoritative save free
consensus between as diverse a variety of citizens as can possibly be
produced." And the idea of democratic liberty has changed with the
democratic citizen himself. "We are deprived," Rorty says, "not of liberty, but of the idea of liberty. For two centuries, we have thought of
liberty through the spectrum of the political sphere that was needed
to organize it. We wanted to be citizens. But citizenship today is only
a convenient means of acting out our ill feeling toward the authorities.
We have lost the foundation of our dignity as free men, the aspiration
of forming a body politic."[20]

This has much to do with the end of the European bourgeois age
that began five hundred years ago and in which the creation of the
United States was a salient event. More precisely, our nation is a product of the eighteenth-century Enlightenment, whose ambitions and
ideals centered on parliamentary democracy, yet in this respect the age
of the Enlightenment, too, is as dead as the era of the bourgeoisie—
the two constituents of the modern age. So, at any rate, argues Jean-
Marie Guéhenno: "The dream of a system of checks and balances,
the parceling out of power between several small autonomous poles,
creates not equilibrium but paralysis. The public debate illuminated by
the light of reason . . . is replaced by a professional confrontation of
interests."[21] So democracy is no longer about the enjoyment of liberty,
whether personal or collective; it is only about interests and the distribution of rewards, generally of a material sort.

In Europe, the reigning intellectual temper is radically post-
Christian and neo-Marxist; in America, it is evangelical Christian
and broadly progressive. In both instances, it is powerfully imbued
with the ideology of multiculturalism, originally imposed by the elite
classes, who have succeeded in shaming or browbeating ordinary people into accepting it, partly as the Weltanschauung of modernity but
also, and more significantly, as a component of basic civility. The result

throughout the Western democratic world is a form of cognitive dissonance at the personal level—while almost everyone professes one thing, very many believe something else without ever being able to admit as much, even to themselves—and a general political incoherence at the public level. Incoherence is unsurprising among the citizens of a postmodern country with no racial, ethnic, or cultural identity; no agreed-on history; no generally accepted system of morality but rather a widespread confusion between the sexes in respect of sexual and generational roles, and other matters; no sense of national values beyond abstract ahistorical principles; no consensus regarding either the nature of law or of the laws themselves; no notion of regional or national obligation; no knowledge of, or feeling for, the past; and only a shallow ideological sense of the future. Western publics (especially in America, where cynicism is still less pervasive than in Europe) are experiencing an epidemic of mass mental confusion, produced by supposedly rational political theories that amount at best to a general, and generalized, pseudophilosophy that spurs voters to vacillate wildly between one candidate, one political party, and the other in a blind quest for a mystical thing called "change"—or protection from change, as the case may be. And they are agitated further by irreconcilable antagonisms created by the so-called culture wars and by demographic fragmentation that, in the not-so-distant future, is likely to result in the balkanization of society.

Jacques Ellul argued the need to reform the democratic citizen rather than democratic institutions, but the prospect for this is not good. The immaturity of the modern democratic mind, apparent in the puerility notable in every aspect of Western culture today, works against it. Mass affluence and a history of relative political and economic stability, both of which tend to shield publics from the harsher realities of private and civic life that prevailed in previous historical eras, have contributed to this generalized juvenility; so has the process of urbanization and suburbanization that has accustomed people to a comfortable existence in a largely man-made, almost wholly artificial, world. Driven by an advertising industry that has turned youth and sex into marketable commodities, the mass media have created a cult of youth, while promoting simultaneously a popular distrust of age and experience and a denial of the wisdom that these things bring, whether in government, scholarship, or the arts. And the culture of leisure that accompanies generalized affluence has encouraged the infantilism endemic to Western society, as contemporary Western dress suggests. (While the bourgeois age lasted, until approximately after the Second World War, children dressed like their parents: girls like smaller versions of their mothers, boys in imitation of their fathers. Today in the classless West ruled by an ideology of sameness, both parents dress like their children—the entire family uniform in a juvenile assemblage of jeans, message T-shirts, ball caps, and sneakers.) Formality, which once prevailed even among the lower classes, is an aspect of human dignity and an expression of the adulthood that everyone seems bent on denying these days, presumably on the assumption that sexual maturity is sufficient to grown-upness while maturity of any other sort simply gets in the way of sexual indulgence.

In the political context, mental and emotional immaturity is apparent in the unrealistic impatience of the democratic citizen who demands from his elected officials instant political results that often enough have little or nothing to do with the "change" that democratic politicians incessantly invoke on the electorate's behalf, and, more broadly, in the growing inability of the voters to weigh and balance political questions, indeed to think politically at all. Most important, ideological thinking—an infallible sign of the hopelessly immature political mind—induces a false spiritualism far more damaging and dangerous than materialism itself. When one considers the extent to which the popular intelligence has deteriorated, and the degree to which formerly homogeneous and relatively simple societies have become heterogeneous and complex ones since the invention of modern democracy two hundred years ago, it seems neither far-fetched nor alarmist to wonder whether the Western democratic publics are any longer governable by democratic means.

Democracy, to succeed, must be more than self-government. It must be the love of self-government, inducing an affection even for government itself. Yet the greater and more expansive government produced by that affection, and by engendered trust, in the end produces love's opposite—hatred of government, and the refusal to cooperate with or tolerate it. There may be no way around this fundamental paradox of the democratic system.

In the literature of democracy and of politics in general, an interesting question is being debated these days. Are the Western democracies approaching an era in which politics will no longer exist?

There is, to start with, the issue of whether democratic capitalism—the market—might not be overpowering democratic politics, economic life, and the political life, and whether politics—even democratic politics—has not come to play a secondary role in public life even as it is becomes conflated with it. Citing the United States as a paramount example, Guéhenno suggests that "in the age of the networks, the relationship of the citizens to the body politic is in competition with the infinity of connections they establish outside it. So politics, far from being the organizing principle of life in society, appears as a secondary activity, if not an artificial construct poorly suited to the resolution of the practical problems of the modern world."[22] His observation is the more apt given the popular ideological claim that "everything is political"—which only serves, of course, to distract people from those issues and activities that are by nature wholly and directly political.

If, for instance, the marital relationship between husband and wife should really be understood as a political one, then it is neither politically irresponsible nor neglectful of a democratic citizen to devote attention, time, and energy to the related sociological, psychological, and ideological issues inherent in the marriage bond at the expense of mastering his government's economic and foreign policies, matters pertaining to the traditional notion of politics. If public life, thus understood, is reduced to an array of more or less disconnected and specialized (from the nonideological point of view) interests and aims, the result could be, as Guéhenno suggests, that "politics, which calls on the active participation of a significant segment of the citizenry, may no longer be the ultimate arena in which these [large] questions are decided." This development would amount to the depoliticizing (or political trivialization) of democracy, which—it has been suggested— might have been democracy's destination all along.[23]

Sir Henry Maine, contrary to Walter Bagehot, who believed monarchy to be the form of government most engaging for the public, thought the people found popular government the most interesting— mainly on account of the party system, which encouraged citizens to follow politics as they would "a never-ending cricket-match between Blue and Yellow."[24] (Or, among the aristocratic politicians themselves, perhaps as a duel. The aisle of Charles Barry's rebuilt House of Commons is said to have been designed, in 1836, to exceed the length of a sword's reach.) But Maine himself disliked and disapproved of the party system—which he called "the wire-pulling system"—because of the temptation it offered to "over-indulgence" in "a passion with elevated minds."[25] James Bryce, a great friend to democracy, nevertheless saw party organization in the United States as a type of "second non-legal government" that had managed to win control over the legal one.[26]

There is a striking contrast between these relatively mild strictures against party from nineteenth-century authors and the scornful condemnation of modern political parties by Jacques Ellul, who condemned personal commitment to a political movement as a surrender of personal responsibility, liberty, and judgment. "There is no longer a living force for political judgment or inspiration; inside the party, there is no longer thought. Old positions are preserved, obsolete thoughts remain what they were, and teams brought to power by different parties follow the same policies because they are conditioned by elements and means that have nothing to do with doctrines. The great choices are outside of party reach." The "false commitment" to party, Ellul concluded, "is probably one of the most striking results of the political illusion."[27] Like Maine, Ellul thought that modern party politics is about team rivalry—only today, the competitive game is taken more seriously by the players than by the majority of spectators, a majority of which, perhaps, has long since ceased to find amusement in the sport.

The complaint against the modern democratic party system is too enormous overall and too extensively enumerated to be discussed at length here. It includes the supposed danger of faction and government instability produced by party government; the shameless "wire-pulling" by the professional politicians, resulting in candidates chosen by professionals instead of by the people; the popular unaccountability that the selection process entails, and the corrupting influence of business, financial, and special interest lobbies; the power of money in deciding elections; the fact of either too many parties in the field or too few of them; the exclusive nature of those parties, which guarantees that many minority interests will be underrepresented or not represented at all; and the tendency for party politics to degenerate into political sport and public amusement. Recent times have also brought objections that these political or sportive rivalries are not sportive enough—that the game, in other words, is rigged, that the two or several parties are at bottom in agreement with one another on all the great issues and their noisy partisan arguments are merely for show.

This nonideological view of democratic politics is common regarding the essentially two-party American system; it is less so regarding the multiparty European arrangements—until recently at least, when the growing power and reach of the European Union has led to the widespread perception of a single bureaucratic interest fixed in Brussels and Strasbourg. The exception appears to be Great Britain, as popular discontent with the alleged lack of choice offered by the two dominant parties, Conservative and Labour, suggests.

The ideological view, on the other hand, holds that party politics—in the United States especially—is ideologically polarized, although opinion divides on the question of whether party polarization accurately reflects the divisions among the electorate. A generation ago, E. J. Dionne published a widely discussed book arguing that American politics has been divided against itself since the "cultural civil war" began in the 1960s and that liberals and conservatives have continued to argue the same issues over and again ever since. The greatest problem with American political life, Dionne argued, involves the failure of liberalism and conservatism, the country's predominating ideologies.[28] In his view, the ideological identity of American politics is an illusion created by the politically motivated formulation of a series of false choices that the parties subsequently present to the electorate. Dependent on elements of their self-absorbed and party-minded constituencies, politicians engage in a type of politics that is largely symbolic rather than substantive. The resulting false polarization prevents the nation from solving its most pressing issues by instituting political gridlock, despite the existence of a nonideological majority that wishes government to be done with the supposedly meaningless liberal-conservative standoff and "move on"—or rather backward, toward what Arthur Schlesinger Jr. in the 1950s called "the search for remedy."

Dionne took care not to conflate "conservatives" with "Republicans" and "liberals" with "Democrats," and his assumption that the majority of Americans are ideologically neutral and pragmatic has become far less tenable in the twenty years since his book was published. Indeed, Barack Obama's election and still more his presidency have hardened ideological and party lines to a degree that makes ideology and party almost the equivalents of one another. "Real" ideological polarization, apparently, is more polarizing even than "false" polarization, and in a deeply divided country "real" party choice is as paralyzing politically as perceived single-party choice can be. (Henry Maine thought party spirit had much in common with religious spirit, and of course history offers numerous examples of religious and party affiliation being one and the same thing.)

Still, there remains the question of fidelity in political representation, the degree to which political parties do in fact represent the people who vote for them. Michael Hardt and Antonio Negri have suggested that, lacking an actual social foundation, "representation" is an artificial construct, whereby democratic representation of mass publics gives way to the manufacture by the people's elected "representatives" of their own constituencies. "Through the mediatic manipulation of society, conducted through enhanced polling techniques, social mechanisms of surveillance and control, and so forth, power tries to prefigure its own power base . . . and simplify the complexity of reality."[29] In these circumstances, no one can say what any particular section of the public believes—or would believe, if it were allowed the chance to decide what it thinks for itself—and democratic representation in the traditional sense becomes unknowable, hence impossible.

The crisis of Western democracy goes deeper than all such considerations. "Underneath the popular anger at not being well represented, one can detect deep anguish at being no longer representable," Pierre Manent suggests. "One can detect the fear that we are no longer a people, or at least are less and less one. This is true whether one understands this fine word 'people' in the sense of a coherent 'society' or in a 'national' sense."[30] Jacques Ellul, Manent's compatriot of a generation earlier, said much the same thing when he questioned whether citizens any longer have the desire to participate in politics. Both men had first in mind their native France but, beyond that, western Europe and North America as well. "Democratic government today resembles a government that neither represents nor governs," Manent says.[31] It does, of course, administer. Or rather, it attempts to do so—though with ever less success, the bureaucracy having, in the interests of democratic "fairness," to a significant extent usurped the place and role of politics.

Two results follow directly from this. The first, as Ellul pointed out, is that democracy has ceased to be a means to limit and control the power of the state; it has become instead the means by which the bureaucracy organizes the masses. The second is that, in the attempt to honor "democratic values," democratic governments have paralyzed democracy, as Manent sees clearly: "In the name of what is sometimes called 'procedural democracy,' we have emptied democracy in its original and proper sense of its substance as the self-government of a political body."[32] In these circumstances, political debate naturally devolves into a question of the individual integrity—a matter of being more procedural than thou—of the political actors involved in a political game in which agreement on the rules is the only point of consensus—the sole recognized "operating standard of a society without a goal," as Guéhenno says.[33] In this way, democracy, obsessed with the moral rigor of human action, judged by the extent to which its moral basis can be generalized, has succumbed to a form of religious fundamentalism.[34]

One perceives here a connection between democracy and religious sentimentalism, and even narcissism. It is the connection between democracy and self-righteousness, as exemplified by Woodrow Wilson. (A democratic people, being by definition a virtuous people, is always morally in the right, even the super-right.) This is why, for liberal democratic publics, human history is always scandalous. Unfortunately, as Manent reminds us, "the requisite morality is simply that of *recognizing political reality*, which means the *objective* character of political bodies and, more generally, of human communities. 'Objective': that means above all that we think independently of what we hope or fear, believe or imagine." (Or like and dislike, of course.)[35]

But the capacity for objectivity and the ability to recognize reality are of no avail in what Guéhenno calls "a world without politics": a world in which the old political rituals alone remain, the political sphere having succumbed at last to its own liberation. (The question of whether a connection exists between the atrophy of religion and the imperial system and the decline of the nation-state is an interesting one.) A half century earlier, Jacques Ellul asserted that in the age of ephemerality the modern politician is no longer capable of making true political decisions but is limited instead to pseudodecisions that, being strictly determined, permit the deciders no leeway: in an age when publics are persuaded that values belong to an outmoded form of politics, the politician may no longer set them above the facts. But facts constrain politics more than values. Thus law and politics—two of man's greatest accomplishments, in which he recognizes forms and objects, assigns names and places, and realizes continuity within universal flux—are replaced by an excessive concern for circumstances, as the politician, hard-pressed by the pseudodecisions of the citizens, is forced into repeated action without delay. (Jouvenel recognized the same thing in what he called "legislative activity," which, rather than resulting from study and meditation, is only the botched product of shortsighted views and self-interest compounded by human passion.)

In this way, politics is removed from the main theater of government and confined to the most superficial actions. Our view of political powers remains the old one, Ellul argues; it persists in accepting at their former value the institutional structures, constitutions, and judicial processes of Western society. But these familiar things have been devalued over time, and the notion that anyone, whether politician or citizen, can modify reality by means of political power, and by participation in the game of politics control the state, is an illusion. Instead, representative government is reduced to rubber-stamping decisions made by panels of experts and at the insistence of pressure groups. And behind everything is the bureaucracy, which no one can understand, let alone control, and which reduces the effect of all political decisions. Bureaucracy, by its omnipresence in the political machines of every country and in every nook and cranny of power, has itself become the state.

"The people will fancy an appearance of freedom," Saint-Just wrote; "illusion will be their native land."

✦   ✦   ✦ Jews

"Suppose Louis XV," Thomas Jefferson wrote to James Madison in 1789, ". . . had said to the moneylenders of Holland, 'Give us money, that we may eat drink and be merry in our day; and on condition you will demand no interest til the end of thirty-four years, you shall then, forever after, receive an annual interest of 15 percent.' The money is lent on these conditions, is divided among the people, eaten, drunk, and squandered. Would the present generation be obliged to apply the produce of the earth and of their labour, to replace their dissipations? Not at all."[36] Nine years later, Jefferson told John Taylor of Caroline that, could he obtain a single amendment to the Constitution, it would be an article removing from the federal government the power to borrow money.

The dangers of profligate spending to any government, or form of government, anywhere, anytime, are obvious: debt has brought down many a government throughout history, the French monarchy in the days of Louis XVI and the Weimar government with the most spectacular results. The huge indebtedness of democratic states in the twenty-first century, incurred by socialist policies resulting in excessive expenditure, put in question the moral and practical responsibility of democratic publics and the restraint of their elected governments. Tocqueville noted a fundamental weakness of the democratic polity when he warned that, although the pursuit of wealth agreed with American civil and political life, a time might come when the two things would be conflated. According to certain modern observers, that time has arrived, greatly facilitated by modern mass media and instruments of direct personal communication such as the personal computer and all its proliferant electronic progeny. "The chief business of the American people is business," said Calvin Coolidge in the 1920s. Today the business of America, and of the other Western democracies, is money, and that is a different thing entirely.

In recent times, economics has taken property, converted it (absent the gold standard) into the abstract form of paper money, and reconverted it again into still more abstract forms like derivatives and floats—illustrating, as Guéhenno says, "how markets severely challenge the power of citizens and the democratic state itself to chart their own course." And modern power, itself an abstraction, is conveyed by money: "the universal passageway" between forms of power. When politics becomes an adjunct to the market, politics as such is abolished: the public interest and the private are no longer considered separate and opposing things, because efficiency in every activity depends on the availability of the greatest amount of information to everyone, in every one of his capacities. Thus the political sphere cannot be independent from all the others. Guéhenno concludes that "corruption is now only an archaic word through which those nostalgic for another age bitterly describe the inevitable value accorded to networked power." The fact explains the scandal-prone nature of modern democracies, which is simply the consequence of money's having become the sole universal measure and means of exchange between modern people.[37]

But governments can scarcely explain this arcane reality to the satisfaction of their publics, accustomed to recognizing corruption according to the old rules and with a natural human instinct for sniffing it out and demanding that the perpetrators be punished. Worse, the politicians have no interest in explaining the new reality (supposing that they have grasped it themselves); instead, they have a very real political interest in concealing it and wielding charges of corruption as a weapon against their political opponents. They have, in short, a motive for fanning class resentments into class warfare—that old, old trick that those in power have used time and again to bring down democratic governments and destroy democracy, along with peace, in their time.

Economic inequalities, in particular those inequalities created and reflected by the power of international finance, have usually been opposed, in the European democracies, by the more or less conventional socialist parties that have maintained a presence within European political establishments since the middle of the nineteenth century. In the United States, populism has been the preferred political alternative to socialism, although, owing to its largely episodic and reactive nature, it has had a far more sporadic career. The People's Party, established in 1892 in response to agricultural depression for the purpose of uniting farm and labor organizations, demanded, among other things, free and unlimited coinage of silver at a ratio of sixteen to one; a national currency issued directly by the federal government (that is, without resort to banking corporations as an intermediary); government ownership and operation of the transport and communications companies; a graduated income tax; the direct election of U.S. senators; and immigration restriction.

Today's imperfect but nearest equivalent of the Populist Party is the Tea Party movement, founded in 2009 during the so-called Great Recession as a tax protest first but also in opposition to the federal bailout of several Wall Street banks, General Motors, and Chrysler. Over the next twelve months, the Tea Party played a crucial role in the election of a Republican successor to Edward Kennedy's Senate seat with the explicit purpose of blocking President Obama's national health-care plan; later, the Tea Party took up the cause of immigration restriction after having deliberately avoided the issue for a full year. So far, European politics has developed no equivalent to the Tea Party— as, indeed, it had none to the Populist Party. Great Britain has the British National Party, France Le Pen's National Front, Austria the Freedom Party, Hungary the Jokke, and Italy the Northern League, but each of these organizations (save perhaps the *Lega Nord*) has a relatively narrow focus—immigration as a threat to national identity— which, for the Tea Party, was distinctly an afterthought.

Between William Jennings Bryan's crusade and the Tea Party, the populist mood and agenda have been represented by George Wallace's third-party presidential bid in 1968, Ross Perot's Reform Party, and Pat Buchanan's pitchfork campaigns in the 1990s. All of these, to a greater or lesser extent, expressed the discontent, anger, and resentment of the Middle American Radicals, a term coined by an American political scientist and popularized by the journalist and historian Samuel T. Francis. Theoretically, at least, "MARs" are the demographic foundation of a New Right, caught between the managerial New Class and the Old Right that, in opposing it, succeeded only in demonstrating its own cultural effeteness and political irrelevance. The New Right is supposed to be nationalist rather than internationalist or anticommunist; to favor the restoration of intermediary institutions between the federal state and the American people; and to demand a strong, populist presidency endowed with the power to break through the liberal oligarchies that would be certain to oppose such a restoration. Middle American Radicals are neither liberal nor conservative; thus they are prepared to accept what Francis described as a new political theory able to win the loyalties and represent the interests of their social base, while rationalizing their quest for social power. (Certain political critics have suggested that the Tea Party and Governor Sarah Palin's wing of the Republican Party, taken together, are the embodiment of the Middle American Radicals, the core of a growing movement that has a chance to "take back" the country for the American people.)

But such a thing is unlikely to happen. Although populism has a long history in the United States, it has been one of co-optation, disappointment, and disaster.

Populist democracy has an inherent social disability. If it is to displace the present-day elite, it must be able to think and act like an elite—socially and humanly speaking an impossibility. Furthermore, a genuine elite never establishes itself by force or at the election booth: it is developed historically and trained up over time to exercise its privileges and assume its proper responsibilities. To repeat, the greatest failure of the ruling elite—the New Class—is that it has never learned, and probably never will learn, how to think like an aristocratic elite instead of as members of a dominant meritocracy, if only because it wouldn't have to.

The ruling class—the managerial state, the New Class, the liberal establishment, call it what you will—across the Western world and among the developing nations rules for the simple reason that it was created by, and reflects, the social and political arrangements underlying modernity: the modern scientific, capitalist, and technological world. So the New Class, comprised of two parts—the mandarins and the high financiers—is ever more securely entrenched. Antidemocratic as it is, it is by now practically unassailable.

It is almost an exercise in sentimentality to rail against the fact, but many contemporary critics have done just that. Of these, Christopher Lasch was among the most passionately trenchant. In *The Revolt of the Elites and the Betrayal of Democracy*, Lasch argued that the course of history no longer favors the leveling of social distinctions but tends to the establishment of a two-class society dominated by the "thinking classes" and the "symbolic analysts" (the latter phrase is Robert Reich's). The dominant class is loyal only to itself and its interests, assured that it well deserves all that it has managed to acquire for its authority and enjoyment; has no sense of generational continuity; and is aware of no responsibility, such as preceding elites (landed aristocracy, the old bourgeois and proprietary classes) felt to exercise true civic leadership, but is determined instead, in its desire to avoid risk and "contingency," to secede from the common world, the common man, and unpleasant reality. It has made noblesse oblige an abstraction by foisting off social costs on the state, which in turn finances social welfare through disproportionate taxation of the lower-middle and working classes. The elites, having lost hope in the project of raising the masses to a level of competence (which Lasch thought carried the original meaning of democracy), are content to entrust them to the "caring classes" operating through (and paid by) the state. Social mobility, he noted, actually buttresses the influence of elites by making plausible the notion that their station in life rests on merit. The journalist Mickey Kaus has suggested that inequality is less a matter of the unequal distribution of money than of the unwarranted power and influence money commands and the difference that money *makes* in America, so much so that democratic self-respect among ordinary people is diminished by the overbearing wealthy. "This is the great unfinished business of liberalism, not to equalize money, but to put money in its place," Kaus believes.[38]

But putting money in its place, beyond the context of an aristocratical society, is like putting feminine beauty in *its* place, and the New Class is not—not at this moment in history, at any rate—removable. This is why, as Christopher Lasch noted, the New Class will go to any length to avoid reference to, or discussion of, class distinctions. It is also why the New Right (the Middle American Radicals, the Tea Party) and now, on the Left, the Ninety-Nine Percent can be counted on to press the class issue to the forefront of the national consciousness, a project in which they are certain to be unwittingly abetted by Wall Street financiers and the party politicians who consort with them. Continuing economic deterioration on the public and private levels ensures class warfare an important role in the economically and socially unstable future of American politics and society.

11

Three against Democracy

Beyond the destabilizing characteristics of modern mass industrial democracies, three general and deep-running tendencies threaten the future of democratic institutions. They are the distortion, circumvention, and eventual destruction, by deceit and stealth, of the original democratic plan of government; the development of scientific technique, which in the long run works more to the advantage of government than of the citizenry (power of whatever sort in time is relentlessly appropriated by Power); and the natural tendency of Power to maximize itself in every form of government—not excluding democratic government.

The notion of a "living Constitution," as it has been developed in the United States over the past century, is scarcely foreign to the many other long-established democracies whose governments are based on written constitutions, or even to Great Britain, with its unwritten plan of government. All constitutions, like that of the United States, are similarly subject to the corrupting effects of ad hoc popular government and, more important still, the determined efforts of "progressive"

public elites. Yet in no country has the doctrine of constitutional organicism been more consciously developed than in America, the paramount symbol of democracy in the world as well as its historical leader—and now, it may be, its bellwether. Going far beyond any other common-law country, the United States is committed to an ideal of judicial activism that has encouraged the legislative form of judgeship to overshadow the common law, and other law as well.[1]

Walter Bagehot was unimpressed by the U.S. Constitution, which he criticized for its cavalier assumption "that the limited clauses of an old state-paper can provide for all coming cases, and forever regulate their future."[2] Bagehot had a point regarding the Constitution's intended historical inflexibility, and it would be interesting to know how he might have proposed coping with it. Given the circumstances of the Constitution's formulation, and the intent and understanding of the men who wrote it, it is certain that whatever alterations to this document posterity deems necessary should be made not by stealth, incoherence, and fudging but by a process as formal as the original one was—a second Constitutional Convention. But democracy in America ceased almost from the beginning (from Chief Justice Marshall's discovery of a constitutional right of judicial review, in fact) to function according to intended constitutional procedure. The new, "pragmatic" jurisprudence has exploited the Constitution of the Founders as a sort of negative entity—or model, or picture—that gives form to its own, positivistic vision of the Constitutional Convention's work. Legal pragmatism and the doctrine of the living Constitution have made over American courts into the complete inversion of the Platonic ideal and converted a deliberately republican document into a profoundly antirepublican one.

Progressive jurisprudence, which began to develop in America in the postbellum period, was progressive not in the liberal sense but rather in the historical one. It found its original inspiration in philosophical pragmatism and social Darwinism, not socialism. But its relativistic understanding of what had hitherto been considered absolute moral truth in no way differed from that of socialism and of liberal progressivism in general.[3] Thus it represented a departure from classical American jurisprudence, from which it differed further in its novel multidisciplinary aspect and also in its newfound awareness of the Left-Right distinction in its political sense.[4]

The new conservative-progressive jurisprudence, like the liberal-progressive jurisprudence that Justice Oliver Wendell Holmes sought to substitute for it, was based on intellectual principles, not material considerations or sociological observation. "The view of courts and legislatures held by conservatives of the progressive era is the view that today is held by liberals, and the view of these institutions held by the early progressives is today held by conservatives," says Bradley C. S. Watson in *Living Constitution, Dying Faith*. After 1937, Franklin D. Roosevelt's Supreme Court, citing "judicial restraint," turned its attention from economic and commercial decisions made by legislatures to favor a concern with "rights" and civil liberties as they have been understood by progressive social Darwinism, such as it came to be interpreted by the Left.[5]

From the beginning of the twentieth century until 1937, the doctrine of substantive due process (deciding cases in the context of an understanding of a legal background consisting of unenumerated rights) held sway in American jurisprudence. The new constitutionalism held the meaning of the Constitution to be inherent solely in terms of historical interpretation. Throughout the Progressive Era, the Supreme Court, despite its reputation as a reactionary bench, was generally supportive of progressive social legislation, both in its decisions and in its willingness to admit information of a sort that only the legislative branch had previously been found worthy to consider. The Brandeis Brief, which introduced, in the 1908 case *Muller v. Oregon*, statistical social and economic data in place of traditional legal arguments to support its contentions, became so thoroughly acceptable to the court that even its opponents imitated its approach—until, with *Brown v. Board of Education* in 1954, Brandeis's method virtually replaced the preprogressive manner of legal reasoning. Louis Brandeis, of course, became a Supreme Court justice, and his proposal for the federal courts to extend the Fourteenth Amendment to both state and local government effectively nationalized the process of state law. Owing to his immense influence on the Supreme Court, Brandeis transplanted the court's earlier activist impulses on behalf of property, individual freedom, and the federalist principle to the social sphere, where they were put in service to social change and the newly discovered "rights" that a changing society was said to demand.[6]

"Legal realism," which Holmes called "the path of the law," took for granted that law is unconcerned with absolute truth or with morals, which seemed to him to be unrelated to law. This assumption denied the desirability, or even the possibility, of a government of laws rather than of men, a concept that had hitherto been considered almost a definition of democracy. Holmes's insistence on what he called "the felt necessities of the times"—necessities more deeply "felt" by lawyers and jurists than by anyone else—ended as the assertion that the law is what the Supreme Court says it is. Moreover, what the court says is the law is determined by the justices' sensitivity to the spirit of the age and whatever they perceive ensures the greatest satisfaction by legal means of any human want no matter what its content might be—a position that directly anticipates the legal pragmatism of Judge Gerald Posner today.

Justice Holmes was expressing this idea in brutal terms when he asserted that he was prepared "to help my country go to hell if that's what it wants"—a sentiment all the more shocking when one considers that Holmes was no mere elitist but was what in those days passed for an American aristocrat, entrusted with the same sense of responsibility for his country that John Adams had felt for the young American republic. But, as Watson explains, "The new jurisprudence was suspicious of the very idea of justice itself."[7] And the less the courts believed in the existence of something called justice, the more they insisted on taking responsibility for it away from the legislative branch and entrusting that responsibility to themselves. Their justification for doing so is plain: an antidemocratic distrust of the mind of the same majority whose wants, needs, and thoughts they claim to fathom with a tender sympathy.

One, no doubt inevitable, result of this dishonesty has been the abuse and deconstruction of language as a necessary cover for the intellectual mayhem modern judges create. Another is the investiture of the American system of justice with a sort of legal nominalism. Still another is the bad philosophy and worse poetry that the system has thrown out over the past decades, the most famous example of which must be Justice William O. Douglas's discovery of "penumbras, formed by emanations," in his majority decision in *Griswold v. Connecticut* (1965), in which the court found a right to "marital privacy" allegedly contravened by the state's anticontraception laws. (In somewhat the same vein, Justice Benjamin Cardozo years earlier had referred to "a semi-intuitive apprehension of the pervading spirit of our law.")[8]

No judicial passage, however, rivals in terms of moral and poetic ecstasy the Supreme Court's assertion, in *Planned Parenthood v. Casey* (1992), of a concept of an Existence Right: "At the heart of liberty is the right to define one's own concept of existence, of meaning, of the universe, and of the mystery of human life. Beliefs about these matters could not define the attributes of personhood were they formed under compulsion of the state."[9] Regarding this astounding statement, one notes, first, that advanced liberalism insists relentlessly on its own concept of existence; second, that its author, and those justices who acquiesced in his work, betray suspicions not only about the existence of justice but also about the possibility of human society itself. One cannot really describe the thoughts it expresses as nihilistic. They are rather, in a quite literal way, demented.

It is not so in England, where the law courts are considered independent in respect of their relationship not to the legislative branch but to the Crown. The British courts must answer to Parliament—unlike the American courts, which are not subject to Congress. (Oddly, the sage and discriminating Walter Bagehot considered the American judicial branch to be its most successful and best designed.) And although the British courts are competent to decide the meaning of laws descending from Parliament, they lack the power of judicial review, so that their legal interpretations, unlike those of the Supreme Court, are not final.

The finality of the U.S. Supreme Court's decisions is guaranteed by its claim to unique competence in defining antecedent principles, and through them to arrive at a decision that cannot further be challenged. According to the Supreme Court in *Planned Parenthood v. Casey*, "Where, in the performance of its judicial duties, the court decides a case in such a way as to resolve the sort of intensely divisive controversy reflected in *Roe* [*v. Wade*] and those rare, comparable cases, its decision has a dimension that the resolution of the normal case does not carry. It is the dimension present whenever the court's interpretation of the Constitution calls the contending sides of a national controversy to end their national division by accepting a common mandate rooted in the Constitution"—in other words, to shut up.[10]

Bradley Watson argues that, although liberal democracies, to survive, must rest on truths and understandings commonly understood and accepted, it is natural to them that their sense of these things should be fluctuating and unstable.[11] This might justify the judiciary's present visionary role in American life, were it not that, constitutionally speaking, it is the role of the legislative branch, not the judiciary, to play Cassandra—to be alert to future dangers threatening the republic. In 1927, Justice Brandeis opined (in *Whitney v. California*) that the sole end of the state is to ensure the full development of human faculties; more recently, Justice William Brennan expressed the opinion that "the demands of human dignity will never cease to evolve."[12] And so the understanding of the U.S. Constitution, as of "democracy" itself, is infinitely flexible, infinitely uncertain; as J. Budziszewski observes, "The very instrument ordained to insure the sober rule of law comes to advance the arrogant rule of men—men who hold office as judges."[13]

Because it is democratically uncontrollable, progressive jurisprudence is fatal to democracy wherever it is permitted to exist. Today this means, first and foremost, the United States—the international guarantor and paragon of democratic societies, and of the rule of law, the world over.

After the World War that immediately followed the first era of progressive jurisprudence, issues of civil and human rights moved to the legal and political foreground in the Western democracies—especially the United States, where what is now called "rights talk" has since become a type of mania. Inevitably, judicial concentration on individual rights and freedom, personal development, and the satisfaction of personal desires did much to mold a society and a political climate that encourage and reward a sense of individual right over social obligation, intransigency over compromise, emotion over reason, intemperance over calmness, and moral absoluteness over compromise. The result is a disordered form of politics in which important questions cannot be frankly debated in public, and trivial ones cannot be decided.

"A tendency to frame nearly every social controversy in terms of a clash of rights (a woman's right to her own body *v.* a fetus's right to life) impedes compromise, mutual understanding, and the discovery of common ground," Harvard law professor Mary Ann Glendon observes. If Walt Whitman were right in saying that comradeship is the permanent basis of democracy, then democracy in America today has no social basis at all.[14] The discovery of a new right leads to the discovery of further new rights, while the disposition to view every issue in terms of rights tends to extend itself to all other political issues by subjecting them to the same stridency of expression and obduracy of attitude. "Rights language," Glendon says, "not only seems to filter out other discourses; it simultaneously infiltrates them."[15] And the endless identification of the new rights of man ends, as Bertrand de Jouvenel observed, by abrogating many of the old rights originally recognized by democracy—for example, A's right to his property versus B's right to public support, or, as mentioned previously, a mother's right to control her body versus her baby's right to be born.

Glendon suggests that one effect of the "rights revolution" is the petrifaction of local governments and political parties, and the widespread distaste much of the American public feels for a system of politics that has become an impotent parody of itself in a time of acute social and political crisis. Influenced by the example of America, much of the world has taken on this obsession with rights, though in a tempered form that often insists also on obligations. Glendon notes that France's Declaration of the Rights of Man, unlike the Declaration of Independence, specifically mentions such obligations, a difference owing perhaps to the possibility that the signers of the Declaration did not really believe their own rhetorical flourishes, the intent of which was to impress a world skeptical of the American colonists' intentions. (On the other hand, the behavior of the citizens of the French Republic in recent times suggests that modern French men and women no longer believe that they are obliged to do, or be, anything.)[16]

The language of "rights talk" is custom-made for sound bites and the electronic media, as Glendon notes. Similarly, the media seem perfectly suited to postdemocratic politics, which is increasingly a type of authoritarianism. Sir Henry Sumner Maine, critical of political democracy as he was, was confident nevertheless that, in a future conflict between democracy and science, democracy would win. Nearly a century and a half later, his confidence does not appear to have been justified.

Contrary to claim, information technology, the electronic media, and computers have not increased the sum total of human knowledge or our stock of intelligible ideas, nor have they raised the level of human wisdom in any appreciable degree. What they have provided us with is facts—and facts, as Chesterton said, are in themselves meaningless—most which have not been verified by any reliable authority. What technology *has* done is to create an illusory (a "virtual") universe experienced at an unmeasurable distance and to dehumanize social and political life, which can only facilitate the arrival of the *really* total state. (This may be in part what Habermas had in mind when he spoke of "the scientization of politics.") Technology of every sort, not just communications technology, in combination makes possible the absolute power of the state, while encouraging the illusion of omnipotence among rulers and ruled alike. (Advanced telecommunications, ephemeral by nature and without physical trace beyond the cyberspace from which they may be instantly obliterated, actually guarantee a radical reduction in information in the form of preserved or available documentation, public and private, as hard copy becomes more and more a thing of the past.)

It appears an accepted fact of our time that the personal computer and the Internet constitute a formidable means by which people with dissident minority opinions, obscure groups, and individuals can make themselves and their ideas known, communicate with one another, build effective organizations, and perhaps effectively challenge established interests by forcing these to take notice of them. Yet Western democratic governments, under cover of responding to terrorist plots and sabotage since September 2001, have betrayed the extent to which they are willing to regulate, interfere with, spy on, and even block the content of the electronic media, whereas frankly nondemocratic governments, like that of China, have demonstrated the ease with which the authorities, if they choose, can do the same. The actions of both the democracies and the authoritarian regimes have put subversives of every sort and level of dissent on notice that cyber-resistance is by no means a secure redoubt for them. And societies developed to a high level of technique in every aspect depend more and more on centralized government to coordinate these aspects one with the other. Moreover, as Jacques Ellul has suggested, the increased role of technique in society encourages politicians to rely on it to solve the most serious problems, while discouraging them from seeking political solutions, a preference in which they are supported by public opinion. There is, finally, the question of biotechnology and its eventual effect on democracy—and on everything else that is human. "Such long old [primordial] fear," said Nietzsche, "finally refined, spiritualized, spiritual—today, it seems to me, this is called science."

Power's aggressive, merciless, and relentless drive to absolute power, as Jouvenel described it, is a process common to Power in every one of its governmental forms and politics in all its multifarious types—including those secondary organizations which Tocqueville valued and from which so many of democracy's professional politicians arise. Democracy, as early modern democrats very well knew, is not exempt from this drive; indeed, democracy's tendency to self-congratulation and complacency makes it particularly susceptible to the lies Power tells, the promises it makes, and the illusions of security and well-being it creates. And beyond political power lies Power in another of its protean forms, which, as a handmaid of Power and even its natural ally, is equally dangerous to democratic institutions. This is the power not of Caesar but of Faust: the Power that seeks to impose its own will and control over nature, as Power seeks to impose its will and control on men. Liberalism in its advanced form combines these two urges, harnesses them, and points them toward the same end. "As such," Nietzsche thought, "it culminates the centuries-old attempt to replace custom and religion by human will and this-worldly reason as the basis of life and thought."

Albert Camus's maxim in respect of modern democratic citizens—that while they seemed to love freedom, in truth they only hated the master—might have served as the epigraph for Jouvenel's *On Power*, in which Jouvenel wrote, "What assists the advance of the state is this: that it is at war with others of men's masters, the abasement of whom tends to be more regarded than its own elevation."[17]

Historiographical skepticism suggests that Jouvenel's account of the historical cycles of political power should be treated as theoretical, a single narrative among many alternative ones. Still, his thesis agrees so well with the historical record as to command the kind of assent that is as much intuitive as it is intellectual. The central argument of *On Power* is at once succinct and compelling. The modern state, following the devolution of power experienced by absolute monarchical government over several centuries, is really the king reincarnate, an omnipotent power center whose function is to further the insatiable urge to destroy all subordinate powers and suppress all local liberties by leveling and standardization. "For two centuries now," Jouvenel writes, "this European society of ours has been seeking [liberty]; what it has found has been the widest, the most cumbersome, and the most burdensome state authority ever yet experienced by our civilization." The development of "this stupendous work of aggression" occurred by a process entirely natural to Power, inherently jealous of any command besides its own, which it seeks to usurp.[18]

In its early phase, the ruler-king challenges the subordinate power, the aristocracy, citing the aim to liberate the common people from the aristocratical grip of their immediate masters. The earliest aristocracy was the clans; the intermediate one was the feudal aristocracy; the landed aristocracy, following the birth of the modern state, was eventually displaced by the capitalist plutocracy. The people are Power's natural allies; they enroll in Power's army and in Power's administrative departments. For a time, Power pleases them. Delighted to be rid of their old masters, they fail to notice that they have acquired a new and increasingly assertive one. Meanwhile, the central administration under the monarchy is becoming the new nobility, as happened in the late Roman Empire. In time, the "statocracy" grows powerful enough to destroy the state from within, and the cycle begins anew, Power having relocated itself in one of the new power cells, thus continuing the process which gives momentum and rhythm to history and human society.

The developing absolutist state weakens and destroys the clannish and feudal aristocracies that oppose it and moves to do the same with the capitalist ones, having concluded that they no longer serve Power's mercantilist interests but their own. Concurrently, "in the interests of the people," the state converts the deliberative parliaments from aristocratic assemblies to popular bodies, thus weakening still further the aristocratic power while extending and strengthening its direct hold on the people. But here something unlooked for by the monarch occurs. By degrees, the assembly acquires the "novel" notion that it represents the nation as a whole rather than a set of particular interests, as the aristocratic parliament had done. In short, it takes on itself the role historically played by the king, whose mission and exactions it assumes. Previously charged with the protection of the citizens, the assembly more and more asserts its responsibility for furthering the public interest through the power of the legislature. In this way, parliament succeeds the king as the representative of all the people through a drastic alteration in the nature of the now "popular" assembly.

With the aristocracy either destroyed or rendered impotent, the legal principle that served previously as the guarantee of the citizen's liberty is replaced by the discretion of a new aristocracy—the parliament—to whom that liberty has been committed in an absolute way. Hence the more complete the destruction of the aristocracy, the more total the tyranny imposed by the revolution will be. The advance of liberty and law, supposedly the accomplishments of "democracy," in reality are the work of the new machinery of government, in which individual wills are no longer sovereign. Sovereignty of the law has become the sovereignty of "the people"—which, in fact and in practice, means the representatives of the people, who thus inherit the rights and duties formerly acquired by the king. The nature of the transfer—and the transformation—of Power is such that it is never suspected, since who can be mistrustful of the people's sovereignty? The people are now said and thought to be equal; yet, Jouvenel notes, "The passion for absolutism is, inevitably, in conspiracy with the passion for equality." Equality among citizens in any case means equal servility in regard to the state. The ground has been prepared for tyranny, which in time provokes revolution. But "there never was a revolution yet which did not result in an accretion of Power's weight."[19]

As parliament transferred the rights of the people to their representatives, so the party system that develops within assembly government transforms a body of independent debaters into an opposition of factions indifferent to principle and caring only for their own selfish interests, a "clearinghouse" by which parcels of votes are bundled together as power and influence. In result, parliament too is relieved of its sovereign powers, which it relinquishes to the party machines. Thus elections become "no more than a plebiscite by which a whole people puts itself in the power of a small gang."[20] Meanwhile, Power—inevitably—is chastening, harassing, and consigning to its place the new capitalist plutocracy just as it did the old feudal aristocracy that had proposed to restrain the monarchy.

"Power has its ups and downs," Jouvenel concludes, "but, looking at the picture as a whole, it is one of continuous advance, an advance which is reflected in the stupendous growth of its instruments, its revenues, its armed forces, its police forces, and its capacity to make laws. . . . What is called the coming of democracy is really the conveyance of the established Power to new owners. . . . As this conveyance or conquest is accompanied by the annihilation or recoil of whatever forces oppose the *imperium*, the position of power in society is in the end more isolated and therefore more powerful."[21]

In time, power cells develop within the body of Power that, like malignant growths, grow and swell until the state is forced to excise them or perish. The cycle, as Jouvenel perceives it, is not only continual but also essentially blind and meaningless. The great question for our time is what will be the nature and shape of the new, growing cells within the body of mass corporate democracy. Jouvenel expected them to come from within the statocracy itself. That may prove to have been an inspired guess, given what looks more and more to be the apparent convergence of the Western democracies and the modern corporate bureaucratic states exemplified by Russia and China. The Obama administration's decision in 2009 partially to nationalize General Motors and Chrysler Corporation and to insert itself into the workings of the largest and most stricken banks, like its drive to control American industry through cap-and-trade policies and similar initiatives, was less, finally, a political decision than it was an organic

one—wholly natural to Power, which is even more a blind and instinc-
tual force than it is a calculating and Machiavellian one.

The power of the modern centralized state is at once enhanced and
restricted by the technological nature of modern society. But these
restrictions do not produce reciprocal gains for democracy. On the one
hand, only the state appears competent to address the enormous challenges presented by societies of unfathomable social and technological
complexity. On the other, the crises produced by this complexity are
beyond the abilities even of the all-powerful state to comprehend and
address (as *New York Times* columnist David Brooks observed during
the environmental catastrophe caused by the explosion of a BP off-
shore oil rig in the Gulf of Mexico in 2010).[22]

In the face of crisis, democratic publics demand their governments
take efficient steps reflecting the efficient (that is, technological) values endorsed by modern democratic societies. As Jacques Ellul noted,
however, when efficiency becomes the principle criterion of political
action and the standard of political legitimacy, this imposes on political
action a new set of limitations. Utilitarian values come to replace moral
ones, and philosophical and political principles seem immaterial to
political decisions. From this, two results follow. The first is the inability of the political sphere to make political decisions, or what Ellul
calls "the illusion of decisions." The second is the entrustment of the
all-powerful state with sole discretion to determine moral value, which
in turn becomes purely a matter of efficiency. ("What the state can do,
the state will do, and what it does will *a priori* become just and true.")[23]

So long as the state is the validator and guarantor of values, Ellul
argued, a contradiction exists between politics and values, and the citizen can act morally with regard to society only outside politics, which
has been totally deprived of its human warmth. (Ellul, who blamed
"the phenomenon of politicization" as much on the growth of popular
participation in government as on the expansion of the state itself,
thought individual action beyond the politic realm essential to dispel-
ling "the political illusion.") "For the autonomy of political affairs to
come to an end it would be necessary that they be subordinated to

common values; that the machinery of parties or the state have no autonomy—that they cease functioning like machines; that acts and decisions inspired by moral reasons be clearly recognized in the eyes of all," Ellul suggested. Yet he saw little chance of that happening among a public educated to think in opposite terms conducive to the end of democracy, and even politics itself.[24]

To return to Chesterton's question, If democracy is not the enthronement of the ordinary man, then what is it? No one, really, has ever been able to answer that question. But it is hard to imagine that Chesterton would have found the answer in the modern leviathan states of the supposedly free and democratic Western world, or in the corporate-state societies that appear poised to develop from them in the course of the twenty-first century.

Part III

The Future of Democracy and the End of History

✦ ✦ ✦

12

The Cold Monster at Bay

Democratic government in modern form is a creation of the nation-state that arose in western Europe in early modern times. Democracy is inseparable from nationality. And so democracy's future depends on the future of the nation-state. Until recently, almost the only people to doubt that the state has a future were, besides anarchists, Marxists of one type or another who argued that the historical dialectic guarantees the withering away of the state apparatus. Today it is no longer Marxists alone who question the relevance, the value, the utility, and the survival of the postmodern state in the age of the global village, global government, the global economy, and the increasing proliferation and reach of internationalist organizations.

As the displacement of the European city-state by the nation-state reduced local residents' capacity for self-government, so the proliferation of transnational authorities is transforming national governments into local ones.[1] A former French ambassador to the European Union, Jean-Marie Guéhenno, has advanced the far more radical proposition that central governments—the traditional loci of power—are beginning to be dissolved by a sort of diffused imperial power, roughly comparable to that of the Roman Empire but based on wholly post-national concepts of space and sovereignty and facilitated by a means of social control that is also postpolitical.

In his view, the watershed events of 1989 marked the end of an era that began not in 1917 or 1945 but in 1789, with the inception of the age of the democratic nation-state.[2] The West has passed from the patrimonial era through the institutional era and into the imperial age, in which territoriality and fixed wealth are being superseded. The imperial age will see the end of nations and of capital cities, all of them replaced by a multicentered and diffuse empire. Together with nationality, institutional power—including bureaucratic power and politics itself—will disappear following the erasure of political boundaries and political principles, which will be replaced by "forms" and "codes." With them, and despite the centrality of a communications system favoring the transmission of information rather than of learning and wisdom, the managerial class that James Burnham described in the 1940s will vanish also.

Like Pierre Manent (is it coincidental that both of these extremely interesting writers are Frenchmen?), Jean-Marie Guéhenno questions whether democracy can exist outside a national structure. For him, in any case, the answer hardly matters, the words *democracy*, *politics*, and *liberty* having come to represent nothing more than a mental reflex by citizens of the postmodern West. Guéhenno does not lament the passing of the institutional age, which he understands as a construct of the Enlightenment, a single episode in human history that solved the perennial problem of free political organization in its own peculiar way. The conditions of the new age require a new idea of freedom, better suited to the dawning historical era.

Guéhenno's outline of the future is worth following in some detail. The modern nation, he argues, is founded on a system of law that reflects the scarcity of physical space and an abundance of human labor that makes the ancient institution of slavery unnecessary. In the postmodern age, access to land has been replaced in importance by access to a network. Guéhenno does not foresee the reorganization of sovereign nations in a revived federal system, however loose, since federations, too, are defined by geographic boundaries. Rather, he envisions an empire, but such an empire as the world has never known: an empire that is "neither a supernation nor a universal republic," and without an emperor at its head. It will consist instead of a multitude of open systems, contrasting with the closed systems of the institutional age, in which formal law and politics based on moral and philosophical principles have been replaced by operating procedure as the governing force. "What is coming into being is not a global political body but an apparently seamless fabric, an indefinite accretion of interdependent elements," he predicts.[3] In this context, power is not the formal, specified power of a prince but inheres in the social entity as the sheer ability to survive.

No matter Guéhenno's allusion to a new definition of freedom: the imperial age, though not constrained by ideological bonds, will not hold freedom in high esteem. On the other hand, it will feel no pressing need to stifle liberty, either. The human element inherited from the institutional age will have fallen into "a deep slumber" and conflict been redefined as "misunderstanding," which the imperial age will seek to avoid by micromanagement. Finally, *liberty*, in the imperial age, will be a meaningless word. "What is liberty in a world of rules? How can power be limited in a world without principles?" Although the empire may be one among several empires, the rules that govern its internal existence will presumably apply to its interimperial relations as well.[4]

The empire Guéhenno foresees will draw no distinction between internal and external security. Its police force will not enforce sovereignty; it will enforce norms. Similarly, distinctions between public and private violence will be blurred; so will those between the domain of the state and of private interests—such as drug cartels. As government dissolves, in surrendering its responsibilities it will learn to rely on private parties to carry them out. World conflicts will become a thing of the past; so will world peace—or any peace. The empire will not develop in a void. It will resemble an "island of order" surrounded by "new barbarians," some of whom will be of its own creation. The empire will not field a soldiers' army; instead it will employ a police force, "ever alert, ever ready to track down the difficult, the unknown, the inexplicable" (all abominations in the eyes of the empire). The empire will be subject to the constant threat of violence, necessitating a race between itself and its enemies to acquire an absolute monopoly over the latest destructive technology. To lose this race would be fatal to the empire. But its death would not be fatal to the new system of power circuits versus the lingering logic of institutional power, because there can be no end to the proliferation of the networks and what Guéhenno calls the "tyranny of progress."

Guéhenno's vision of a postnational age is intellectually intriguing and even plausible historically speaking, if in a somewhat abstract way. The "circuits" he describes, conveying information and organizing and focusing mental power to advance the agenda of international corporations and agencies, private and public, are observable and already well advanced. So are the private armies and the proxy ones (some of them employed by the U.S. government), the global police force without borders (Interpol), and the drug cartels, most of them really joint venture companies owned and operated by a combination of private and public interests, as in Mexico. In other respects, however, the institutional system today seems surprisingly resilient, though no doubt Guéhenno would argue that periods of resurgence are expectable in the course of an age's protracted demise.

One thinks of the present state and possible future course of the European Union (EU), which was experiencing resistance from its respective publics even before the debt crisis struck the Continent in 2010. To secure the signing of the Lisbon Treaty (2007), essentially intended to centralize further the Union by amending the Maastricht Treaty and the Treaty of Rome, the EU's headquarters in Brussels undertook a series of dishonest ploys, the most notable of which was the determined resubmission of the treaty—in the wake of threats and other scare tactics employed by national politicians, as well as by

EU officialdom—to the national legislatures that had rejected it, the Irish among them. The EU was never a popular project in either sense of the term, nor is there anything "democratic" about it. Rather, the idea behind the EU is "basically fascist" (Sir Oswald Mosley was the only British politician to support the notion of Europe as a nation), its system of popular representation quite undemocratic.[5] And it is even less popular today, when the financial crisis has revealed the persistence of nationalist feeling in Europe and made plain the impossibility of yoking together, under a common political and financial system, still-independent nations living at differentiated social, economic, and political levels.

Liberal Fascism

Only several years earlier, Guéhenno had pointed to what he described as the confused debate over European sovereignty at a moment in history when the age of political networks has broken down. This "is for the best if it is a question of getting beyond the conflict between nations, and for the worst if one still dreams of free and voluntary citizens."[6] Today Europe may be shrugging off the postnational dream as the Continent faces what some observers are describing as the beginning of a great European depression that defies a unified response by the economically disparate European nations. Still, the logic of a world in which geographical boundaries are being to one degree or another made irrelevant by "circuits" of communication, and real wealth significantly replaced by the abstract kind, is certainly perceptible. Indeed, it is already being experienced around the world, from Boston to Borneo.

"State," said Nietzsche, "is the name of the coldest of all cold monsters." The philosopher loathed the national state for many reasons, not least the vital role it played in creating the democratic government and democratic society Nietzsche scorned. One can imagine him embracing the coming empire described by Jean-Marie Guéhenno as a world set free at last from the old assumptions, the old Christian morality, the old obsession with absolutes. Pierre Manent thinks that the nation-state played a role in modern Europe identical to that of the city-state in classical Greece; the two are the only political forms, he says, that have succeeded in uniting civilization and liberty. Yet almost overnight, it seems, Europe has lost its understanding of the meaning and importance of the democratic nation. "Today democracy turns actively and aggressively *against* the state," Manent argues.[7] Tocqueville feared the power, the sovereignty, of the people. Today the very concept of a people needs to be questioned. This is because pure democracy, which is held up to Western publics as a kind of Holy Grail, is in fact "democracy without a body," in Manent's wonderful phrase. Bodiless democracy has its attractions for the modern European mind to the degree that it views the old European body as a historical monster—the stinking, lumbering embodiment of predemocratic times, guilt-burdened and marinated in racism, militarism, cultural arrogance, religious intolerance, superstition, and tyranny. Sloughing off this old body, European civilization seeks to escape its historical identity and to assume a new, abstract body, shining and pure as the sun. This is the body progressive Europeans today call "Europe."[8]

This development is supposed to represent democracy arrived at its final limits. Nations, for pure democrats, are too self-limited in every respect, including their democratic identities. But the fact of a particular, flesh-and-blood people involved in the process of self-rule is the fundamental condition for democracy. Since 1945, Manent says, Europe has worked to create "a non-national democracy whose sole political program is to retain its innocence."[9] It forgets that it was the sovereign state and democratic government working together that created a high order of mass civilization characterized by order and liberty, and it is oblivious to the reality that, by abasing politics and elevating bureaucratic procedure, it has created governments that are ever less sovereign, on the one hand, and, on the other, increasingly less representative. The preservation of the nation is essential to the continuance of "the European adventure.[10] But are these things still possible? Jacques Ellul, in the 1960s, perceived the state as being still engaged in "political activities," however attenuated. Yet the trend is in the antipolitical direction. Even should Guéhenno's empire of the future never materialize, could bodiless democracy survive the civilization it has destroyed?

Democracy thrives on peace, at home and abroad. As a rule, the most successful democracies have developed gradually, over a lengthy period—British democracy, for example, and its North American offshoots. Democracies that owe their existence to revolution and war usually follow at a remove from it—for instance, democracy in France, which was realized under the constitutional monarchy of the Bourbons—while those that victors impose on the losers, like the democratic government installed in Germany after the Treaty of Versailles, tend to be both fragile and short-lived. Yet the young twenty-first century promises to be even more violent and unstable than its predecessor was. We live in a world that is increasingly resentful and angry, ever more lawless, confused, aggressive, violent, and chaotic—hardly a field likely to produce an abundant democratic harvest.

The early nineteenth century believed in universal education as the engine of enlightenment and mutual understanding that would deliver peace between the peoples of the world; the present century has a similar faith in electronic communications. It counts on nearly instant communication to correct misunderstandings and misapprehensions between governments and peoples around the world, and to make every culture the collective goodwill ambassador to every other culture. Through mass communications the recognition of our common humanity across cultural, institutional, and ethnic boundaries will finally be achieved. To meet and to know the Other, at last, is to love him.

The reality is, far more often than not, the opposite: to become acquainted with the Other is to loathe him. A glaring and obvious example is the hatred much of the Muslim world has conceived for the Western world through the global communications system that has swamped Muslim peoples with the popular culture of the West. It seems unreasonable to suppose that their dislike has anything to do with "democracy" as such, beyond the fact that Muslim nations naturally resent being relentlessly bombarded by the Western democracies with exhortations to liberalize their form of government and society. (Democracy is not something easily dramatized and conveyed to popular audiences by television, movies, and rock music.) America's pro-Israeli policies in the Mideast for the past sixty years are the most direct, and probably by far the greatest, cause for the ill will it has gained among Muslims. Still, there is a broader explanation. Muslims and many other non-Western peoples find America and American culture vulgar and distasteful, as sophisticated Europeans for two hundred years have done; more important, they are offended by their irreligious aspect. Western publics would doubtless have a similar reaction to the electronic portrayal of ordinary life in Iraq, Haiti, Kenya, and China were it not for the self-imposed constraints of reflexive political correctness. Europeans in the sixteenth, seventeenth, eighteenth, and nineteenth centuries—the age of exploration—certainly responded with fascinated horror to the representations of savage cultures transmitted to them by the Gutenberg press, rotogravure, and still photography. It is only societies in love with novelty and profoundly uncomfortable with themselves and their traditions for whom the unfamiliar, the foreign, and the exotic fail to breed contempt, or something stronger.

Critics might argue that if non-Western cultures truly disliked the West, they would not come here in their millions. But that argument would overlook the fact that Third World immigrants have been willing to subordinate—for now—the cultural repugnance they feel for the West to pursue Western affluence, Western goods, and the Western technology that alerted them to our comfortable existence in the first place. (Their stubborn nonassimilation in Europe, and in particular Great Britain, France, and Germany, should be taken as a warning that they are unlikely to repress their distaste for much longer.)

At any rate, the global prevalence of American television, movies, rock music, and the Internet are but one aspect of the situation. Rifle cartridges encased in paper packets allegedly greased with pork fat ignited the Indian Mutiny of 1857. The Zimmermann Telegram nearly sparked war between the United States and Germany in January 1917 (and facilitated America's entry into the Great War three months later). The reproduction of a cartoon drawing of Muhammad launched an international crisis several years ago that might easily have led to real unpleasantries in Europe and elsewhere. And when Pope Benedict XVI, speaking in Regensburg, delivered a lecture that Muslims found heretical, within twenty-four hours a Roman Catholic nun was murdered in the Near East. Modern communications permit too fast, too emotional, and too unconsidered a response to nearly instantaneous news reports. Had the sailing ships of the day not required two months to cross the Atlantic, the American Republic might well have gone to war with France very early in its history. An efficient global communications system does not promote restraint. It encourages immediate and unreflective action, the more so in an age when all action, political and otherwise, is a form of propaganda, and propaganda a type of action.

Modern communications have another, less direct, less palpable, and less immediate—but extremely unsettling—effect on global relations. The secularist modern culture they transmit induces a relaxation of the social and religious standards and rules of religious, premodern cultures—as, for example, has been happening in Iran since the 1970s—but it greatly offends ancient or traditional cultures and radicalizes their supporters. The result is a confrontation between a spirit of absolute toleration and one of absolute intolerance in circumstances conducive to the spread of moral relativism, and even nihilism, internationally—a tendency the recent history of the United Nations reflects.

The process is aggravated by the secular, relativistic, and nihilistic content of American popular culture, which promotes immorality, irreligion, irresponsibility, antiauthoritarianism, lawlessness, and Mammon. This encouragement to moral and institutional chaos is increasingly evident in the explosive proliferation of lawless activities around the world—terrorism, the drug trade, human smuggling, brutal private armies (like the Lord's Resistance Army in Uganda) that terrorize innocent civilians, gunrunning, piracy off the Horn of Africa, and romantically barbaric antigovernment insurgencies around the world, many of whose perpetrators seem to be self-consciously acting out a variety of internationally popular myths created by Hollywood's studios. Such activities are significantly responsible for the world's many failed and failing states, of which the most notorious are Somalia and Mexico, whose violent and bloody existence embodies the national myth of blood, violence, cruelty, lawlessness, machismo, and revenge.

Moral relativism and irreligion are one result of the international proliferation of popular Western culture, manners, mores, and values. Another and opposite one is the pervasive radicalization of religion and the stiffening of morals, moralism, and intolerance. As the historic religion of the West decreases in faith, confidence, fervor, and evangelistic impulse, others of the world's religions—Islam, Hinduism, Sikhism, Sufism, and Jainism—increase in all these respects. (Judaism, of course, is not a proselytizing or crusading faith, though in the context of the increasingly inflammatory Middle East, it is a militant one.) The situation enhances religious rivalries that merge with the ethnic and racial conflicts responsible for so much bloodshed and unrest among the non-Western peoples as well as between those of the East and West, and the political instability these things create. And a history of social, economic, and political failure on the part of the former colonies, along with the multiculturalist ideology of Western oppression that is a creation of the West itself, aggravates resentments that are a legacy of colonial times.

Informing all these forces promoting international chaos are the many nationalist and "liberation" movements—from the Balkans to

Chechnya to Tibet to Quebec—inspired by Woodrow Wilson's obsession, a century ago, with national self-determination and compounded by various indigenous rebellions, among them those of President Juan Evo Morales Ayma in Bolivia, the Zapatista Army of National Liberation in Mexico, and the Uighars in western China. It is a measure of the degree to which liberation politics has achieved respectability that, during the papacy of John Paul II, liberation theology became a significant force within the Church of Rome. All these things are part of the "clash of civilizations" described and predicted by Samuel Huntington, whose unpopular message was at the time contradicted or played down by partisans of Francis Fukuyama's vision of the "end of history."

Rhymes with

✦ ✦ ✦

The world does not grow old gracefully: that is the conclusion Paul Theroux has reached after a life of global travel, much of it in the Third World. Whether or not global warming caused by human activity is a factor, earth's climate is changing perceptibly—as it has been changing for five billion years, though far more gradually. In religious terms, there is no such thing as "too many people." But for science, human overpopulation is an ecological reality. The Green Revolution, of which so much was expected fifty years ago, has failed. Famine is common in the Third World, nowhere more acute than in Kenya, which, as a colony under British rule, was by comparison a paradise. Long before the end of the twenty-first century, fresh water may be at a greater premium than oil is today. Arable land has already reached that point. The sands of the Sahara advance inexorably southward, year by year. If the poles, from whatever cause, should melt out, rising seas will deluge the most densely populated regions of the earth. Throughout the world, rural people are migrating from the countryside to the exploding cities, where living conditions are nearly intolerable, owing to poverty, overcrowding, and the absence of sanitation facilities. They are migrating to neighboring countries with a marginally better standard of living and also to the nations of the West, all of which are experiencing environmental difficulties of their own: water, land, and air pollution, lack of territorial space, and a depletion or exhaustion of natural resources, including farmland.

This is not to predict an environmental doomsday, the collapse of civilization, or a cataclysmic die-off among the human race, whether by warfare or natural causes, though none of these things is inconceivable. What is foreseeable is an age of extreme global instability that will impose a radical need for enhanced political and social order at the national and international level: a need that the eroding institution of the nation-state, to say nothing of "democracy," will be hard pressed to meet. All that the modern world boasts of as its major accomplishments—its impressively large societies and economies of scale, its bewildering and diverse social structures, its self-encumbered political systems, and its incomprehensible technological complexity—will make democratic solutions to the problems created by advanced civilization seemingly impossible, and perhaps impossible in fact. Scale and complication are enemies of democratic polities, as the ancients understood. Yet scale, complication, and abstraction, at ever higher levels, are the human future if the world continues on the path along which—pressed especially by its great democracies—it is now moving.

13

The Future of Democracy

Tocqueville thought two types of people unsuited to democracy: the excitable and the apathetic. James Bryce believed that the best political philosophers and the best legislators come from a people remarkable for good sense and self-control—for example, the Roman and the English peoples, whom history shows to have been both practical and of sound judgment, able to recognize wisdom in the men who proposed to lead them and willing to follow them afterward. Bertrand de Jouvenel considered individual good sense and self-control requisite to the stable, fixed, and predictable habits necessary for successful resistance to Power. Sir Henry Maine thought that Englishmen's propensity to assemble did much to lay the foundation of constitutional government in England by the spontaneous formation of local assemblies. One historian of democracy has pointed to a popular sensitivity to condescension as a characteristic useful to democratic development. Reinhold Niebuhr credited the "ultimate presuppositions" on which Judeo-Christian culture rests as having being conducive to the growth of democratic ideas; Protestant principles since the Reformation have been similarly noted. The American Founders thought of themselves not as examples of the new race of man Crèvecoeur believed Americans to be but as men whose moral and intellectual roots struck deep into the European past: most important, England's Glorious

Revolution, the Whig tradition, and that of the English, Scots, and French Enlightenments, in addition to English common law.

As with individuals, so with the societies they comprise. Thus the personal autonomy the Roman patriciate enjoyed took many generations to decline into anarchy or tyranny, owing to the strength of Rome's established folkways and rituals. The English were able, early in their history, to develop a "calm national mind" characterized by mutual confidence among the electors and an assurance that the opposition would not seek, in defeat, the destruction either of their political system or of society as a whole.[1] In the global democratic age, by contrast, even a relative historical pessimist like Samuel P. Huntington hesitated to affirm the cultural specificity of democracy, which he thought conceivably applicable to all the world's societies save for the most extreme (those dominated by Confucianism or Islam). George Kennan, representative of an earlier generation and endowed with the wider experience a diplomatic career gave him, denied that evidence exists for the proposition that democracy is the natural form of rule beyond the relatively narrow perimeters of northwestern Europe and North America. "[There is no reason] to suppose that the attempt to develop and employ democratic institutions would be the best course for many of these peoples [beyond the early perimeters]," Kennan wrote.[2]

Twenty years ago, Huntington suggested that the process of global democratization occurred in a succession of democratic "waves." According to this schema, the first wave occurred between 1828 and 1926, the second from 1943 to 1962, and the third from 1974 to 1989. These democratic eras, Huntington argued, were interrupted by two reverse waves, occurring from 1922 to 1942 and 1958 to 1975. The stark dates alone evoke an approximate sense of the nature and sequence of the historical events that Huntington's enumerated periods frame.

Huntington denied that a single factor could explain democratic development anywhere; instead, he saw many elements operating together and differing from country to country, from one historical era to the next. Thus the first wave of democratization, in the nineteenth century, was produced by economic and social development in the West; by favorable social and economic conditions in those countries the British colonized; by intellectual liberalism and the Protestant religion; and by the Allied victory in World War I. The victory of the democratic powers in 1945 and the process of decolonization that ensued largely explain the second wave, Huntington thought, while the third wave is attributable to all sorts of factors, including the democratic mystique and the seeming implausibility of monarchical legitimacy; Marxism's economic failures; the spread of affluence and literacy; the growth of an international middle class; and the influence of the liberalized Catholic Church after Vatican II.

Huntington emphasized that the "conditions" for democratization are separate from, and dependent on, its "causes"; in his view, conditions favorable to democracy were irrelevant in the absence of a set of political leaders determined to realize the potential of these conditions. "In the fifteen years following the end of the Portuguese dictatorship in 1974," he wrote, "democratic regimes replaced authoritarian ones in approximately thirty countries in Europe, Asia, and Latin America. In other countries, considerable liberalization occurred in authoritarian regimes. In still others, movements promoting democracy gained strength and legitimacy. Although obviously there were resistance and setbacks, as in China in 1989, the movement toward democracy seemed to take on the character of an almost irresistible global tide moving from one triumph to the next."[3]

Two decades later, it would be an exaggeration to say that the world has experienced another reverse wave of antidemocratic reaction (although this has not made it a less violent and chaotic place). Nevertheless, the global democratic tide Huntington described in the final decade of the twentieth century today seems hardly irresistible, while a number of more recent tendencies, unfavorable to the spread and growth of democracy (though not necessarily to a degree of liberalization), have developed. Democracy has suffered a setback since the early 1990s, despite the events known as the Arab Spring.

"The percentage of countries designated as free has failed to increase for nearly a decade and suggests that these trends may be contributing to a developing freedom stagnation," Arch Puddington of Freedom House wrote in 2006. In Puddington's estimation, a "pushback" against democracy is occurring as refractory regimes take steps against various groups representing the cause of human rights, measures that democratic governments have not widely protested. Some observers—most notably Francis Fukuyama—argue that the reaction against democracy is a direct negative response to President George W. Bush's aggressive policies in promoting democracy around the world, by force of American and allied arms if necessary. "Bush's arrogance has turned people off the idea of democracy," according to the coeditor of the *Journal of Democracy*.[4] Yet he concedes that democracy is not working well in many developing countries. For example, Haiti held elections in 2006, prompting Freedom House to give the country high marks. But elections have not altered Haiti's status as a failed state. "The basic problem confronting the developing world today," Fareed Zakaria claims, "is not an absence of democracy but an absence of governance."[5]

Democratic world-historical optimists like Francis Fukuyama should consider several basic questions:

1. Is the popular majority of every society politically interested and motivated toward political activity?

2. Is democracy what people, everywhere in the world, really want?

3. Is the fact of a particular people's wanting a particular regime, such as democracy, good reason to believe that they will eventually get it?

4. Are a society's history and cultural traditions conducive to grasping democratic principles and establishing a workable democratic structure?

5. Is the habit of individual and collective self-control sufficiently developed in a particular society to allow its members to cooperate, peacefully and efficiently, in reaching an agreed-on end?

6. Is democracy a coherent or a self-contradictory idea?

7. Is democracy an inherently self-perpetuating or self-destructive form of government?

Proponents of the view that liberal capitalist democracy is the global future argue that liberal democracy is, after all, the system of government the majority of the world's people *want*. But even if that proposition were self-evident, what people have wanted throughout history has only occasionally been what people *got*, and even then often by sheerest accident—a fact that economic affluence and the power of the democratic myth have tended to obscure in modern times. The reason is not, for the most part, the refusal or failure of predemocratic forms of government to respond to popular desires and demands, or the forces of reaction or corruption in democratic government itself, but simply the susceptibility of all human plans (collective ones especially) to distortion and ultimate failure, usually according to the law of unintended consequences. Indeed, one is tempted to argue that what people most want is precisely what they never get. Nicholas D. Kristof, a columnist for the *New York Times*, claims that it is "condescending and foolish to suggest that people dying for democracy [in the Arab world and elsewhere] aren't ready for it."[6] But a willingness to die for something is not necessarily relevant to one's capacity to attain and manage it, as a man's willingness to die for the woman he loves is irrelevant to the question of whether he would know what to do with her when he finally got her. I recently came across a remark by a Tunisian democrat commenting on the elections for his country's constitutional assembly. "Today," this man said, "we got our freedom, and our dignity, from the simple act of voting." Such political naiveté, however touching, is simply not the stuff from which democratic governments are made.

Beginning in the 1980s, books on the global spread of democracy have conscientiously compiled lists of countries that had recently acquired democratic governments, or lost them. Usually the criterion has been whether those governments were democratically elected ones or not. Of course, there are democratically elected governments—and then there are democratically elected governments. The purpose of this chapter is not to make a scorecard and calculate probable additions and subtractions in the future; it is to evaluate those features of modern (and modernizing) societies that appear to favor, or discourage, the expansion and survival of democratic government around the world. There is space here for a few generalized assessments.

The type of low-grade, interstitial but pandemic and ceaseless conflict foreseen by Jean-Marie Guéhenno is being realized today by the failed states. The spectacular example is Mexico, which is often praised as a successfully democratizing country (delivered only a decade ago from seventy years of one-party rule by the Institutional Revolutionary Party, when Vicente Fox won the Mexican presidency in 2000) but which in fact is collapsing from within under the unseeing gaze of the world. In January 2009, Stephen J. Hadley, President George W. Bush's departing national security adviser, warned that escalating violence between the Mexican government and the drug cartels threatened Mexico's democratic government.[7]

The present bloody catastrophe is rooted in—and is beginning to resemble—the Mexican civil war, which lasted, effectively, from 1910 until the murder of President Obregón in 1928. Like the civil war, it is rooted in the character, the habits of mind, and the folkways of historic Mexico, which are an amalgam of Spanish and Indian cruelty and violence, as well as many fine qualities of Mexican civilization.[8] The media (like the Mexican government and the U.S. State Department) persist in describing the present conflict as a more or less clear-cut battle between the government and the cartels, blurred by corrupt government placemen working behind the lines on both sides. But knowledgeable observers claim that the situation is far more complicated and even more chaotic: a sort of national free-for-all in which innumerable elements of the Mexican population are mixing into the fray in fierce and bloody competition to grab what they can for themselves. In the context of Mexican history, the possibility that the present Mexican government could ultimately assert control seems a faint one; the likelihood that democracy, such as it is in Mexico, could survive, much less create truly democratic institutions and habits, seems almost nil. This is why Bush's retiring CIA director predicted that Mexico could rival Iran or Iraq as a challenge for President Obama, especially should the drug wars spill across the border into the United States. "There is a wave of barbarity that is heading toward the United States," a Mexican professional man told an American reporter. "We are an uncomfortable neighbor."[9]

What is happening in Mexico, the southwestern writer Charles Bowden says, is not a breakdown in order; it is the coming new order in that country. The WikiLeaks revelations of November 2010 showed a country that had deteriorated to the point where even the State Department began to perceive the gravity of the situation, though it maintained an optimistic demeanor in public.

New York Times correspondent Jeffrey Gettleman has filed vivid stories from the failed states of East Africa and the Horn for many years. Two centuries after the United States defeated the Barbary states of North Africa—which for decades had demanded, and received, tribute from the United States and Britain to ensure their shipping from depredations by the Muslim pirates of Barbary—the supposedly anachronistic profession of piracy has resumed in the Indian Ocean off the African Horn, where former Somali fishermen in small boats pursue and board large merchant ships and even private yachts, commandeer and bring them into port, and demand ransom money for their crews, as in the good old days of yore. Some of the proceeds go to enrich the formerly impoverished pirates, who divert substantial amounts to the radical Islamic revolutionaries who have nearly destroyed the moderate Somali government elected to rescue the country from the warlords, the clans, the religious radicals, and the Ethiopians.

It is hard to imagine a more apt example, or image, of postcolonial and postmodern barbarism, operating almost with impunity between the great world empires—just as Guéhenno predicted. The threat is not limited to international shipping or the Horn: Somalia, thanks to the largesse afforded by piracy, has become a training ground for Muslim radicals and a source for terrorists sent forth to promote jihad around the world, including neighboring countries such as Kenya—since independence a model for developing African nations, but today experiencing political gridlock, ethnic warfare, and economic crisis, a state perhaps in the early stages of disintegration and collapse.

A report by McKinsey & Company claims that between 2000 and 2008, African economies developed twice as fast as they had done during the previous two decades.[10] Nevertheless, despite the notable success of South Africa and Botswana, state building in Africa has been largely a failure. A student of African politics argues that, fifty years ago, the world was in so great a hurry to grant sovereignty to the former colonies of the Dark Continent that it conferred recognition as something granted from outside, not earned from within. Thus sovereignty was neither accompanied by popular accountability nor built up from a proper social contract. The proposed solution is drastic but not unprecedented: the donor countries that have supported African regimes for so long must derecognize the worst of them in an attempt to compel their rulers to seek legitimacy from their own people.[11] It is unlikely that such a policy would create a more democratic Africa. The result might be even greater political and social chaos than exists there today.

Many failed states in the age of democratization had democratic institutions imposed on them, either at the time of their creation, like those of Africa, or at a later stage in their development. This suggests how dangerously destabilizing the democratic imperative can be, encouraging many countries, like Pakistan, to attempt democracy prematurely. In 1956, Pakistan declared itself an Islamic republic operating under a constitution; it succumbed two years later to a military coup, from which it has never recovered. Today its effective dissolution—not just as a democracy but also as a nation—threatens catastrophe for its neighbors, most of them as dysfunctional as itself or simply, like Afghanistan, politically and socially unformed. Pakistan, whose judicial branch is at swords' point with the legislative and executive bodies, whose intelligence service acts often either independently of or against the military, and whose religious radicalism, intolerance, and violence are endemic, is virtually ensured a future as a failed state. Meanwhile, Pakistan's perennial hatred and suspicion of India have made it a spoiler in the political affairs of the subcontinent and its contiguous regions—including Afghanistan—and those of the West, a role with potentially devastating consequences for Asia and the West, Great Britain and the United States in particular. These consequences are likely to work against democratic development in the region: certainly in Afghanistan and possibly in India, where democratic institutions are vulnerable to compromise by security concerns about Pakistan, its often bellicose and unstable neighbor.

A more recent example of a failed state threatening to destabilize central Asia further is Kyrgyzstan, a liberated republic of the USSR. As a supposedly independent "democracy" of sorts, Kyrgyzstan has served as a pawn in the new Great Game between Russia and the United States, torn nearly in two by a pair of giants attempting to gain decisive influence there. It is a wholly artificial state lying athwart a deep ethnic divide, a victim of history thrust into the unsought role of guarantor of war or peace in its own, highly flammable, neighborhood.

Although the list of failed or failing states is extensive and various, one thing may broadly be said about them here. As democracy's golden age—the era following World War II—fades, the world is likely to be littered with the remains of more, rather than fewer, failed democracies, whether real or pretend, each one of which would have the destructive potential of a half-extinguished campfire abandoned to smolder in the depths of a dry pine forest.

The number of failed democratic states in history has been over-matched by the many failed democratic revolutions—democratic, that is, in the sense that their alleged aim was the establishment of democracy, or simply more democracy. Year in, year out, the daily news offers a chronicle of such events, the large majority of which pass within months beyond the memory of everyone but politicians, political scientists, and historians. Some of these revolutions seem to have been doomed to failure from the start, others fated to enjoy at least a partial success. But history is the record of surprises, and revolutions are a tricky business to make odds on. Today's world is filled with anger, resentment, jealousy, discontent, and dissatisfaction, all awaiting exploitation by unfocused aspiration and raw ambition.

Probably no morning has dawned in the past hundred years without the newspapers writing that somebody, somewhere, is either demanding democracy or fighting for it. Today these stories are being filed from Bangkok, Kabul, Istanbul, Prague, Kiev, Tbilisi, Teheran, Tunis, Benghazi, Cairo, Bahrain, Amman, Damascus, and many of the world's great capitals (including Beijing, Moscow, London, and Washington). So many words, so much conflict—but to what end?

The Color Revolutions in Georgia and Ukraine, both former Soviet republics located in what the Russian government calls its Near

Abroad, are examples of democratic revolutions whose architects have in mind a basic plan for the governments they wish to create but who are thwarted by international politics, history, geography, foreign meddling, and personal rivalries, as well as the character of their peoples. In Ukraine's disastrous presidential elections of 2004, Viktor A. Yushchenko, running as the candidate of the Our Ukraine party, nearly died of poisoning but managed to finish the race, which he went on to lose to Viktor F. Yanukovich. After Western observers concluded that the balloting had been fraudulent, a second election was held, and this time Yushchenko prevailed. After a series of political crises the president's popularity collapsed, while Yanukovich recovered his. In the parliamentary elections of 2007, Yushchenko hired American political operatives (three of them with connections to Bill Clinton, Arnold Schwarzenegger, and Mitt Romney)—giving an adviser to the former prime minister, Yulia V. Tymoshenko, an opening to describe her made-over opponent as belonging to "the same old Soviet and post-Soviet political culture."[12] Today Tymoshenko is ill and in prison on dubious charges of corruption, and is waging a hunger strike.

The so-called Arab Spring is the most dramatic international political occurrence since the fall of the Soviet Union in 1991. It began with the self-immolation of a fruit vendor in Tunis in January 2011 and the flight of President Zine El Abidine Ben Ali to Saudi Arabia, and it continued with the overthrow of Hosni Mubarak in Egypt. There followed a bloody street revolution in Bahrain, the deposition and murder of Libyan ruler Mu'ammar Gadhafi by native rebels with the aid of a NATO bombing campaign, and the insurgency against Syrian president Bashar al-Assad and the dominant Alawite minority that has ruled the country for decades. Although Western democrats hoped the Middle East would be transformed in the image of the democratic West, the Arab Spring was being called, a year after it sprung, the Arab Winter. Oddly, the revolution has proved most successful in Tunisia, although even there the Muslim influence is pressing on the government. At the other extreme, Bahrain is deadlocked between the opposition and the monarchy. Otherwise, the developing

officially, "The Arab Spring Towards Democracy"

story has gone against optimistic expectations of democratic sentiment realizing itself in solid democratic institutions. Events in Libya, Egypt, and Syria are precisely what skeptics over the past two centuries would have predicted.

The Arab Spring is proof that vague democratic aspirations on the part of people who have never experienced democratic government are insufficient to establish it. It also shows that a country's unwilled history is more powerful than its hoped-for future, and that religion is a vastly more powerful force than democratism in traditional societies. By the spring of 2012 the crisis in Syria had become so complex and chaotic that the Western capitals, looking to interpose themselves in the carnage, could not identify a clearly defined opposition to back against Assad, whose government, as al-Qaeda in Iraq joins the insurgents fighting to overthrow the regime, is not demonstrably less desirable than any conceivable replacement for it. No wonder that Francis Fukuyama, writing in *The Spectator* a year before the Egyptian revolution, admitted that history still had a few more surprises up its sleeve, including what he described as the capitalist autocracies in Venezuela and Russia. He did not consider the likely collapse of "democratic" government in Iraq following the American military's withdrawal from the country (after nearly nine years' engagement) or NATO's failure to prevail in Afghanistan, where the British in the nineteenth century and the Soviets in the 1980s were ignominiously defeated. Whatever the political outcome in the Middle East and western Asia, it is unlikely to be the establishment of authentically democratic government anywhere.

The historian Mark Lilla has warned that the West, which learned to separate religion and politics only after centuries of national and civil strife, should not expect the Muslim world to do the same. Christian political theology, Lilla reminds us, had a long "afterlife" in the West (Germany especially) that lasted as a political force until the end of World War II. Friedrich Gogarten, a collaborator of Barth's, wrote after Hitler's accession to power, "Precisely because we are today once again under the total control of the state, it is again possible, humanly

speaking, to proclaim the Christ of the Bible and his reign over us."
(Meanwhile, Kevin Phillips frets about what he calls the "Republican
theocracy" in the United States, meaning a voting bloc of American
evangelical Christians.)[13]

Democrats looked for great things from Russia following the dissolution of the Soviet Union in 1991, though optimism was greater among
Westerners than the Russian people, who have learned over centuries
that pessimism is the highest form of realism. Two decades after the
restoration of the historical Russia, democracy is no more realistic a
prospect there than the restoration of the Romanovs. If any people has
autocracy embedded in its DNA, that people is the Russians. Culture
is destiny, and Russian culture is finally not that of European Russia—
the Russia of Tolstoy, Dostoyevsky, Turgenev, and Solzhenitsyn—but
of the Russia of the East. American Cold Warriors expected the Russian masses to accept "democracy" and "freedom" once the triumphant
Western powers liberated them from the tyranny of the communist
state. In fact, no such thing has happened, and no such thing is likely
to happen. A very good reason why is that Russians (save for the czar-
ist upper classes of the enlightenment period) do not, and never have,
admired western Europe and America, or even liked them very much.
The history of the post-Soviet era suggests that Cold War hostilities
between the USSR and the United States were an expression less of
ideological disagreement than of nationalist rivalry between major
powers (as John Lukacs has argued since the 1950s), which explains
why the two countries remain mutually antagonistic decades after the
Soviet empire's collapse.

   In the postdemocratic world, a noisy minority will always be around
to agitate on behalf of "freedom," "democracy," and "human rights,"
as it does in Russia today. Nevertheless, the Russian majority is, as the
2012 elections showed, prepared to settle for the corporate national-

ist authoritarian government that Vladimir Putin has fashioned during his two terms as president and his prime ministerial tenure under
President Dmitry Medvedev—and now is fashioning as president
again. In Putin's Russia, where nostalgia for the Stalinist regime lin-
gers, political and economic power are one and the same thing, as they
were under the czars. The columnist Ralph Peters has described this
mode of government as "tolerant totalitarianism," which he attributes
to Putin's recognition that "a post-modern dictatorship needs to make
only a single compromise to prosper: It has to halt at the front door. . . .
'I get the political power, you get material and social freedoms. Behave
in the streets and I'll stay out of your sheets.'"[14] Putin's government
has never repudiated, or apologized for, the crimes of the Stalin era,
as other governments have done following the replacement of previous
criminal regimes. Instead, Putin has been at pains to ignore and paper
over the history of Stalinism, glorifying its successes while keeping the
Stalinist archives (including those of his previous fiefdom, the KGB)
under seal, a notable departure from the more open practices of the
1990s. The new Russian nationalism is a nationalism of the oligarchs,
not of the new bourgeoisie. But the people, broadly speaking, seem
content with their bargain.

Following the death of Aleksandr Solzhenitsyn in the summer
of 2008, the great novelist (who thought writers under a dictatorship the equivalent of a second government) was revered, but he was
not mourned. "The relatively subdued response," the *New York Times*
observed, "raised the question of whether Mr. Solzhenitsyn's life and
work still resonated in a Russia that is far different from the Soviet
Union it replaced."[15] The Russian government, a democrat might easily conclude, had fobbed off on the people off a liberalized authoritarianism instead of democracy. But did the Russian people ever wish for
democracy? Solzhenitsyn himself was no democrat, and he abhorred
what he perceived as the moral decadence and materialism of the
world's greatest democracy while living in exile in the United States
before the communist government of his native country fell.

Taking Vladimir Putin's Russia for its model, the Central Politburo of the Communist Party of China has pursued a similar course toward a softer totalitarianism that combines social and economic relaxation. Thus it has maintained material supremacy and nationalist hegemony by giving 1.5 billion people the opportunity to cooperate in the construction of a superstate. As in the case of Russia, the number of dissidents in China demanding democracy in the Western sense of the word remains proportionately few, despite the international media attention they receive; unlike his Russian counterpart, the typical Chinese dissident lives abroad—chiefly in the United States, which, as China's biggest debtor, is not strategically well positioned to press for democratic reform in the People's Republic. Although the Chinese regime is almost certain to liberalize further, democratic reform, as in Russia, is unthinkable for the foreseeable future. Putin and Hu Jintao, the Chinese head of state, are working toward their own goals in directing their countries, which appear to be on convergent courses toward a more efficient corporate nationalism: the refinement of the state as a diversified corporation and of the national economy as a collective business enterprise, almost wholly owned and operated by the state, in which workers and citizens are one solid and indistinguishable thing.

If "democracy" has experienced a setback over the past twenty years, "freedom" has made certain advances, as Fareed Zakaria argues in *The Future of Freedom* (2007). Indeed, Zakaria believes that, since 1990, freedom has achieved greater progress than democracy. The Chinese state has relaxed its grip on its citizens in a number of ways, including permitting a few private companies to operate alongside the giant state-owned ones and allowing a degree of union activity. In Russia in the fall of 2010, President Medvedev vetoed a law proposed by his governing party, United Russia, that would have placed further restrictions on street protests—a move that encouraged the humorless or thickheaded leader of the outlawed Bolshevik Party to protest, "We still live in a police state." (Since his reelection as president in March 2012, Vladimir Putin has signed a bill imposing drastic fines on participants in unsanctioned street demonstrations.) Simple freedoms, Zakaria insists, are not to be despised, whether they are realized by democratic elections or granted by oligarchs. One can have freedom without democracy, and the United States errs (he thinks) by recognizing as legitimate, and rewarding, only those governments that advance toward civic freedom by means of the ballot box.

The problem, Zakaria suggests, is not the absence of democracy but ineffective government—the acknowledged democracies included, where democratic procedure and excessive inclusivity have severely compromised the ability of governments to govern. Recalling what he terms "liberal autocracy"—for example, constitutional monarchy in the nineteenth century—Zakaria notes that liberalism and democracy are not synonymous. He seems to prefer liberalism—more constitutional liberalism, less intrusive (direct or participatory) democracy. But Zakaria fails to appreciate fully how radically Western liberalism changed in the second half of the twentieth century. "Liberalism" and "constitutionalism" overlapped, but they were never the same thing, and each served as a necessary check on the other. Today advanced liberalism has merged with the Western concept of democracy, which it is bent on destroying. In these circumstances, if (advanced) liberalism should collapse, democracy would fall with it. At least, it would in Western countries. Paradoxically, the less democratically developed non-Western nations, where advanced liberalism has yet to penetrate, might have a future advantage in this respect.

Fareed Zakaria appears to favor a softer version of the Chinese national corporate state as a model for a postdemocratic world. "Dictators have tended over time to become arrogant and corrupt. Can China escape the fate of other autocracies and keep up its extraordinary track record [in development]? If it does, it will be seen by many countries around the world as a viable model for modernization, one that rivals the American-centric model that speaks of democracy and economic freedom as intertwined."[16]

Zakaria's insistence that government needs to be efficient as well as free has special relevance for the present fiscal crisis in the United States and the European Union, which is fundamentally about the affordability of liberal social democracy and its viability as a functioning form of government and a type of modern society. At issue is a simple question: Does democratic socialism, the direct descendant of political democracy, work, or does it not? The answer may come from Greece, which invented democracy 2,500 years ago and has survived in its modern instauration to press the idea of democratic governance to its most irresponsible and destructive limits and itself into political paralysis and social chaos. Today Europe and the state of California are collapsing simultaneously into the fiery sunset of the Golden West.

During Supreme Court justice Elena Kagan's confirmation hearings in 2010, Senator Tom Coburn, an Oklahoma Republican, expressed his "absolute fear" that Americans are less free than they were thirty years ago. A fellow senator, Democrat Amy Klobuchar of Minnesota, countered, "Were we really more free if you were a woman in 1980?" (when no woman justice sat on the Supreme Court, and the U.S. Senate included a single woman).[17]

Senator Klobuchar's concept of political and social freedom is faulty. It is also very contemporary, very widespread, and very dangerous. There was, of course, no federal law in 1980 denying a woman the right to run for the Senate or to be seated in that august institution if she won a place there. It is only that, in those days, American society (like Western society as a whole) was not as habituated to the idea of females running for the office of senator or getting themselves nominated to the Supreme Court as it is in the twenty-first century. Social conventions and expectations, however stultifying they may be, do not amount to a denial of freedom to anyone. What may very easily lead to a loss of freedom is President Obama's insistence that the justices he nominates must possess "the empathy to understand what it's like to be poor, or African-American, or gay, or disabled, or old." As Thomas Sowell asked during the confirmation proceedings of Justice Kagan's immediate predecessor on the bench, Justice Sotomayor, "Didn't we spend decades in America, and centuries in Western civilization, trying to get away from the idea that who you are determines what your legal rights are?"[18] Referring to the court's decision in *Kelo v. the City of New London* (2005), permitting local politicians to seize private property and transfer it to other people in the interests of "public use," Sowell said simply, "That's not a 'living Constitution.' That's a dying Constitution."

"Here," Gerald Ford asserted on August 9, 1974, "the people rule"—a quote William Kristol appropriated for a column during the presidential election of 2008.[19] But it is not true. Here, as in every other mass democracy, the people vote. That is all. They make themselves heard, to a limited extent. They interfere with the plans of their masters, occasionally to some avail, with either good results or bad ones. But they do not rule, and they never did (and never will). Even so, the Constitution previously guaranteed them considerably more freedoms than they have today, which was Senator Coburn's point. Many of these freedoms have been abrogated in recent decades by the federal government, while others have been violated by the state governments, strongly encouraged and often coerced by Washington, D.C.

In every aspect of American life, governmental control over the citizenry has been expanded and extended into such areas as education, religion, alcohol, diet and nutrition, gun ownership, the use of private property, transport (drivers' licenses and the standardization of road signs), provisions for disabled and handicapped people, "hate crimes," and personal rehabilitation. At the institutional level, the federal government has assumed control of the national health system, federalized mortgage lending, and effectively nationalized the largest banks and two of the largest automotive corporations. The point is not whether these things are good or bad but whether they further, or limit, the freedom of a supposedly democratic people.

Tocqueville warned of democracy's potential to create an extensive bureaucracy for the purpose—or at least with the effect—of exercising "an immense, tutelary power, which takes sole charge of assuring [the people's] enjoyment of watching over their fate. It is absolute, attentive to detail, regular, providential, and gentle." Although one may object that the gigantic Western bureaucracies that governments have created over the past two centuries correspond with Tocqueville's prediction solely in terms of their absoluteness, still they come close enough in other respects to qualify as an example of the "soft despotism" Paul A. Rahe foretold in a recent book.[20] Rahe rightly notes that America is forfeiting all the characteristics and conditions that Tocqueville thought made it "exceptional." He fails to add that, to the extent that America ever *was* exceptional, it is probably now the more vulnerable for it, not less.

The United States, from the time of its creation until now, has been in the vanguard of the democratic revolution: first as example, then as encourager, now as enforcer. The two administrations of President George W. Bush and the neoconservative democratic globalists who staffed it were never able to appreciate Churchill's remark that democracy is the worst of all forms of government, except the others, or the plain truth that a democratic government is necessarily an incomplete one. For these people, democracy can be only a positive good, never a negative one. Democracy is for them a religion, and here is something truly new in the world: the Jacobins, with their Rights of Man, were violent atheists. This universalization of democratic thought in the decade since 2001 has done much to discredit democracy as an idea (and ideal) and with it Francis Fukuyama's famous thesis. As a result, the United States is less and less the acknowledged model democratic nation in the world. Indeed, one wonders whether America can any longer serve as a model for itself.

A multicultural nation is a contradiction in terms. It follows that the multiculturalist ideology is fatal to the nation-state. In a startling book published in 1949, Wyndham Lewis, the English painter, novelist, and critic, described the United States as the world's first multicultural country (he did not, of course, employ the modern terminology).[21] Lewis offers an interesting echo of Orestes Brownson, who predicted that the young and dynamic United States would eventually incorporate Canada and Mexico within its boundaries. America, Lewis thought, was in the process of creating a human type he celebrated as "cosmic man," or what Ben Wattenberg called the "first universal man": "the sum of all assimilation, a cosmic fruit, indeed . . . a perfectly eclectic, non-national, internationally minded creature, whose blood is drawn—more or less—from all corners of the earth, with no more geographical or cultural roots than a chameleon."[22] To Lewis, the United States seemed an imperfect "advance copy" of "a future world order."[23] Americans would come to despise the imperialist doctrine known as "Americanism," and the older nations of the world, taking notice, would in time renounce notions of sovereignty and racial pride. America after the Second World War, Lewis noted, was, paradoxically, universalistic and imperialistic at the same time. But it would not remain so, he predicted. Instead it would use "the raw human material of Socialism" to build a new international, or anyway internationalized, society.[24] "America is much more a psychological something than a territorial something. . . . In a sense [American patriotism] may be said to be abstract. The United States is rather the site for the development of an idea of political and religious freedom than a mystical *terre sacrée* for its sons, upon the French model. They will fight for brotherhood, rather than, possessively, for a mother earth."[25] In *America and Cosmic Man*, Wyndham Lewis anticipated the doctrines of the First Universal Nation and the Proposition Nation and yoked them to the immemorial utopian ideal of the Brotherhood of Man.

Pitirim Sorokin, writing two decades before Lewis, would have disapproved of this sentimentality. "Any great culture, instead of being a mere dumping place of a multitude of diverse cultural phenomena, existing side by side and unrelated to one another, represents a unity or individuality whose parts are permeated by the same principle and articulate the same basic value."[26] Until recently, the argument was going Sorokin's way. Charles Frankel, a dean of American liberal philosophy in the decades following World War II, thought it a dangerous theoretical error to confuse a liberal society comprising many publics, none of which dominates the others, with a society lacking an organized public to serve as an independent judge whose role is to monitor the decisions taken by that society's ruling groups. "The conditions most favorable for polyarchy [pluralist democracy] are comparatively uncommon and not easily created," according to Robert Dahl. Roland Stromberg argues that both too much and too little pluralism work against democracy. In the case of the United States, the relentless erosion of our common cultural foundations is pushing the country toward cultural anarchy: "Today's popular term *identity* is a terribly impoverished substitute for the older term *community*."[27]

As almost everyone agrees, the United States confronts many grave, even critical problems. Among these are its loss of status as sole superpower, the rise of powerful international competitors (in subcontinental Asia, eastern Asia, and Latin America especially), and the nation's relative decline as an economic and even a military power. There are also its dissolving manufacturing base and national indebtedness to foreign creditors, China in particular; a vague but widening perception, at home and abroad, of America's transformation from a can-do society to a can't-do one (epitomized in the popular mind, whether fairly or not, by the BP oil spill in the Gulf of Mexico); economic crisis induced by irresponsible and dishonest business practices in the private sphere and matched by equally irresponsible fiscal and monetary policies in the public one; overextended and overambitious government at the federal, state, and local levels, which has left government attempting everything and succeeding at almost nothing; popular dissatisfaction and impatience with incumbent politicians, existing governmental institutions, and the practice of party politics; and the corrosive doctrine of multiculturalism that almost no one dares to criticize, much less defy, at least in public.

In *The Servile Mind* (2010), Kenneth Minogue builds on an earlier work, *Alien Powers: The Pure Theory of Ideology*, to explain how modern democracy erodes the moral life and how multiculturalism comports with servility. Western politicians, Minogue argues, no longer assume, as they did in the nineteenth and early twentieth centuries, associations of independent self-motivated individuals; rather, they see societies of vulnerable people in need of protection by the state. Meanwhile, *democracy* has become a term justifying the belief that the moral as well as the political life must be democratized. Hence the appearance of what Minogue somewhat clumsily terms "the politico-moral": an ideal that, in the past generation or so, has moralized politics and politicized morality, and currently, he thinks, provides the current direction of our moral world. The designers and builders of modern democracies carefully present their constructs as symbols of social inclusion, clubs with memberships of scores or millions of people, not a single one of whom can be permitted to suffer "discrimination" without reprisal and correction by the state. In this context Minogue wonders whether the moral life and ultimately freedom itself are compatible with the moralizing state, which forms the basis for the new-model democracy that amounts, throughout the Western world, to the latest of many successive "democratic" revolutions.

Minogue views the future of the individual as Western tradition understands him as the central issue of our age. Obviously, the politico-moral project is a perfectionist enterprise. The "monism of perfection," once achieved, would anneal Western civilization with those innumerable cultures, past and present, that have identified the one right way of life and refuse to tolerate any other. Yet the political-moral itself does not, Minogue thinks, qualify as a religion itself. Instead it is an attempt to divinize society by making it the source of all that we rely on, including our ideas, our power, and our sense of self-identity and human belonging.[28]

Ten years after the 1960s expired, liberalism seemed at death's door, exhausted by the achievement of the tasks it had set itself. Advanced liberalism (of which politico-moralism is an ingredient) succeeded it in the 1980s, absorbing democracy or becoming annealed with it. Thus the future of democracy in the United States is tied to the future of modern liberalism. And the future of both looks to be disastrous—unless democracy, perceiving the inevitable at last, discovers both a will and a way to free itself from liberalism.

Democratic theory has always assumed a special relationship between liberalism and modernity, supposing either that they are one and the same thing or that they must inevitably accompany each other. Alan Wolfe has reaffirmed the second proposition: "Modernity is a brute fact of contemporary social life" whose course is humanly irreversible. Because liberalism has proved itself most capable of managing modernity, being of all political philosophies most in accord with the way the modern world functions, it will endure.[29] (Wolfe does not consider the possibility that modernity's course might be *unintentionally* reversible—a far more likely possibility that corresponds with the way history actually works.) The chief reason for Wolfe's confidence in the staying power of liberalism is what he perceives to be the modern citizen's belief that he inhabits a world of his own making, a world he understands he never could have made without the aid of liberalism to buttress and defend its assumptions: a mode and habit of looking at the world he will consequently never renounce.

Democracy needs reality to sustain it, as fire needs oxygen. But the new, advanced liberalism is founded on an illusory concept of metaphysics, human nature, the essence of the good, and the nature of evil. Moreover, liberalism not only fails to sustain society in its sense of reality; it works actively to deprive it of any apprehension of the real. "The liberal regime can exist only because it is incomplete," says James Kalb. It lives off illiberal values and the preliberal values of the past. "The victims of liberalism destroy those [pre-liberal] patterns, and in the end will destroy liberalism itself."[30]

Critics of liberalism have noted during the past two centuries that liberal politics are essentially opposition politics and that liberalism's chief contributions to the sum total of human happiness have been negative ones, most of them achieved during the nineteenth and early twentieth centuries, when liberal parties mainly had the opposition role in government. Liberalism in power, on the other hand, undermines both itself and the society it rules. Too rigid in theory and in procedure, "liberal modernity" (in Kalb's phrase) lacks the ambiguities and the subtleties to renovate its principles, even when these are obviously destructive of its aims. By "raising consciousness" everywhere, liberalism constantly reveals new illiberalities, which it is then obliged to remedy. In the attempt, it creates new inequalities that must also be corrected. Thus liberalism is constantly radicalizing itself in ways that cause its fundamental irrationality and oppressiveness to be felt, lessening its attractiveness and causing it to resort eventually to group assertiveness in the absence of a common culture, and force and rhetoric to prevail in spite of the unprincipled nature of its actions. In the end, "the burdens of moral and intellectual decline outweigh their benefits to the regime." Inevitably, Kalb concludes, "When it proves impossible to base human relationships on further extensions of equal freedom, the regime will face insuperable problems."[31] At this point the issue will be whether liberal culture can survive the collapse of the liberal regime. Perhaps the answer is no—in the absence of a regime in place to reward it. If the answer is yes, then it is hard to see how the old regime could be replaced by a democratic one. Kalb, recalling how the collapse of the Soviet Union brought on rule by mafia and dangerous demographic decline, speculates that the same thing could happen to the United States.

Come what may, the great question remains: what is the probable future of democracy in a world in which the United States is either no longer a democratic nation itself or else too badly weakened by its commitment to democratic ideology to promote and defend something like the real thing abroad?

14

After Democracy

All governments grow within their various forms, fail, and die at last by overreaching—by becoming, that is, too much themselves.

There have been times during the present age when something like a democratic recession seemed to be occurring. Being a human institution, democracy is never stable, yet it is hard, from the vantage point of the early twenty-first century, to perceive a global movement toward or away from democratic institutions. For every dictatorship that, like Cuba, shows signs of relenting, there is a democracy, like Venezuela, that is pressed into dictatorship. Even so, Father John Courtney Murray's warning, more than six decades ago, that the monism that distinguished the pre-Christian West seems to be returning in the post-Christian era—as it attempts to restore by totalitarian means, including the suppression of Christian individualism and particularity, the lost unity of the ancient world—needs to be heeded today.[1]

More significantly, the conditions of life in the postmodern world characterized by mass society, mass politics, the corporate state and the corporate economy, economies of scale, mass culture, mass communications, the dominance of technique no one can grasp in its entirety, and the nearly infinite complexities of globalization are inherently opposed to the more personalized and less complicated and distracted societies, built to a far smaller scale, from which democratic institutions and habits arose. It is true that today democracy faces no ideological enemy of comparable strength, such as communism or fascism; yet that, really, was Daniel Bell's point when, in the 1950s, he described the implications of the "end of ideology." More than a half century later, democracy attempts to fill the vacuum by becoming an ideology itself. This may help to explain the vague dissatisfaction so many democratic citizens express with their governments, in form and in practice.

Paradoxically, the more public satisfaction with democratic institutions wanes, the greater the enthusiasm of democratic "leaders" for "democracy" waxes. The reason is obvious: democratic ideology constrains and harasses democratic publics while strengthening their governments and the politicians who run them. The democratic ideology is profoundly undemocratic, and democratic peoples have begun to notice the fact. The world, Roland Stromberg thinks, "has entered a post-democratic phase—not necessarily non-democratic, but searching for some 'new structure' [T. S. Eliot's phrase] in which democracy can live."[2] Consequently, democratic publics' want of respect for their governments will probably intensify to the point where the legitimacy of those governments is dangerously compromised. Although democracy at present may appear to be globally indispensable, it is difficult to say how long this perceived indispensability will endure.[3]

What people in the past have called democratic government and democratic society existed for millennia before the advent of the Industrial Revolution in the eighteenth (some say the seventeenth) century. That does not change the fact that modern democracy and industrialism are inextricably interrelated and mutually dependent: the twin pillars of the Western world in the modern age. It has been plain for a couple of decades now that the West is confronting still another in a series of crises that have occurred over the past century, each of which has threatened its survival. The present crisis has political, economic, social, and religious elements, all of them related to the inadequacy of the two institutions on which our present world stands: mass democracy and industrial consumerism (or consumerist industrialism).

It was Karl Marx who popularized the term *contradiction*, as in "the contradictions of capitalism." Two results followed from this. The first is that contradiction became a suspect, if not discredited, concept at the political center and on the Right, which perceived it (correctly) as an example of vulgar pseudo-intellectualism, as well as a false political insight. Yet it is a perfectly valid, indeed an undeniable, one, if for *contradiction* one substitutes the word *entropy*. Every system— inorganic, biological, social, economic—runs down in time, collapses, dies, and is replaced by something else. Political philosophers have debated from the beginning of recorded history which political and economic systems "work" and which do not. The sole verifiable answer is that no setup works over the long term, though many do in the short run. It is also true that some systems, being grounded in metaphysical reality and in human nature, are intrinsically superior to others. As Tocqueville observed, democratic government answers in many ways to human nature and the human condition—but so, in other ways, does aristocratic government. One pays one's money and one takes one's choice, but one cannot enjoy the advantages of both choices together. There have been periods in history when imperial, monarchical, constitutional-monarchical (or mixed), republican, and democratic governments have operated effectively and with benefits to society at large. All, in time, weakened and yielded to one or another of the several political systems human ingenuity has devised. It is no good saying which—democracy, republicanism, monarchy, or tyranny—is the "best" form of government, or which, for that matter, is the worst. There is a time for everything, as Ecclesiastes says, though that time may not last very long. Hence one can plausibly argue that democracy, for a couple of centuries now, has proved the best of all imaginable systems for the organization of human society in the modern world.

The problem is the second of the two pillars on which the world stands, industrialism: a system of rationalized mechanical production on a large scale, which does not answer in any way to nature, human nature, or the laws of natural or political sustainability. Industrialism is a Faustian project, a result of Francis Bacon's dictum that knowledge is power. Naturally, power is what industrialism expends, produces, and acquires for itself. A power of this magnitude requires an equal power to oppose it, and the only power capable of doing so is government, which, in a democratic age, means democratic government. But democratic government was originally designed to reduce and disperse power, not to augment and centralize it. Theoretically, it is possible for local government to regulate industrial power, yet the size and geographical reach of modern industrial corporations and of communications and transport systems, as well as the cost of regulatory action, make it nearly impossible in practice. One leviathan requires another to confront it effectively, but the leviathan state is either the totalitarian state (the Soviet Union) or the corporate authoritarian state (the People's Republic of China).

Modern democracy and industrialism, which once worked so well together, now work against each other. Mass industrial society, by nature hedonistic, selfish, and narcissistic, is no longer a society comprising independent persons or autonomous social institutions and arrangements suited to, or capable of, democratic self-government; the social-democratic welfare state that was created in response to industrialism is hostile to free enterprise and efficiency in industry, preferring instead the corporate statist or social model, neither of which is efficient in terms of profit or production in the long run. Moreover, the self-serving closeness of industry to government, and of government to industry, has discredited both in the eyes of the public, which persists in its naive belief that the Western nations remain, in spite of everything, "democracies," or that they can somehow regain their lost democratic identities. Western citizens demand the goods that both socialist government and industrialism deliver, but they are jealous and resentful of the interlocking, reinforcing powers of industry and government. Finally, the environmentalist Left has succeeded in compromising industrialism's reputation as the bearer of prosperity and progress and the means by which humanity can somehow transcend itself, as a growing number of people associate it with climate change and environmental degradation, whether or not they are ultimately willing to forego its benefits.

Mass disillusionment is always a potent cause for generalized anger, unrest, and disruption, especially when the grounds for disillusionment are real.[4]

James Bryce, observing that Frenchmen, Englishmen, and Americans took for granted an active interest in politics, assumed that this preoccupation is as natural to men everywhere as it is undying. Yet, for a millennium after the Roman Republic, the most civilized European peoples devoted their time to the arts and to learning, abandoning politics to kings and their henchmen. "Free government," Bryce predicted, "is not likely to be suppressed in any country by a national army wielded by an ambitious chief. If any people loses its free self-government this will more probably happen with its own acquiescence. But oligarchy springs up everywhere as by a law of nature."[5] Bryce was concerned by the fact that people in Europe and North America early in the twentieth century cared less for democracy as the promise of liberty than for democracy as an engine for procuring for the masses the objects of their desires. (He would not have been surprised by the political indifference of Chilean young people who, more than twenty years after General Pinochet's political Waterloo in the referendum he called in 1988, ignored the presidential election held in December 2009. Only 9.2 percent of Chileans eighteen to twenty-nine years old were registered to vote at the time.)[6]

"The ancient world, having tried many experiments in free government, relapsed wearily into an acceptance of monarchy and turned its mind quite away from political questions," Bryce wrote. "More than a thousand years elapsed before their long sleep was broken."[7] A century after Bryce, Harvey Mitchell concludes that citizens the world over are less concerned with democratic community than with an efficient government, an emphasis that has helped to make the growth of Tocqueville's "soft despotism" a global phenomenon. (Mitchell speculates that the domination of government by economics has much to do with this, and he is almost certainly right.)[8] Be that as it may, Bryce was convinced that the fate of popular government is bound inextricably to what he called "the moral and intellectual progress of mankind as a whole."

Samuel P. Huntington conceded the possibility that his "third wave" of democratization could be followed by a third reversal, noting that in many cases the first two waves were succeeded by forms of authoritarianism hitherto unknown to history. These, he suggested, might be suited to "wealthy, information-dominated, technology-based societies."[9] Huntington thought China a candidate for a postmodern authoritarian regime—as Russia clearly is, and perhaps, in time, the United States as well. In the 1960s and '70s, "convergence"—the tendency of the Soviet system and the American one to draw together, as the USSR adopted elements of the capitalist system and the United States aspects of the communist one—was a much-debated scenario. Today the two countries, and China, seem to be converging toward a corporate nationalist system. Huntington expected that China, if it stuck to its commitment to authoritarianism and expanded its control in east Asia, would in time exercise a powerful negative influence on the growth of democracy in the region (though in the end, he believed, time was on the side of democracy there).

Robert Dahl notes that the history of democracy recounts as many failures as successes: temporary victories followed by major defeats, "and sometimes . . . utopian ambitions followed by disillusionment and despair."[10] Dahl predicts that a group of stable democracies will continue to exert great influence in the world and that even nondemocratic regimes will pay homage to democracy and democratic principles. Still, he expects many of these regimes to continue in power, even as some authoritarian governments become polyarchic.[11] He considers democratic governments to have limited ability to create democracy in other countries, although he recognizes the possibilities for pursuing policies that work toward a change in conditions conducive to polyarchy's growth. A more realistic forecast may be that, as modern capitalism and Enlightenment ideas continue to diverge—most significantly, in the United States—democracy will become increasingly a victim of hostile forces.[12] Huntington rightly observed that the universalism inherent in Western thought guarantees friction between it and other civilizations, yet the West cannot hope to dominate the world, any more than it can separate itself from it. (After quoting from Lincoln's "House Divided" speech, he questioned how long an increasingly interdependent world can remain divided between democracy and authoritarianism—a complete non sequitur.)[13]

At any rate, the future of democracy cannot be realistically assessed by toting up recent electoral triumphs and authoritarian coups, as so many writers have done. Optimists looking forward to a democratic future typically focus on the emergence of "democracy" in one previously authoritarian country or another, but they are not so keen-eyed when it comes to discerning tyrannical tendencies emerging in existing "democracies"—the United States among them. Less significant than where previous or present despotisms are going is the direction in which present-day "democracies" are headed. To repeat: the future is not a matter of "what people want"; what counts, finally, are the nature and tendencies of the public (and private) environments in their totality, and the implications these have for the survival of democracy in a mass-technological world that has no real care for the individual and none at all for the small in scale. Democracy is beset by many problems, the majority of which insoluble by political means, democratic or otherwise, yet democratic government is unable to recognize them as such. (One recalls Bertrand de Jouvenel's "myth that there is a solution.") Many kings, but few presidents, have understood that government and politics are chiefly a matter of muddling through—or "carrying on," as the British say.

Modern democratic citizens demand far more from politics than political activity, and thinking about politics, can realistically bear. Jacques Ellul put his finger on the problem—and the theoretical solution. "It is necessary to 're-invent' a situation in which life's true problems are not posed in political terms," and in which all questions of morality are referred to the state.[14] True political life, Ellul thought, depends on tension, which the omnipresent and monolithic state is unwilling to countenance. Fundamental to politics is the tension between private versus political life—which is, however, only one among many tensions. Tension, Ellul thought, is the only means of containing the state within its valid framework. Man must rediscover himself to restore authenticity in human life and in society. (He did not say that this will or can happen; he said only that, if it does not, "More or less quickly, the political illusion, which is transitory in nature, will dissolve into ashes, and what will be left will be an organization of objects run by objects.")[15]

We must rid ourselves of large ideas and grand syntheses and devote ourselves to "the restitution of man," on which the return of democracy depends. "The problem used to be: 'For democracy to live, the citizen must have civic virtues.' . . . Today, the problem is: 'The growth of politics destroys man in his innermost being. And yet nothing can be done without man.'"[16] The citizen must remain, at one level of his being, a political animal, if what Habermas described as a depoliticized public addicted to theater is to be avoided. But that public is already with us, and growing larger with every election cycle.[17]

Ellul would not have contemplated the demise of "organized democracy" (which he compared, alternately, with the medieval feudal system and Vichy France) with sorrow or regret. He considered democracy in any era an inefficient political system but, more important, one that runs counter to man's instincts, which do not conform with the admonition that the price of liberty is eternal vigilance. This book is a brief neither for nor against democracy, and so I shall suggest here only that democracy—taken even as a political ideal—seems to represent not the end of history but the end of a historical age that is now passing, after the bourgeois era and that of the West, which gave democracy birth. (There are many things one ought to be philosophical about, politics most of all.)

Should the democratic age be lamented, if and when it does pass? That is not a proper historical question, of course. And so we retreat to the world of impressions and return at last to the pair of works discussed at the beginning of this book, and to the two countries, France and the United States, they describe.

Was Alexis de Tocqueville's France less free and "democratic" than the modern French nation on the eve of the Great War—or more so? Was the young republican democracy Tocqueville observed in the early 1830s a freer society and a more democratic nation than the superpower his compatriot Bernard-Henri Lévy discovered nearly two centuries later—or a more politically and socially constrained civilization? Which is more important, democracy or freedom? Or are they the same thing? The democratic nations of the modern world have been grappling with that question, and attempting to put the answer into practice, for more than two centuries. Do we still agree with that answer? Do we really know what the proper question is, *and* the correct answer? Perhaps it no longer matters, as we plunge deeper into the postmodern age, which, in its wholly impersonal way, is hostile to both democracy and freedom, and to humanity itself.

What is democracy? As we have seen, the word has no simple or universally agreed-on definition. One thing seems plain to this writer: whatever democracy is, there is likely to be a great deal less of it in the decades and centuries to come.

Coda

Because of Francis Fukuyama's book, for the past twenty years the future of democracy has been associated in the mind of the reading public with the "end of history."

The view of the liberal classes is essentially that of the English middle class at the end of the nineteenth century, the apex of Pax Britannica. As the historian Arnold Toynbee described it, "History, for them, was over. And they had every reason to congratulate themselves on the permanent state of felicity which this ending of history had conferred on them."[1] For the liberal classes today, all that remains of history is a wrap-up in which maximum equalized satisfaction is attained domestically, while the levers of liberal power (international organizations backed by military power, mass communications regulated by liberals) are worked to produce a global liberal empire.

For one antiliberal, the historical prospect is the opposite: the end of liberal society, brought on by the contradictory and illusory aspects of liberal thought. James Kalb writes, "While history is not over, a particular history—the progressive development of Western society toward a particular ideal for rational order—appears finished."[2] The scenario recalls Vico's myth of the leveling materialist age of men, which, having realized its aims, collapses like a dying star into chaos and is followed by an age of gods and heroes of the sort Carlyle demanded. There are, indeed, as the theologian Reinhold Niebuhr wrote, cumulative moments in history.

Fukuyama's notion of the end of history stands dangerously close to the ages-old desire to escape history altogether. Niebuhr, a wise and gentle man, described an eschatology that, though professedly Christian, speaks to the secular as well as to the religious understanding. Allowing that history becomes progressively inclusive and complex as the human race increases in knowledge and in technique, Niebuhr perceived the danger of "a more positive disorder" in the higher order that realized human freedom creates. In Christian terms, the name for this evil is Antichrist, for which the modern secular equivalent can be universal despotism, nuclear war, or environmental collapse. Historical culminations, Niebuhr saw, are a curse as well as a blessing. Liberal philosophies, led astray by their determination to read history as a redemptive process, have either denied these evils or refused to recognize their effects. Yet it is "obvious that history does not solve the basic problems of human existence but reveals them at progressively new levels." This is a sophisticated expression of the saying that historical problems are never resolved, they are simply succeeded by new dilemmas. The belief that man can resolve his problems or transcend them through history, Niebuhr thought, develops from the sin of pride: man's pride, the pride of Adam.

One does sense that historical visions such as Fukuyama's are rooted in fear—the existential fear that history might have no meaning and man himself might be much less than a puppet, rather an empty illusion. But, from the Christian perspective, "history is not meaningless because it cannot complete itself; though it cannot be denied that it is tragic because men always seek prematurely to complete it."[3]

Is it possible that the mood of vague apprehension pervading *Democracy in America* reflects Tocqueville's fear that the nature of democracy is to push forward, thoughtlessly and relentlessly, toward that premature completion of history of which Reinhold Niebuhr spoke?

Notes

Preface: Two Books

1   Graham Robb, *The Discovery of France* (New York: Norton, 2007). Unless otherwise noted, all quoted material from here until the next endnote is from Robb.

2   Bernard-Henri Lévy, *American Vertigo* (New York: Random House, 2007). All quoted material hereafter is from Lévy.

Chapter 1: From Tocqueville to Fukuyama

1   Hugh Brogan, *Alexis de Tocqueville: A Life* (New Haven, CT: Yale University Press, 2008), 4.

2   This and subsequent quotations from *Democracy in America* are drawn from Alexis de Tocqueville, *Democracy in America*, ed. J. P. Mayer, trans. George Lawrence (Garden City, NJ: Doubleday Anchor Books, 1969).

3   Francis Fukuyama, *The End of History and the Last Man* (New York: Free Press, 2006; first published 1992).

4   Alexandre Kojève, *Introduction to the Reading of Hegel: Lectures on the Phenomenology of Spirit*, ed. Allan Bloom, trans. James H. Nichols (Ithaca, NY: Cornell University Press, 1980).

Chapter 2: The Momentum of Monarchy

1   Ernest Kantorowicz, *The King's Two Bodies* (Princeton, NJ: Princeton University Press, 1997), 48.

2   Ibid., 9.

3   Ibid., 23.

4   See W. F. Butler, *The Lombard Communes: A History of the Republics of North Italy* (New York: Haskell House Publishers, 1969).

5   Sir Henry Sumner Maine, *Popular Government* (Lightning Source, offprint of the 1885 edition).

6   Frances Trollope, *Domestic Manners of the Americans* (New York: Dodd, Mead, 1927).

7   Edmund Burke, *Reflections on the Revolution in France* (Indianapolis, IN: The Liberal Arts Press, 1955).

8   Roland N. Stromberg, *Democracy: A Short, Analytical History* (Armonk, NY: M. E. Sharpe, 1996), 29.

9   Quoted in Albert Camus, *Notebooks 1951–1959*, trans. Ryan Bloom (Chicago: Ivan R. Dee, 2008).

10 Walter Bagehot, *The English Constitution* (New York: Cosimo Classics, 2007; first published in 1867).

11 Quoted in Harvey Mitchell, *America after Tocqueville: Democracy against the Difference* (New York: Cambridge University Press, 2002), 24.

12 Ibid., 41.

13 Paul A. Rahe, *Soft Despotism, Democracy's Drift: Montesquieu, Tocqueville, and the Modern Prospect* (New Haven, CT: Yale University Press, 2009), 278.

14 Michael Drolet, *Tocqueville, Democracy, and Social Reform* (New York: Palgrave Macmillan, 2003), 95.

15 Ibid., 230–35.

16 See Rahe, *Soft Despotism, Democracy's Drift*, 3–10, 271–73.

17 See Alan S. Kahan, *Aristocratic Liberalism: The Social and Political Thought of Jacob Burckhardt, John Stuart Mill, and Alexis de Tocqueville* (New Brunswick, NJ: Transaction Publishers, 2001; first published in 1992).

18 Ibid., 158.

Chapter 3: Democracy's Forked Road

1   John Dunn, *Democracy: A History* (New York: Grove-Atlantic, 2005), 18.

2   Orestes A. Brownson, *The American Republic* (Wilmington, DE: ISI Books, 2003; first published in 1865), with an introduction by Peter Augustine Lawler, xlv.

3   Pierre Manent, *Democracy without Nations? The Fate of Self-Government in Europe* (Wilmington, DE: ISI Books, 2007), 97.

4   Ibid., 95–101.

5   Brownson, *The American Republic*, 78–82. Brownson, by the time *The American Republic* (a book he insisted superseded and corrected all his previous writings) was written, had become a Catholic. His political theory may indeed sound

extreme to modern ears, including Catholic ones. Hence it is interesting to read a modern historian asserting, in no uncertain terms, that bourgeois society and its successors—enduring representations of Hobbes's bourgeois emancipation and composed of modern men regarding themselves as wholly independent and autonomous beings—are inherently atheistic. See Barry Cooper, *The End of History: An Essay on Modern Hegelianism* (Toronto: University of Toronto Press, 1984), 383–84.

6   Dunn, *Democracy: A History*, 120.

7   Maine, *Popular Government*, 4.

8   Mitchell, *America after Tocqueville*, 7.

9   Dunne, *Democracy: A History*, 125–26.

10 Claude Polin, "The Idea of Socialism," *Chronicles: A Magazine of American Culture*, August 2006, 19–24.

11 Claude Polin, "Democracy: The Enlightened Way," *Chronicles: A Magazine of American Culture*, June 2006, 19–25.

12 Claude Polin, "Tocqueville's America and America Today," *Chronicles: A Magazine of American Culture*, October 2004, 17–23.

13 Donald W. Livingston, "The Natural History of the Watchman State," *Chronicles: A Magazine of American History*, August 2006, 14–16.

14 Manent, *Democracy without Nations?*, 12–14.

15 Stromberg, *Democracy*, 40.

16 Dunn, *Democracy: A History*, 153.

17 In respect of "reforms," the case of Germany is both unique and highly complex. Jonathan Steinberg has described how "Bismarck sprang the idea of universal suffrage on a startled German public in 1863 [only] in order to prevent King William from going to a congress of princes called in by the Emperor of Austria. It worked. The Austrian move failed. Prussia unified Germany and universal manhood suffrage became the franchise for the new Reichstag, the lower house of parliament in the new German Empire." Thus Bismarck, who despised socialists and the Catholic influence, laid the foundations for a modern middle- and working-class democracy that eventually produced parliamentary majorities consisting of what the chancellor described as "enemies of the Reich." Bismarck, of course, was no democrat. Steinberg denies that he was a nationalist as well. See Jonathan Steinberg, *Bismarck: A Life* (New York: Oxford University Press, 2011), 8.

18 Stromberg, *Democracy*, 44, 49, 153, 64.

19 Ibid., 48–49.

20 Ibid., 45, 50, 53.

21 Stromberg, *Democracy*, 57, 65, 69, 70; and see A. N. Wilson, *The Victorians* (New York: Norton, 2002), 271, on "the aristocratic balance."

22 Juliet Nicolson, *The Great Silence: Britain from the Shadow of the First World War to the Dawn of the Jazz Age* (New York: Grove Press, 2011).

23 Stromberg, *Democracy*, 76–77.

24 Ibid.

25 John Lukacs, *The Legacy of the Second World War* (New Haven, CT: Yale University Press, 2010), 22–25.

26 See Claude Polin, "The Enigmatic Professor Strauss, Part II," *Chronicles: A Magazine of American Culture*, August 2007, 42–44.

27 Godfrey Hodgson, *The Myth of American Exceptionalism* (New Haven, CT: Yale University Press, 2010), 3, 9.

28 Ibid., xvi; see also 3–35.

29 Frank Prochaska, *The Eagle and the Crown: Americans and the British Monarchy* (New Haven, CT: Yale University Press, 2008), 17–18, 13, 14, 12.

30 Ibid., 43.

31 Ibid., 62.

32 See Donald W. Livingston, "The Declaration of Independence and Philosophic Superstitions," *Chronicles: A Magazine of American Culture*, January 2007, 14–19. See also Richard Hofstadter, *The American Political Tradition and the Men Who Made It* (New York: Knopf, 1948).

33 J. O. Tate, "Founders, Keepers," a review of *Revolutionary Characters: What Made the Founders Different* by Gordon S. Wood, *Chronicles: A Magazine of American Culture*, January 2007, 32.

34 Hodgson, *The Myth of American Exceptionalism*, 43.

35 Clyde Wilson, "Cincinnatus, Call the Office!" *Chronicles: A Magazine of American Culture*, June 2006, 14–15.

36 See Clyde Wilson, "Please Tread on Me," *Chronicles: A Magazine of American Culture*, August 2005, 20–22.

37 See Jack Beatty, *The Age of Betrayal: The Triumph of Money in America, 1865–1900* (New York: Vintage, 2008).

38 Hodgson, *The Myth of American Exceptionalism*, 81.

39 See H. L. Mencken, *Notes on Democracy* (New York: Knopf, 1926), 209.

40 Ibid., 210–11.

41 G. D. Lillibridge, *Beacon of Freedom: The Impact of American Democracy upon Great Britain, 1830–1870* (Philadelphia: University of Pennsylvania Press, 1955), xv.

42 Ibid., xiii.

43 Ibid., 4, xiv.

44 Quoted in Lewis, *America and Cosmic Man* (London: Nicolson & Watson, 1948), 13.

45 Ibid., 13.

46 Dunn, *Democracy: A History*, 158.

47 Stromberg, *Democracy*, 158.

48 Hodgson, *The Myth of American Exceptionalism*, 100, 99.

49 Charles Frankel, *The Democratic Prospect* (New York: Harper Colophon Books, 1962), 178–79.

50 Ibid., 17.

51 Samuel Francis, *Beautiful Losers: Essays on the Failure of American Conservatism* (Columbia: University of Missouri Press, 1994), 7.

52 Samuel P. Huntington, *The Third Wave: Democratization in the Late Twentieth Century* (Norman: University of Oklahoma Press, 1991), 284.

53 Dunn, *Democracy: A History*, 158.

54 Quoted by Samuel Francis, "Enthusiastic Democracy," *Chronicles: A Magazine of American Culture*, February 2004, 32–33.

55 Quoted by Hodgson, *The Myth of American Exceptionalism*, xiii.

56 Manent, *Democracy without Nations?*, 83.

Chapter 4: What Is Democracy?

1 Bertrand de Jouvenel, *On Power: Its Nature and the History of Its Growth* (Boston: Beacon Press, 1962; first published in 1945), 276.

2 Jacques Ellul, *The Political Illusion* (New York: Knopf, 1967), 226; Huntington, *The Third Wave*, 6; Christopher Lasch, *The Revolt of the Elites and the Betrayal of Democracy* (New York: W. W. Norton, 1995), 106; Alan Wolfe, *The Future of Liberalism* (New York: Vintage, 2010); and Kenneth Minogue, *The Servile Mind: How Democracy Erodes the Moral Life* (New York: Encounter Books, 2010).

3 James Bryce, *Modern Democracies*, 2 vols. (New York: Macmillan, 1921), vol. 1, 23.

4 Ibid., 23.

5 J. Budziszewski, *The Line through the Heart: Natural Law as Fact, Theory, and Sign of Contradiction* (Wilmington, DE: ISI Books, 2009), 182.

6 Barry Cooper, *The End of History: An Essay on Modern Hegelianism* (Toronto: University of Toronto, 1984), 8.

7 See Orestes A. Brownson, *The American Republic* (Wilmington, DE: ISI Books, 2003).

8 Pitirim Sorokin, *The Crisis of Our Age* (New York: Dutton, 1941), 318.

9 Walter Bagehot, *The English Constitution* (New York: Cosimo, 2007; first published in 1867), 39.

10 Claude Polin, "Western Political Models and Their Metaphysics, Part II: On the Differences between a Republic and a Democracy," *First Principles Journal*, May 26, 2010, http://www.firstprinciplesjournal.com/articles.aspx?article=1408.

11 Bagehot, *The English Constitution*, 271.

12 Dunn, *Democracy: A History*, 149.

13 See James Kalb, *The Tyranny of Liberalism* (Wilmington, DE: ISI Books, 2010).

14 Ibid., 20.

15 Ibid., 220.

16 Ibid., 240–42.

17 Bertrand de Jouvenel, *On Power: Its Nature and the History of Its Growth* (Boston: Beacon Press, 1962), 220.

18 Ibid., 159.

19 Kalb, *The Tyranny of Liberalism*, 77.

20 Ibid., 32.

21 Ibid., 94, 103.

22 As quoted in Chilton Williamson Jr., *The Conservative Bookshelf: Essential Works That Impact Today's Conservative Thinkers* (New York: Citadel Press, 2004), 109–16. See James Burnham, *Suicide of the West* (New York: The John Day Company, 1964).

Chapter 5: "Fit Your Feet"

1 Frankel, *The Democratic Prospect*, 17, 174.

2 Gary Hart, "Just Another Word," *New York Times Book Review*, March 22, 2009, 14–15.

3 Jean-Marie Guéhenno, *The End of the Nation-State* (Minneapolis: University of Minnesota Press, 1993), 67.

4 Jacques Ellul, *The Political Illusion* (New York: Knopf, 1967), 79, 238–39, 70–71.

5 Chilton Williamson Jr., "Contradiction and Collapse," *Chronicles: A Magazine of American Culture*, September 2011, 32–33.

6 See Geoffrey Gorer and Henry B. Mayo, quoted in Stromberg, *Democracy*, 123, 161.

Chapter 6: The King's Second Body

1 G. K. Chesterton, "Why I Am Not a Socialist," reprinted in *Chronicles: A Magazine of American Culture*, August 2006, 50–52.

2 See Donald W. Livingston, "Republicanism, Monarchy, and the Human Scale of Politics," *Chronicles: A Magazine of American Culture*, August 2005, 14.

3 See Claude Polin, "Tocqueville's America and America Today," *Chronicles: A Magazine of American Culture*, October 2004, 17–23.

4 See Polin, "Western Political Models and Their Metaphysics, Part II."

5 Livingston, "Republicanism, Monarchy, and the Human Scale of Politics," 14.

6 Ibid., 15–16.

7 Polin, "Tocqueville's America and America Today," 17.

8 Ibid., 17–23.

9 Ibid., 21–22.

10 Ibid., 22.

11 Polin, "Western Political Models and Their Metaphysics, Part II."

Chapter 7: The Business of Aristocracies

1 Matthew Arnold, *Democratic Education* (Ann Arbor: University of Michigan Press, 1962), 18.

2   Ibid., 24.

3   Quoted in John Lukacs, *Last Rites* (New Haven, CT: Yale University Press, 2009), 43.

4   Clive Bell, *Civilization* (New York: Harcourt, Brace & Co., 1928), 233.

5   Ibid., 234–35.

6   Josef Pieper, *Tradition: Concept and Claim*, trans. and with a preface by E. Christian Kopff (South Bend, IN: St. Augustine's Press, 2010), 62.

7   Ibid., 27.

8   Quoted in ibid.

9   Albert Camus, *Notebooks 1951–1959* (Chicago: Ivan R. Dee, 2008), 132.

10 Jouvenel, *On Power*, 188.

11 Maine, *Popular Government*, 42.

12 Bagehot, *The English Constitution*, 89.

13 Ibid., 38.

14 Ibid., 3–4.

15 Ibid., 54.

16 Ibid., 92.

17 Arnold, *Democratic Education*, 6–7.

18 Ibid., 18.

19 Ibid., 93; and see David Cannadine, *The Decline and Fall of the British Aristocracy* (New Haven, CT: Yale University Press, 1990).

20 Lasch, *The Revolt of the Elites and the Betrayal of Democracy*, 44–45.

21 For an excellent critique of meritocracy and a defense of class distinctions and tradition, see T. S. Eliot, *Notes Toward a Definition of Culture* (New York: Harcourt, 1949).

22 Jouvenel, *On Power*, 348.

23 Maine, *Popular Government*, 188.

Chapter 8: Christianity: The Vital Spot

1   Manent, *Democracy without Nations?*, 68–69, 23.

2   See Donald Livingston, "David Hume: Historian," *Chronicles: A Magazine of American Culture*, September 2008, 16–19.

3   Kenneth Minogue, *Alien Powers: The Pure Theory of Ideology* (Wilmington, DE: ISI Books, 2008), xxvi. Kevin Phillips claims that Christian theocratic pressures have made the GOP over into "America's first religious party." But the fundamentally ideological nature of modern Republican "conservatism" is suggested by former vice president Dick Cheney's support for the homosexual-rights agenda, including the right of homosexuals to marry one another. See *Kevin Phillips, American Theocracy: The Peril and Politics of Radical Religion, Oil, and Borrowed Money in the Twenty-first Century* (New York: Viking, 2008).

4   Minogue, *Alien Powers*, 3.

5   Ibid., xxiii.
6   Ibid., xxv.
7   See Guéhenno, *The End of the Nation-State*, 55.
8   David Novak, *In Defense of Religious Liberty* (Wilmington, DE: ISI Books, 2009), 87.
9   Ibid., 87.
10 Ibid., 101.
11 Ibid., 101–2.
12 Quoted in Budziszewski, *The Line through the Heart*, 156.
13 Ibid., 182.
14 Ibid., 179–80.
15 Emile Perreau-Saussine, *An Essay in the History of Political Thought* (Princeton, NJ: Princeton University Press, 2012).
16 Robert P. Kraynak, *Christian Faith and Modern Democracy: God and Politics in the Fallen World* (Notre Dame: University of Notre Dame Press, 2001).
17 See Chilton Williamson Jr., "Obama and the Bishops," *Chronicles: A Magazine of American Culture*, April 2012, 34–35.
18 Huntington, *The Third Wave*, 76, 84.
19 Polin, "Western Political Models and Their Metaphysics, Part II."

Chapter 9: Speechless Democracy

1   Sorokin, *The Crisis of Our Age*, 311.
2   Lasch, *The Revolt of the Elites and the Betrayal of Democracy*, 162.
3   Ibid., 174.
4   Ellul, *The Political Illusion*, 55–56.
5   Guéhenno, *The End of the Nation-State*, 29.
6   Jodi Dean, *Publicity's Secret: How Technoculture Capitalizes on Democracy* (Ithaca, NY: Cornell University Press, 2001), 2–3.
7   Ibid., 13.
8   See Mitchell, *America after Tocqueville*, 234.
9   Dean, *Publicity's Secret*, 151.
10 Walter Lippmann, *Liberty and the News*, foreword by Ronald Steel, afterword by Sidney Blumenthal (Princeton, NJ: Princeton University Press, 2008), 23.
11 Chilton Williamson Jr., "Democracy and the Internet," *Chronicles: A Magazine of American Culture*, March 2012, 34–35.
12 Lukacs, *Last Rites*, 71.
13 Ellul, *The Political Illusion*, 98.
14 Ibid., 103.
15 Ibid., 112.
16 Ibid., 134.
17 Manent, *Democracy without Nations?*, 29.

Chapter 10: Democracy and Modern Man

1 Quoted in Chilton Williamson Jr., *The Immigration Mystique: America's False Conscience* (New York: Basic Books, 1996), 31.

2 Office for National Statistics (UK), cited in Simon Rogers, "The UK's Foreign-born Population: See Where People Live and Where They're From," *Datablog* (blog), *The Guardian*, May 26, 2011.

3 Richard Cummings, "Rivers of Blood: Immigration and Terror in a Time of Chaos," *Chronicles: A Magazine of American Culture*, October 2005, 26.

4 Ibid., 27

5 Christie Davies, "The Muslim Conquest of Britain," *Chronicles: A Magazine of American Culture*, September 2004, 38–39.

6 See Michael Cosgrove, "How Does France Count Its Muslim Population?" *Le Figaro*, April 7, 2011; "Muslim Population by Country" (Chart), *The Future of the Global Muslim Population*, The Pew Forum on Religion and Public Life, January 2011. As *Le Figaro* explains, precise estimates of France's Muslim population are difficult to obtain because "the compilation of official statistics based on religious beliefs is not permitted by French law." As a result, "what few estimates there are vary widely." In June 2010, France's Interior Ministry offered the estimate of five to six million Muslims in France.

7 Alberto Carosa, "From Invasion to Conquest: Illegal Immigration into Europe and the United States," in *Immigration and the American Future*, ed. Chilton Williamson Jr. (Rockford, IL: Chronicles Press, 2007), 255–56.

8 See Christopher Caldwell, *Reflections on the Revolution in Europe: Immigration, Islam, and the West* (New York: Doubleday, 2009).

9 Carosa, "From Invasion to Conquest," 253.

10 Ibid., 253–54.

11 Caldwell, *Reflections on the Revolution in Europe*, 13.

12 Ibid., 330.

13 Giuseppe Germano Bernardini, "We Will Dominate You," *Middle East Quarterly* 4, no. 4 (December 1999), http://www.meforum.org/448/we-will-dominate-you.

14 Carosa, "From Invasion to Conquest," 269.

15 Caldwell, *Reflections on the Revolution in Europe*, 330; and see Pascal Bruckner, *The Tyranny of Guilt: An Essay on Western Masochism* (Princeton, NJ: Princeton University Press, 2010).

16 Caldwell, *Reflections on the Revolution in Europe*, 330.

17 Ibid., 222. One notices that Caldwell is alert to the distinction between the older liberalism and "democracy."

18 Bagehot, *The English Constitution*, xi.

19 Lukacs, *Last Rites*, 84.

20 Quoted in Mitchell, *America after Tocqueville*, 289.

21 Guéhenno, *The End of the Nation-State*, 122.

22 See Mitchell, *America after Tocqueville*, 4; and Guéhenno, *The End of the Nation-State*, 19.

23 Guéhenno, *The End of the Nation-State*, 30.

24 Maine, *Popular Government*, 149.

25 Ibid., 148.

26 Quoted in Lewis, *America and Cosmic Man*, 38.

27 Ellul, *The Political Illusion*, 168, 171.

28 See E. J. Dionne, *Why Americans Hate Politics* (New York: Simon & Schuster, 1991).

29 Michael Hardt and Antonio Negri, *Labor of Dionysus: A Critique of the State Form (Theory Out of Bounds)* (Minneapolis: University of Minnesota Press, 1994), 271.

30 Manent, *Democracy without Nations?*, 37.

31 Ibid., 39.

32 Ibid., 41. (Emphasis in original.)

33 Guéhenno, *The End of the Nation-State*, 68–69.

34 Manent, *Democracy without Nations?*, 41, 44.

35 Ibid., 44.

36 Quoted in William Quirk, "Just One More Thing: Repudiating the National Debt," *Chronicles: A Magazine of American Culture*, May 2009, 17–18.

37 Guéhenno, *The End of the Nation-State*, 23, 101–9.

38 Mickey Kaus, *The End of Equality* (New York: Basic Books, 1992), 131.

Chapter 11: Three against Democracy

1 Bradley C. S. Watson, *Living Constitution, Dying Faith: Progressivism and the New Science of Jurisprudence* (Wilmington, DE: ISI Books, 2009), 114.

2 Bagehot, *The English Constitution*, 60.

3 Watson, *Living Constitution, Dying Faith*, xx.

4 Ibid., xx.

5 Ibid., 17, 21–22.

6 Ibid., 145.

7 Ibid., 122, 128, 129.

8 Quoted in ibid., 149.

9 Quoted in Budziszewski, *The Line through the Heart*, 140.

10 Ibid., 142.

11 See Bradley C. S. Watson, *Civil Rights and the Paradox of Liberal Democracy* (Lanham, MD: Lexington Books, 1999).

12 Watson, *Living Constitution, Dying Faith*, 5.

13 Budziszewski, *The Line through the Heart*, 131.

14 Mary Ann Glendon, *Rights Talk: The Impoverishment of Political Discourse* (New York: Free Press, 1991), xi.

15 Ibid., 177.

16 Sir Henry Sumner Maine argued that natural law and natural rights belong to the purview of jurisprudence, not of government. Rousseau and Bentham, he thought, were really after governmental, not legal, reform. In Maine's view, Bentham was the first Englishman to perceive how civil jurisprudence could be reconstructed and adapted to its stated ends by means of the powers of the legislature. He added, "That because you can successfully reform jurisprudence on certain principles, you can successfully reform Constitutions on the same principles, is not a safe inference." Maine, *Popular Government*, 168.

17 Jouvenel, *On Power*, 158.

18 Ibid., 317, 159–60.

19 Ibid., 177, 215.

20 Ibid., 275.

21 Ibid., 236–37.

22 See David Brooks, "Drilling for Certainty," *New York Times*, May 28, 2010.

23 Jouvenel, *On Power*, 43, 81.

24 Ibid., 93.

Chapter 12: The Cold Monster at Bay

1 See Robert Dahl, *Democracy and Its Critics* (New Haven, CT: Yale University Press, 1989), 319 20.

2 Guéhenno, *The End of the Nation-State*, x.

3 Ibid., 59.

4 Ibid., 125.

5 A. N. Wilson, *Our Times: The Age of Elizabeth II* (New York: Farrar, Straus and Giroux, 2008), 92.

6 Guéhenno, *The End of the Nation-State*, 54.

7 Manent, *Democracy without Nations?*, 30–31, 9, 17.

8 Ibid., 15, 82.

9 Ibid., 14, 31–32.

10 Ibid., 67–68, 33, 69.

Chapter 13: The Future of Democracy

1 Bagehot, *The English Constitution*, 257, 254; and Frankel, *The Democratic Prospect*, 176.

2 Quoted in Huntington, *The Third Wave*, 288–89.

3 Ibid., 21.

4 Quoted in Fareed Zakaria, *The Future of Freedom: Illiberal Democracy at Home and Abroad* (New York: W. W. Norton, 2007), 260.

5 Ibid., 262.

6 Nicholas D. Kristof, "Unfit for Democracy?" *New York Times*, February 27, 2011.

7 "Mexican Collapse?" *Washington Times*, January 22, 2009.

8 See Frank McLynn, *Villa and Zapata: A History of the Mexican Revolution* (New York: Basic, 2002).

9 See Charles Bowden, *Murder City: Ciudad Juárez and the Global Economy's New Killing Fields* (New York: Nation Books, 2010).

10 See McKinsey & Company, "Lions on the Move: The Progress and Potential of African Economies," June 2010, cited in Celia W. Dugger, "Report Optimistic on Africa Economies," *New York Times*, June 23, 2010.

11 Pierre Englebert, "To Save Africa, Reject Its Nations," *New York Times*, June 12, 2010.

12 Clifford J. Levy, "Ukrainian Prime Minister, Once Seen as Archvillain, Reinvents Himself," *New York Times*, September 30, 2007.

13 Mark Lilla, "The Politics of God," *New York Times Magazine*, August 19, 2007; Mark Lilla, *The Stillborn God: Religion, Politics, and the Modern West* (New York: Knopf, 2007).

14 Ralph Peters, "Czar Vlad's Tolerant Tyranny," *New York Post*, February 2, 2009.

15 Clifford J. Levy, "Nationalism of Putin's Era Veils Sins of Stalin's," *New York Times*, November 27, 2008.

16 Zakaria, *The Future of Freedom*, 269.

17 Cheryl Gay Stolberg and Charlie Savage, "In Another Day of Republican Quizzing, Kagan Sticks to Careful Script," *New York Times*, October 29, 2008.

18 Thomas Sowell, "Obama and the Law," *Laramie Boomerang*, October 29, 2008.

19 William Kristol, "Here the People Rule," *New York Times*, October 20, 2008.

20 Paul A. Rahe, *Soft Despotism, Democracy's Drift: Montesquieu, Rousseau, Tocqueville, and the Modern Prospect* (New Haven, CT: Yale University Press, 2009).

21 See Lewis, *America and Cosmic Man*.

22 Ibid., 203.

23 Ibid., 30.

24 Ibid., 17.

25 Ibid., 27.

26 Sorokin, *The Crisis of Our Age*, 17.

27 Robert Dahl, quoted in Stromberg, *Democracy*, 169; Stromberg, *Democracy*, 169, 135–36; see Dean, *Publicity's Secret*, on the "fantasy" of a "public" and its dangers in a diverse society: "The nation can no longer provide the fantasy of unity necessary for the ideal of a public," owing to globalization, migration, immigration, and so forth (p. 156); and Manent, *Democracy without Nations?*, 79.

28 See Kenneth Minogue, *The Servile Mind: How Democracy Erodes the Moral Life* (New York: Encounter, 2010).

29 Alan Wolfe, *The Future of Liberalism* (New York: Knopf, 2009), 254.

30 Kalb, *The Tyranny of Liberalism*, 144.
31 Ibid., 142–43, 150.

Chapter 14: After Democracy

1   Peter Augustine Lawler, "Introduction," in Orestes Brownson, *The American Republic: Its Constitution, Tendencies, and Destiny* (Wilmington, DE: ISI Books, 2003), xcviii–xcvix.
2   Stromberg, *Democracy: A Short, Analytical History*, 171.
3   Dunn, *Democracy: A History*, 183.
4   Chilton Williamson Jr., "A Disillusioned World," *Chronicles: A Magazine of American Culture*, January 2012, 34–35.
5   Bryce, *Modern Democracies*, vol. 2, 603.
6   Alexei Barrionuevo, "Chile's 'Children of Democracy' Sitting Out Presidential Election," *New York Times*, December 13, 2009.
7   Bryce, *Modern Democracies*, vol. 1, 12.
8   Mitchell, *America after Tocqueville*, 288.
9   Huntington, *The Third Wave*, 316.
10 Dahl, *Democracy and Its Critics*, 312.
11 Ibid., 315.
12 Mitchell, *America after Tocqueville*, 3–4.
13 Huntington, *The Third Wave*, 312, 29.
14 Ellul, *The Political Illusion*, 206, 186.
15 Ibid., 223.
16 Ibid., 227.
17 Mitchell, *America after Tocqueville*, 3–4.

Coda

1   Arnold Toynbee, quoted in Huntington, *The Clash of Civilizations*, 301.
2   Kalb, *The Tyranny of Liberalism*, 18, 286.
3   Reinhold Niebuhr, *The Nature and Destiny of Man: A Christian Interpretation* (New York: Charles Scribner's Sons, 1941–43), 315–21.

Acknowledgments

The author wishes to thank the following persons for their contributions to the publication of this book: Tony Outhwaite of JCA Literary Agency in New York City; Jed Donahue, editor in chief of ISI Books; and Bill Kauffman, for his careful copyediting work.

Index

Abbey, Edward, 134
absolute power, 176
absolutism, 178
Adams, Henry, 57
Adams, John, 52, 54, 142
Adams, John Quincy, 4
advanced liberalism: Existence Right,
    171; future of the U.S. and, 218–
    20; global liberalism and, 78; power
    and, 79, 81; survival of Western
    civilization and, 82
Aeneid (Virgil), 143
Afghanistan, 205, 208
Africa: failed states, 203–5
Age of Betrayal, The (Beatty), 58
Age of Jackson, The (Schlesinger), 55
Age of Revolutions, 39
Alain-Fournier, xvii
Alien Powers: The Pure Theory of Ideology
    (Minogue), 217–18
al-Qaeda, 208
America and Cosmic Man (Lewis), 216
American democracy: capitalism and,
    65–66; democratic idealism and,
    42; as ideological democracy, 41;
    immigration and, 141–42; issues of
    scale and, 92–94; Lévy's account of,

xviii–xxii; Maine on, 26; modern
    complaints of assaults on, 10–11;
    modern obsession with rights,
    173–74; nationalist-ideological
    tradition in, 54–63; new elite and
    the global economy, 111; New Left
    and, 66; notions of freedom and,
    96; selfishness and, 97–98; state
    sovereignty and, 95–98; Tocqueville
    on American materialist values
    and ambitions, 96–97; Tocqueville
    on the factors maintaining and
    advancing, 7–9; Tocqueville on
    threats to, 11; Tocqueville's initial
    views of, 3–4; universalism and,
    63–68, 215; WASP aristocracy,
    108–9. *See also* United States
American empire, 92–93
American exceptionalism: capital-
    ist economics and, 65; history of,
    50–51; liberal Protestantism and,
    49–50; Russell on, 49
American Founders: debate on
    immigration, 142; later aware-
    ness of change in America, 55;
    notions of democracy, 73;
    as "political atheists," 114;

American Founders (*continued*)
power of the chief executive and,
52; republican political ideal of, 95;
self-conception of, 197–98; views
of the American republic, 11–12

American Vertigo (Lévy), xix, xx, xxii

ancient "democracies," 37

ancients: Athens, 37, 101, 102; decline
of the Roman patriciate, 198;
Greek city-states, 94; tradition and,
103

Aquinas, Saint Thomas, 103

Arab immigrants, 146

Arab Spring, 207–8

Arendt, Hannah, 71, 80

aristocracy: Arnold on, 106–7; association with landholding, 111;
Bagehot's defense of, 27–28, 105–6;
Carlyle on, 21; destruction of,
79–80; faults of, 106–7; importance
to the future of democracy, 112;
impossibility of in the modern
world, 111–12; in Jouvenel's theory
of power, 177–78; meritocracy and,
107–8; "parliamentary aristocracy,"
80; rise of the plutocracy and, 105,
106; role in opposing despotism,
104; Tocqueville as an aristo, 1–2;
Tocqueville's views of, 41, 106;
twentieth-century perceptions of,
104

aristocratic liberalism, 33–35

Aristotle, 73, 94

Arnold, Matthew, 22, 100, 101, 105,
106–7

Aron, Raymond, 96

Articles of Confederation, 95

artists: rejection of democracy, 44

Assad, Bashar al-, 207, 208

assemblies. *See* legislatures; parliaments

atheistic Left, 113–14

Athens, 37, 101, 102

Atlantic Monthly, xviii

Augustine, Saint, 122

Austria, 48, 162

authority: tradition and, 103–4

autocracy: "liberal autocracy," 212;
Russia and, 209

autonomous politics, 86–87

Babeuf, François-Noël, 41

Bacon, Francis, 109, 223

Bagehot, Walter: on the American
judiciary, 171; on the British Constitution, 27; on the British monarchy and aristocracy, 27–28, 105–6,
107; on change in the "spirit" of
politics, 149; criticism of the U.S.
Constitution, 168; on democracy's lack of self-criticism, 90; on
the educative role of the British
Parliament, 132; on establishing a
democratic government, 76; forms
of government identified by, 71; on
republics, 76; view of the U.S. as an
elective monarchy, 52

Bahrain, 207

Bancroft, George, 52

Barbary states, 203–4

Baseball Hall of Fame, xxi

Beatty, Jack, 58

Beaumont, Gustave de, xviii, 3

Bell, Clive, 101, 102

Bell, Daniel, 222

Belloc, Hilaire, 46, 91

Ben Ali, Zine El Abidine, 207

Benedict XVI, 193

Bentham, Jeremy, 25, 26

Berlusconi, Silvio, 135

Bernanos, George, 101

biotechnology, 175

Bismarck, Otto von, 48

Blackstone, Sir William, 15

Blair, Tony, 144

Bolshevik Party, 211

Boumediene, Houari, 146

Bowden, Charles, 203
Brandeis, Louis, 169–70, 172
Brennan, William, 172
British National Party, 162
Brogan, Hugh, 1, 3, 12
Brooks, David, 180
Brown, Gordon, 144
Brownson, Orestes A.: on the Age of
    Revolutions, 39; on the American
    Founders as "political atheists," 114;
    on the "best" system of govern-
    ment, 75, 76, 89; on Catholicism
    and the rescue of the United States,
    121; on commercial society, 97;
    definition of republic, 138; on
    despotism, 38; on the primary work
    of republics, 100
Brown v. Board of Education, 169
Bryan, William Jennings, 58
Bryce, James, 74, 154, 197, 225–26
Buchanan, Pat, 162
Budziszewski, J., 74, 121, 172
Buonarroti, Philippe, 41
Burckhardt, Jacob, 34, 35, 47, 101–2
bureaucracy, 159, 214–15
Burke, Edmund, 19–20, 27
Burnham, James, 78–79, 82, 148
Bush, George H. W., 67
Bush, George W., 62, 67, 200, 215
Bush Doctrine, 62

Caldwell, Christopher, 145–46, 147,
    148
Camp of the Saints, The (Raspail),
    144–45
Camus, Albert, 23–24, 104, 176
Canada, 120–21
Cannadine, David, 107, 112
capitalism: American exceptionalism
    and, 65
capitalist aristocracy, 110
capitalist democracy, 65–66
Cardozo, Benjamin, 171

Carlyle, Thomas, 21, 22, 24
Carter, Jimmy, 66–67
Catholic Church: democratization and,
    124; liberalism and, 121–22, 123,
    124–25; response to mass immi-
    gration in Europe, 147; Second
    Vatican Council, 121, 122, 123,
    124; socialism and, 42
Cavour, Camillo di, 21
Cecil, Lord Robert, 45–46
centralization: in nineteenth-century
    France, xi–xviii; Tocqueville's con-
    cerns about, 8, 33
Charles, Prince of Wales, 144
Chateaubriand, François-René de, 3
Chesterton, G. K., 46, 72, 91, 174, 181
Chile, 225
China, 210–11, 212, 226
Christianity: Christian ideal of
    government, 99; Christian kings,
    38; church-state conflicts and the
    origins of democracy, 38–40; as the
    enemy of ideology, 117; implica-
    tions of mass immigration for,
    147; liberalism and, 113, 121–25;
    "nationalization" of during the
    Reformation, 38–39; Nietzsche on,
    23, 24; notions of human dignity,
    122–25; significance to democracy,
    115; socialism and, 42; Tocqueville
    on Christianity and democracy, 40.
    See also Catholic Church
Christian nations: secularization, 116
Christian political theology, 208–9
Christie, Agatha, 114
Chrysler Corporation, 179
Churchill, Winston, 215
civilization: as the aim of govern-
    ment, 99; definitions of, 100–101;
    democracy and, 82, 83, 101,
    102; as high culture, 113; perspec-
    tives on the essential elements
    of, 101–2; as a process, 102;

civilization (*continued*)
Sorokin's typology of, 128–30;
threat of the "mass man" to,
127–28; tradition and, 102–3
Civilization: An Essay (Bell), 101
civil rights: liberalism and, 121;
modern obsession with, 173–74;
Tocqueville's views of, 28–29
civil society. *See* civilization
class warfare, 161, 165
Clérel family, 2
climate change, 195
Clinton, Bill, xxi, 67
Coburn, Tom, 213
Cold War, 64–65, 209
Coleridge, Samuel Taylor, 20
Color Revolutions, 206–7
Commentaries on the Laws of England
(Blackstone), 15
communication "circuits," 188, 189
communications industry, 135. *See also*
electronic communications / media;
mass communication
communicative democracy, 134–40
Comte, Auguste, 20
Conservative Party (Great Britain), 44
Considerations on France (Maistre), 22
*Considerations on the Romans and Uni-
versal Empire* (Montesquieu), 32
Constitutional Convention, 73, 168
constitutional liberalism, 212
constitutional monarchy, 112
constitutional organicism: doctrine of,
167, 168
constitutions: Bagehot's defense of the
British Constitution, 27; corrupting effects on, 167–68; notions of a
"living Constitution," 167. *See also*
U.S. Constitution
consumerist industrialism, 223
contradiction, 223
Coolidge, Calvin, 160
corporate capitalism, 132

corporate nationalist state, 226
corruption, 161
"cosmic man," 216
Crèvecoeur, Hector St. John de, 50
culture: religion and, 113, 125

Dahl, Robert, 72, 217, 226–27
Davies, Christie, 144
Dean, Jodi, 135, 136
debate. *See* political debate
debt, 159–60
Declaration of Independence, 174
Declaration of the Rights of Man, 174
deferential rule, 76
democracy: absence of absolute
principles in modern democracies, 94–95; as an artificial society,
125; ancient "democracies," 37; as
antitraditional, 103; as the "best"
government, 75–78; Burke on,
19–20; challenges of modern global
instability and, 195–96; Chesterton
on, 91; Christianity and, 38–40,
115; church-state conflicts in the
origins of, 37–40; civilization
and, 82, 83, 101, 102; during the
Cold War, 64–65; compared to a
republic, 77; critiques of democratic
society, 87; danger of progressive
jurisprudence to, 172; definitions
of, 71–74; democratic tyranny, 81;
depoliticizing trends, 153–59; elite
in, 110; as the end of a historical
age, 229; entropy of systems and,
223; European concept of "pure"
democracy, 62; Europe's approach
to extending democracy, 68; Fukuyama on, 5–7; fundamental paradox
of, 152–53; Maine on the history
of, 16–17; human consciousness
and, 85, 86; ideology and, 119, 222;
impact of science and technology
on, 174–75; importance of ideals

to, 100; industrialism and, 222–25; issues of scale and, 92–94; justice and, 78; Left and, 115; liberalism and, 78–82, 212; liberal reformism and, 43–44; liberty and, 112; mass communication and, 191–95; "mass man" and, 128; mass media and, 134–40; as a means, not an end, 43, 75, 90; Mencken on, 60–61; meritocracy and, 107–10; monarchy and, 40–41, 75–76, 112; nation-state and, 185, 189–91; peace and, 191; perspectives on the future of, 112, 167, 225–29; in political thought following World War II, 4–5; in a postmodern world, 221–22; "Power" and, 176; progress and, 85–90; religion and, 26, 37–40, 116, 119–25; self-righteousness and, 158; skepticism toward and reactions against, 20–26, 43–49, 92, 199–200; social justice and, 78; state sovereignty in modern democracies, 95–98; Tocqueville on, xviii, 1, 4, 13, 28–29, 31–33, 40; totalitarianism and, 87; tradition and, 108; "without nations," 49; Zakaria on, 212. *See also* American democracy

Democracy in America (Tocqueville): on the factors maintaining and advancing American democracy, 7–9; on the future of democracy, xvii; importance of the formative circumstance of American democracy, 4; lack of impact in its own time, 35; political prophecy in, 1; on self-destructive tendencies in democracy, 13; on threats to American democracy, 11; Tocqueville's aim in writing, 12, 28

democratic citizens: Bryce's description of, 74; changes affecting the character of, 141; fundamental paradox of democracy and, 152–53; future of democracy and, 228; immigration and, 141–49; impact of money on democratic self-respect, 164; modern changes in and condition of, 149–52; perspectives on the characteristics of, 197–98

democratic idealism, 42

democratic ideology. *See* ideological democracy

democratic revolutions, 206–9, 215

democratic socialism, 49, 213. *See also* socialist democracy

democratic tyranny, 81

democratization: failed states, 202–6; Huntington's theory of "waves" of democratization, 124, 198–99, 226; problematic nature of, 200–202. *See also* global democratization

Denmark, 147

départements, xv

despotism: aristocracy's role in opposing, 104; "soft despotism," 215, 226

Dionne, E. J., 156

Discovery of France, The (Robb), xxii

Disraeli, Benjamin, 43

Distributists, 46, 91

Đjilas, Milovan, 108

Domestic Manners of the Americans (Trollope), 17–19

Douglas, William O., 171

dress and fashion, 152

drug cartels, 187, 188, 202

Dunn, John, 37, 67, 72

Eagle and the Crown, The (Prochaska), 53

East Africa, 203–4

economic inequalities: American populism and, 161–63; class warfare and, 165; European socialist parties and, 161; New Class and, 163–65

Edward VII, 53

efficiency, 180

Egypt, 207, 208

electronic communications / media: absolute power of the state and, 175; global effects of, 191–95; Internet, 135–40, 175. *See also* mass communication; mass media

Eliot, T. S., 23, 104, 109, 222

elites: in democracies and meritocracies, 110; Lasch on, 128; liberal-managerial elite in the U.S., 110, 111; New Class, 108, 163–65; social mobility securing influence of, 164

Elizabeth (the Queen Mother), 53

Ellul, Jacques: on autonomous politics, 86–87; condemnation of modern political parties, 154–55; on the confusing of political and social affairs, 116; on the contradiction between politics and moral values, 180–81; on the crisis of Western democracy, 157; on democracy, 72; on efficiency and political action, 180; on the increased role of technique in society, 175; on liberty and reflection, 132; on the modern obsession with news, 134; on modern politicians and pseudo-decisions, 158; on the modern view of political powers, 159; on the nation-state, 191; on the need to reform the democratic citizen, 151; on political facts, 139; on true political life, 228; on the "vacuity of ideology" in the 1960s, 118

empire: American empire, 92–93; French Empire, 32; in Guéhenno's imperial age, 187–89

End of History and the Last Man, The (Fukuyama), 5–7, 20

England: American influence on, 64; Arnold on the aristocracy, 106–7; Bagehot on the English political system, 76; Bagehot's defense of the monarch and aristocracy, 27–28, 105–6, 107; "calm national mind" of, 198; doctrine of "the King's two Bodies," 15–16; law courts, 171; spontaneous formation of local assemblies, 197. *See also* Great Britain

English Constitution, The (Bagehot), 27–28, 105

Enlightenment, 150

environmentalist Left, 225

equality: absolutism and, 178; Tocqueville on, 28–29

Espionage Act (1917), 60

establishments: the American WASP establishment, 108–9; conservative nature of, 110

ethicists, 118

"Eurabia" project, 146

Europe: approach to extending democracy, 68; concept of "pure" democracy in, 62; immigration concerns and dangers, 144–49; multiparty system, 155; "non-national democracy" and, 190–91; opposition of socialist parties to economic inequalities, 161; socialist-democratic versus nationalist-ideological divide in the U.S., 41–42, 61–63

European Economic Community (EEC), 7, 49, 146

European Union (EU), 49, 62, 155, 188–89

evangelical Christians, 209

Existence Right, 171

expansionism: American, 55–57

Faguet, Émile, 21

failed states, 202–6

faith. *See* religious faith

Fallaci, Oriana, 146
famine, 195
fantasy literature, 131
Federalist Papers, 132, 141–42
Federalists, 33
First Amendment, 60
First Reform Act (Great Britain), 25
Flaubert, Gustave, 20
Florence (Italy), 94
folk culture, 130
Ford, Gerald, 214
France: Burke on the French monarchy, 19; Declaration of the Rights of Man, 174; democracy in the wake of the French Revolution, 40, 44; growth of the power of state sovereignty in, 95–96; Maistre on the French Republic, 22; mass immigration and, 144–45, 147; Montesquieu's views of the French Empire, 32; National Front, 162; nineteenth-century processes of nationalization and centralization in, xi–xviii; origins of socialism, 42; *regroupement familial* policy, 145; selfish democracy in, 96; significance of the aristocracy in, 104; Tocqueville on the threat of centralization in, 8; Tocqueville's political career, 12; Tocqueville's views of contemporary political history in, 13, 30–31. *See also* French Revolution
franchise, 111. *See also* suffrage
Francis, Samuel T., 78–79, 162, 163
Frankel, Charles, 65, 66, 86, 217
Frankfurt School, 5
Franklin, Benjamin, 51–52
freedom: American democracy and, 96; Catholic notions of human dignity and, 124–25; in Guéhenno's imperial age, 187; Kierkegaard on, 22; modern advances, 211–12; modern condition in the U.S., 213–14; U.S. Constitution and, 214
Freedom House, 200
freedom of religion, 120–21, 147
French Revolution: atheistic Left and, 113–14; Maistre on, 22; Tocqueville on, 37
Fukuyama, Francis: on democracy and history, 4–7; on the future of democracy, 208; on reactions against democracy, 200; view of fixed identities in democratic societies, 10; view of liberal capitalist democracy, 71; view of the aims of government, 99
Furet, François, 46
Future of Freedom, The (Zakaria), 211

Gadhafi, Mu'ammar, 207
Galbraith, John Kenneth, 65
General Motors, 179
George III, 52, 53
George VI, 53
Georgia (former Soviet republic), 206–7
Germany: immigration and, 145; National Socialists and World War II, 48, 49
Gettleman, Jeffrey, 203
Gilbert, W. S., 103
Gilded Age, 58
Gladstone, William Ewart, 44
Glendon, Mary Ann, 173–74
global democratization: American nationalism following the September 11 terrorist attacks and, 67–68; case of China, 210–11; case of Russia, 209–10; democratic revolutions, 206–9; failed states, 202–6; Huntington's theory of democratic "waves," 124, 198–99, 226; problematic nature of, 200–202. *See also* democratization

global economy, 111
global police force, 188
global warming, 195
Gogarten, Friedrich, 208–9
"Good Man Is Hard to Find, A"
 (O'Connor), 110
government: Bryce on the future of
 free government, 225–26; corruption, 161; money and, 159–61;
 perspectives on the aim of, 99–100;
 possible forms of, 71; preference for
 "mass man," 132
Gramsci, Antonio, 114
Grand Meaulnes, Le (Alain-Fournier),
 xvii
Great Britain: American influence on,
 63–64; Bagehot on the educative role of the Parliament, 132;
 Bagehot's defense of British Constitution, 27; Bagehot's defense of
 monarchy and aristocracy, 27–28,
 105–6, 107; British National Party,
 162; decline of the aristocracy and,
 112; "half-way" democracy in,
 45–46; House of Commons, 154;
 law courts, 171; Maine on legislative change in, 25; mass immigration and, 143–44, 147; party
 system, 155; tradition of rights in,
 77. *See also* England
Great Conclave (1962–65), 124
Great Depression, 61
Great Silence, The (Nicolson), 46
Great War. *See* World War I
Greece, 213
Greek city-states, 94
Greeley, Horace, 57
Grégoire, Abbé Henri, xiii–xiv
Griswold v. Connecticut, 171
Guéhenno, Jean-Marie: on the future
 of the nation-state, 185–89; on a
 government of checks and balances,
 150; on the influence of markets

on democracy, 160–61; on political
 debate in a procedural democracy,
 158; on politics in "the age of networks," 153, 154
Guicciardini, Francesco, 33
Guizot, François, 3

Habermas, Jürgen, 136, 174–75
Hadley, Stephen J., 202
Haiti, 200
Hall, Capt. Basil, 19
Hamilton, Alexander, 95, 142
Hardt, Michael, 156–57
"hate speech," 147
Heath, Edward, 143
Hegel, Georg Wilhelm Friedrich, 6, 20
Hemingway, Ernest, 60
Henry VIII, 113
high culture, 113
Historical Fragment (Burckhardt), 34
History of the Revolution (Thiers), 3
History of the United States (Bancroft), 52
Hitler, Adolf, 48, 49
Hodgson, Godfrey, 50, 51, 65
Hofstadter, Richard, 54
Holmes, Oliver Wendell, 169, 170
House of Commons, 154
Hu Jintao, 211
human consciousness: democracy and,
 85, 86; modernity and, 86
human dignity: in Christianity, 122–25
humanism, 34
human nature: classical and Christian
 views of, 125; republican government and, 94; viewed in liberal
 democracies, 123–24
human rights. *See* rights
Hume, David, 95, 116
Hungary, 162
Huntington, Samuel P.: belief in
 general applicability of democracy,
 198; "clash of civilizations" concept,
 149, 195; on the future of democ-

racy, 226, 227; theory of "waves" of global democratization, 124, 198–99, 226; view of democracy as procedural, 72
hypernationalism, 49, 63

idealistic culture, 128, 129
ideals: democracy and, 100
ideational culture, 128, 129, 130
ideological democracy: distinguished from socialist democracy, 41; politics and, 117–18; religion and, 121; undemocratic nature of, 222
ideology: Christianity as the enemy of, 117; definitions of, 117, 118; democracy and, 40, 119, 222; multicultural, 116–19; political Right and, 116; politics and, 117–18
"illiberal liberal religion," 121
immigration, 141–49, 192–93
Immigration Act of 1965, 142
imperial age, 186–89
Indian Mutiny of 1857, 193
indigenous rebellions, 195
industrialism: democracy and, 222–25
inflation: of the supply of ideas, 136–37
injustice: civilization and, 102
inquiétude, 31–33
institutional age, 186
intellectual aristocracy, 107–8
intellectual democracy, 107–8
intellectuals: nineteenth-century objections to democracy, 20–26
internationalism: American, 67–68
international nationalist movement, 48
Internet, 135–40, 175
Iran, 193
Iraq, 208
Iraq War, 67
Italy, 145, 162

Jackson, Andrew, 55, 64
Jacksonian democracy, 55

Jacobins, 215
Jay, John, 141–42
Jefferson, Thomas, 54–55, 57, 63, 142, 159, 160
Jesus Christ, 103, 140
John Paul II, 124–25, 195
Johnson, Samuel, 100–101
journalism, 133–34, 137–38
Journal of Democracy, 200
Jouvenel, Bertrand de: on absolute power, 176; on the capitalist aristocracy, 110; on democracy, 72; on the development of "Power," 79–90, 176–79; on the identification of new rights of man, 173; on "legislative activity," 159; on the myth of a "solution," 227; on personality traits necessary to resist "Power," 197; on "Power" as command, 86; on the root of modern despotism, 74
Judaism, 49, 194
judicial activism, 168–72
Julius Caesar, xii
jurisprudence: progressive, 168–72
justice: democracy and, 78; Maine on, 25

Kahan, Alan S., 35
Kalb, James, 79, 81, 82, 219, 220
Kant, Immanuel, 122
"Kantian Christianity," 122–23
Kaus, Mickey, 164
Kelo v. the City of New London, 214
Kennan, George, 64–65, 198
Kennedy, John F., xxi
Kenya, 195, 204
Kidd, Benjamin, 45
Kierkegaard, Søren, 22
kings: Christian kings, 38; in Jouvenel's theory of power, 177–78; nature of "Power" and, 79–80. *See also* monarchy

"King's two Bodies" doctrine, 15–16
Klobuchar, Amy, 213
Kojève, Alexandre, 7
Kraynak, Robert P., 122
Kristof, Nicholas D., 201
Kristol, William, 67, 214
Krüger, Gerhard, 103
Kyrgyzstan, 205–6

Lamartine, Alphonse de, 30
Lamoignon des Malesherbes, Chrétien-Guillaume, 2
landholding systems, 111
Lasch, Christopher: on the aristocracy of talent, 107–8; on democracy, 72; on democracy and media, 134; on public debate, 132–33, 134; on the ruling elite, 128; on two-class society, 164
Lassalle, Ferdinand, 45
"Last Man." *See* Nietzsche
Lavisse, Ernest, xvii
law courts: British, 171. *See also* jurisprudence
Le Bon, Gustave, 45
Le Bras, Hervé, xii
Left: democracy and, 115; environmentalist, 225; in the French Revolution, 113–14; multiculturalism and, 116–17; revolt against Christianity, 114–16; success in the West since World War II, 115
legal pragmatism, 168. *See also* progressive jurisprudence
legal realism, 170
legislatures: Jouvenel on "legislative activity," 159; "Power" and, 80. *See also* parliaments
Leo XIII, 115
Lévy, Bernard-Henri, xviii–xxii
Lewis, C. S., 72, 101, 131
Lewis, Wyndham, 20, 64, 215–16
"liberal autocracy," 212

liberal democracy: critiques of, 87; Fukuyama on, 71; history of suffrage, 87–88; human consciousness and, 85, 86; modern European skepticism toward and reactions against, 43–49; New Left and, 87; progress and, 85–90; proletarian citizens in, 88–89; religion and, 119–25; view of human beings in, 123–24
liberalism: anti-Christian and anti-monarchical prejudice, 113; Burnham on the weakness of, 82; Christianity and, 113, 121–25; critics of, 219; dangerous characteristics of, 81; democracy and, 78–82, 212; dynamics in the undermining of society and itself, 219–20; as the enemy of Western civilization, 82; future of the U.S. and, 218–20; inflation of the supply of ideas and, 136–37; managerial liberalism, 78–79; mass immigration and, 146–47; modernity and, 219; notions of human nature and, 81–82; the popular press and, 137; "Power" and, 79–81, 176; religion and, 82, 119–25; Zakaria on, 212. *See also* advanced liberalism
liberal Protestantism, 49–50
liberal reformism, 43–44
liberal republicans, 31–33
"liberation" movements, 194–95
liberation theology, 124, 195
liberty: aristocratic liberalism and, 34; Carlyle on, 22; democracy and, 112; European extension of democracy and, 68; in Guéhenno's imperial age, 187; importance of reflection to, 132; modern changes in the idea of, 150; Montesquieu on, 31, 32; "sociology of liberty" concept, 33–34; Tocqueville on, 34

Libya, 207, 208
Lilla, Mark, 208
Lincoln, Abraham, 63
Lippmann, Walter, 133–34, 137
Lisbon Treaty, 188–89
"living Constitution," 167, 168
Living Constitution, Dying Faith (Watson), 169
Livingston, Donald W., 94, 95
L'Osservatore Romano, 123
"lost generation," 60
Louisiana Purchase, 54
Lukacs, John, 48, 65, 131, 139, 209

Maastricht Treaty (1993), 49
Macaulay, Thomas, 20
Madison, James, 54–55, 73, 95
Maine, Sir Henry Sumner: on aristocracy, 104, 112; on the conflict between democracy and science, 174; on democracy as monarchy inverted, 40–41; on the difficulty of democracy, xxi; distrust of popular democracy, 24–26; on the English character, 197; on the history of democracy, 16–17; on "intellectual democracy," 107; on the party spirit, 156; on the party system, 154; on "political innovation" and science, 44–45; views of American democracy, 26, 52
Maistre, Joseph de, 21–22
Mallarmé, Stéphane, 44
managerial liberalism, 78–79, 81
Managerial Revolution, The (Burnham), 78–79
Manent, Pierre: on the creation of the European nation-state, 38, 39; on the crisis of Western democracy, 157–58; on democracy and government, 73; on democracy and national structure, 186; on democracy and the nation-state, 190; on

democracy from 1848 to 1968, 43; on the European extension of democracy, 68; on "pure" democracy, 62; on the secularization of Christian nations, 116; on speech and community, 140
manifest destiny, 55–57
Mann, Horace, 133
Marcuse, Herbert, 5
Marinetti, Filippo Tommaso, 44
markets: effect on politics, 160–61
Marshall, John, 168
Marx, Karl, 223
Marxism, 116, 118, 119
mass communication: failure of, 139–40; global effects of, 191–95. *See also* electronic communications/media
mass culture, 130–32
mass industrial society, 223, 224–25
"mass man": mass culture and, 130–32; threat to civilization, 127–28
mass media: creation of mass culture and, 131–32; critique of, 134–40; infantilism of modern society and, 151–52. *See also* electronic communications/media
mass social democracy, 87
Mayo, Henry B., 89
McKinsey & Company, 204
Medvedev, Dmitry, 210, 211
Mencken, H. L., 60–61, 97, 137
Mérimée, Prosper, xvi
meritocracy: American WASP establishment, 108–9; as an intellectual aristocracy, 107–8; elite in, 110; nature of, 109
messianic democratism, 62
Mexican immigration, 142–43
Mexican War, 56
Mexico, 194, 202–3
Middle American Radicals, 162, 163, 165

Mill, John Stuart, 20, 35, 133
Miller, Perry, 49–50
Millerites, 26
Minogue, Kenneth: on democracy, 72, 217–18; on the effects of liberalism, 81; on ideology, 118; on multiculturalism, 116–17, 119, 217–18
Mitchell, Harvey, 226
mob, 23–24
modernity: human consciousness and, 86; liberalism and, 219; Nietzsche's criticism of, 23–24
monarchy: American attitudes toward, 51–54; Bagehot's defense of British monarchy, 27–28; Burke on the French monarchy, 19; Christian kings, 38; democracy and, 40–41, 75–76, 112; Franklin on, 52; Maine on, 16; in Jouvenel's theory of power, 177–78; liberalism's prejudice against, 113; revolt against secular authority, 113. *See also* kings
money, 159–61, 164
monism, 221
Monroe Doctrine, 59
Montesquieu, 31, 32, 74
moral life, 218
moral relativism: mass communication and, 193–94
moral values: politics and, 180–81
Morgenthau, Hans, 64–65
Morley, Sir John, 64
Mosley, Sir Oswald, 189
Mubarak, Hosni, 207
Muller v. Oregon, 169
multiculturalism: as an expression of Western self-hatred, 119; impact on the modern West, 116, 118; mass immigration and, 147; modern democratic citizen and, 150–51; nation-states and, 215–18; radical skepticism of, 118–19; religion and, 116–17

Murray, John Courtney, 73, 221
Muslims and Muslim immigration, 144–49, 192
mythmaking: in America, xxi

nationalism: American democracy and, 54–63; effect of World War II on, 49; Hitler and, 48; Russian, 210
nationalist movements, 48, 194–95
nationalization: of Christianity, 38–39; in nineteenth-century France, xi–xviii; by the Obama administration, 179–80
national socialism, 45, 47–48
nation-states: Arnold on the importance of ideals to, 100; democracy and, 185, 189–91; Guéhenno on the future of, 185–89; multiculturalism and, 215–18; "non-national democracy" and, 190–91; origins in Europe, 38–39; secularization, 116
Naumann, Friedrich, 45
Nazi-Sozis, 48
Negri, Antonio, 156–57
Netherlands, 145
neutralism, 121
"New Christianity," 42
New Class, 108, 163–64
"new imperial age," 86
New Left, 78, 87
New Right, 162–63, 165
news, 134
New World Order, 67
Nicolson, Harold, 47
Nicolson, Juliet, 46
Niebuhr, Reinhold, 197, 232
Nietzsche, Friedrich: concept of the "Last Man," 24, 127; criticism of modernity, 23–24; on liberalism, 176; on man's fate, 128; on the nation-state, 189–90; on science, 175; on the tradition of aristocracy, 104; Overman, 23

nihilism, 193–94
Ninety-Nine Percent, 165
Nixon, Richard, 66
"non-national democracy," 190–91
Norman Anonymous, 15
Novak, David, 120
Novus Ordo Mass, 124

Obama, Barack, 119, 156, 179–80, 213
obligations, 174
O'Connor, Flannery, 110
offensive democracy, 62
*Old Regime and the French Revolution,
    The* (Tocqueville), 1, 30, 37
oligarchy, 102
online journalism, 137–38
On Power (Jouvenel), 176–79
Ontario (Canada), 120–21
Ortega y Gasset, José, 127, 128
Overman, 23
overpopulation, 195

Paine, Thomas, 50, 52, 63
Pakistan, 205
Palin, Sarah, 163
"parliamentary aristocracy," 80
parliaments: Bagehot on the educative
    role of, 132; in Jouvenel's theory of
    power, 177–79; party system and,
    178–79. *See also* legislatures
participatory journalism, 137–38
party system. *See* political parties
Patriotic Gore (Wilson), 80
pays, xii, xiii
Pearson, Karl, 45
Péguy, Charles, 118–19
People's Party, 58, 161–62
Perot, Ross, 162
Perreau-Saussine, Emile, 122
Perry, Rick, 93
personal computers, 175
Peters, Ralph, 210
Phillips, Kevin, 209

"philosophic age," 116
physiocracy, 30
Pieper, Josef, 103
Pinochet, Augusto, 225
piracy, 204
Planned Parenthood v. Casey, 171, 172
Plato, 73, 94
Plowden Reports, 16
plutocracy, 105, 106, 108
Polin, Claude, 41–42, 95–96, 97, 125
"political atheism," 39
political debate, 132–34, 158
political economy: Tocqueville's views
    of, 30
political liberty, 32
political parties: complaints against,
    154–55; in Jouvenel's theory of
    power, 178–79; polarization of
    party politics, 155–56; questions of
    fidelity in political representation
    and, 156–57
political rights: Tocqueville's views of,
    28–29
politico-moralism, 72, 218
politics: autonomy of, 86–87; class war-
    fare and, 161; corruption, 161; effect
    of money and markets on, 160–61;
    efficiency and political action, 180;
    Jacques Ellul on the true political
    life, 228; ideology and, 117–18; mass
    media and, 134–40; moral values
    and, 180–81; pseudodecisions,
    158–59; trends in the depoliticizing
    of democracy, 153–59
Pompidou, Georges, xiv
popular culture: critique of, 130–32;
    global impact of American/West-
    ern popular culture, 192–94
Popular Government (Maine), 24
popular press, 137
populism, 58, 72, 161–63
positivism, 43
Posner, Gerald, 170

Powell, J. Enoch, 143

power cells, 179–80

power/"Power": as command, 86; complexity of technological societies and, 180; democracy and, 29, 95, 176; drive to absolute power, 176; industrialism and, 223; Jouvenel's theory of the development of, 79–90, 176–79; liberalism and, 79–81, 176; money and, 160; personality traits necessary to resist, 197; power cells, 179–80; Tocqueville on power in democracy, 29

press, 133–34, 137

"procedural democracy," 157–58

Prochaska, Frank, 53

progress: liberal democracy and, 85–90; Maine's criticism of, 24–25

Progressive Era, 169

progressive jurisprudence, 168–72

progressivism, 59, 169

proletarian citizens, 88–89

propaganda, 139

Proudhon, Pierre-Joseph, 20

Puddington, Arch, 200

"pure" democracy, 62

Puritans, 49, 50

Putin, Vladimir, 210, 211

Rahe, Paul A., 215

Raspail, Jean, 144–45

Rawls, John, 72–73

Reagan, Ronald, 5, 62, 67

Red and the Black, The (Stendhal), 115

Reflections on the Revolution in Europe (Caldwell), 146

Reflections on the Revolution in France (Burke), 19

Reform Act of 1832 (Great Britain), 64, 77

Reformation, 38–39, 113

regroupement familial policy (France), 145

Reich, Robert, 164

religion: church-state conflicts and the origins of democracy, 37–40; concept of the privatization of, 120; culture and, 113, 125; democracy and, 26, 37–40, 116, 119–25; effects of mass immigration on, 146–47; effects of the loss of traditional religious faith, 149–50; liberalism and, 82, 119–25; mass communication and the radicalization of, 194; multiculturalism and, 116–17; republics and, 94, 125

religious faith: modern assault on, 9–10; Tocqueville on American religious faith, 8–9

religious freedom, 120–21, 147

Renaissance, 33–34

Renaissance (Burckhardt), 101–2

Renan, Ernest, 20–21, 101

representation: political parties and, 156–57

Republican Party, 116

"Republican theocracy," 209

republics: Bagehot on, 76; Brownson on the primary work of, 100; Brownson's definition of, 138; compared to democracy, 77; issues of scale and, 92–94; mass media and, 138; religion and, 94, 125; republican political ideal of the American Founders, 95

Revolt of the Elites and Betrayal of Democracy, The (Lasch), 164

Revolt of the Masses, The (Ortega y Gasset), 127

revolutions: Chesterton on, 91; democratic, 206–9, 215; "Power" and, 79; Tocqueville on the revolutions of 1848, 42–43

Right, 116

rights: in Great Britain, 77; modern obsession with, 173–74; obligations and, 174; "right of insurrection," 39

Rights of Man, 19, 215
Robb, Graham, xi–xiii, xv, xvi, xvii, xxii
Rockefeller, John D., 57
rock music, 131
Roosevelt, Franklin Delano, 61
Roosevelt, Theodore, 53, 59
Roosevelt Corollary, 59
Rorty, Richard, 150
Rosanbo, Louise de, 2–3
Rousseau, Jean-Jacques, 26, 31–32, 94, 96
royalty: American attitudes toward, 51–54; Bagehot on, 76. *See also* monarchy
ruling class. *See* elites
rural migration, 195–96
Rush, Benjamin, 52
Russell, Bertrand, 49
Russia, 209–10, 211

Saint-Just, Louis Antoine de, 159
Saint-Simon, Henri de, 42
Sarkozy, Nicolas, 147
scale, 92–94
Schlesinger, Arthur M., Jr., 55, 65, 66, 156
Scholastics, 122
Schumpeter, Joseph, 72
science and technology: impact on democracy, 174–75; national socialism and, 45
secession, 93
Second Reform Act (Great Britain), 46
Second Vatican Council, 121–24
secularization: of modern nations, 116
Sedition Act (1918), 60
self-government: Bryce on the future of, 225–26; popular press and, 137
selfish democracy: in America, 97–98; in France, 96; welfare state and, 97
self-righteousness: democracy and, 158
sensate culture, 128–30

Servile Mind, The (Minogue), 217–18
Seventeenth Amendment, 59
Siegfried, André, 47
Sieyès, Abbé Emmanuel-Joseph, 28, 29
Sixteenth Amendment, 59
slavery: civilization and, 102
Smith, Adam, 101
Social and Political Condition of France before the Revolution (Tocqueville), 30
Social Contract, The (Rousseau), 94, 96
socialism: American popular antipathy to, 42; "mass man" and, 128; nature and origins of, 41–42; as a threat to democracy, 40; World War I and, 46–47
socialist communities, 42
socialist democracy: distinguished from ideological democracy, 41; origins of socialism, 41–42; in the U.S., 58–59
Socialist Party of America, 58
social media, 135. *See also* Internet
social mobility: as securing the influence of elites, 164
"social monarchy," 45
sociology, 45
"sociology of liberty," 33–34
"soft despotism," 215, 226
Solzhenitsyn, Aleksandr, 210
Somalia, 194, 204
Sombart, Werner, 58
Sorel, Georges, 44
Sorokin, Pitirim, 75, 128–30, 216
sovereignty: of the people, 86; state sovereignty, 95–98
Soviet Union: Cold War and, 209; collapse of, 67; convergence with the U.S., 226
Sowell, Thomas, 213–14
Spain, 145
Spanish-American War, 59
Spanish language, 142

Spectator, The, 208
Spencer, Lady Diana, 53–54
Spengler, Oswald, 47
Stalinism, 210
state secession, 93
state sovereignty, 95–98
statocracy, 80, 177
Stein, Gertrude, 60
Stendhal, 20, 115
Stromberg, Roland N.: on artists' rejection of democracy, 44, 47; on democracy and personal liberties, 72; on parliamentary politics in Great Britain, 45; on pluralism and democracy, 217; on the postdemocratic world, 222; on the production of democratic regimes, 20; view of democracy as a means to another end, 43, 75
Students for a Democratic Society (SDS), 5
substantive due process: doctrine of, 169
suffrage: as "a stake in society," 111; expansion under Jackson in America, 55; history of, 87–88; proletarian citizen and, 89; Tocqueville's views of, 29
Sun Also Rises, The (Hemingway), 60
Syria, 207, 208

Taine, Hippolyte, 20
Tate, J. O., 54–55
Tea Party movement, 162–65
technique and technocratic development, 134, 175
technology. *See* science and technology
telecommunications. *See* electronic communications/media
terrorist attacks: American internationalism and, 67–68
Texas, 55
theology: liberation theology, 124, 195; as "the science of tradition," 102–3

Theroux, Paul, 195
Thiers, Adolphe, 3
"third wave" democratization, 124, 226
Third World: famine in, 195; immigration, 142–43, 144, 192–93
Tocqueville, Alexis de: aim of in *Democracy in America*, 12, 28; on American materialist values and ambitions, 96–97; on American public debate and discourse, 133; on American pursuit of wealth, 160; on American sensitivity to criticism, 18; aristocracy and, 1–2, 41, 106; aristocratic liberalism and, 33, 34, 35; on capital cities as a threat to representative government, 8; concerns about centralization, 8, 33; debate on the political sympathies of, 1; on democracy and bureaucracy, 214–15; on democracy and Christianity, 40; on democratic tyranny, 81; development of political thought in, 3; on the English aristocratical system, 41; on the English heritage of Americans, 53; on the factors maintaining and advancing American democracy, 7–9; family history, 2–3; fears of conformity in America, 131; on the French Revolution, 37; on the future of democracy, xviii, 4, 13, 31, 32–33, 40; on the importance of the character of a people, 50; on inquiétude and democratic society, 32; lack of impact in his own time, 35; Lévy's opinion of, xviii–xix; on personality characteristics unsuited to democracy, 197; as a political prophet, 1, 4, 15, 33; political views of, 12–13, 28–31, 33, 34, 35; on the revolutions of 1848, 42–43; on self-destructive tendencies in democracy, 13; travel to America,

3–4; views of contemporary French political history, 13, 30–31; views of the American republic, 11–12

Tocqueville, Bernard de, 2

Tocqueville, Hervé de, 2–3

Todd, Emmanuel, xii

Tolkien, J. R. R., 131

totalitarianism: in China, 211; democracy and, 87

tourism: in nineteenth-century France, xvi–xvii

Tracy, Baron Destutt de, 40

tradition: authority and, 103–4; civilization and, 102–3; nature of, 103; problem of transmission in a democracy, 108

transportation: French national development and, xv–xvi

Treaty of Guadalupe Hidalgo, 56

Treaty of Rome (1957), 49

Trollope, Mrs. Frances, 17–19

Tunisia, 207

Turkish immigrants, 145

Twain, Mark, 57

two-class society, 164

Tymoshenko, Yulia V., 207

Ukraine, 206–7

United States: Articles of Confederation, 95; attitudes toward royalty, 51–54; class warfare in the future of, 165; Cold War and, 209; Constitutional Convention, 73, 168; convergence with the Soviet Union, 226; democratic revolution and, 215; foreign policy following Vietnam, 66–67; global democracy and, 67–68; global economy and, 111; ideological Right in, 116; immigration and, 141–42; impact of the New Left on, 66; influence on Great Britain, 63–64; Lewis on the future of, 216; liberalism

and the future of, 218–20; liberal-managerial elite in, 110, 111; manifest destiny, 55–57; modern assault on religious faith, 9–10; modern complaints of assaults on, 10–11; modern condition of freedom in, 213–14; modern obsession with rights, 173–74; nationalism and, 54–63; New Class elite, 163–65; New Right, 162–63; peacetime reaction to World War I, 60–61; polarization of party politics, 155–56; popular antipathy to socialism, 42; populism in, 161–63; as a product of the Enlightenment, 150; progressive jurisprudence in, 168–72; pursuit of wealth and, 160; republican political ideal of the American Founders, 95; secondary role of politics in public life, 153; socialism in, 58–59; socialist-democratic versus nationalist-ideological divide with Europe, 41–42, 61–63; Tea Party movement, 162, 163, 165; Tocqueville on American materialist values and ambitions, 96–97; Tocqueville's views of the American republic, 11–12; Frances Trollope's observations of, 17–19; universalization of democratic thought and, 215; WASP establishment, 108–9. *See also* American democracy

universalism: American democracy and, 63–68, 215

universal suffrage, 29, 88, 89

Univision network, 142

U.S. Constitution: Bagehot's criticism of, 168; corrupting effects on, 167–68; doctrine of constitutional organicism, 167, 168; freedoms and, 214; progressive jurisprudence and, 168–72

U.S. Supreme Court: and issues of
social and political freedom,
213–14; progressive jurisprudence
and, 169–71, 172
utilitarianism, 43
utopianism, 6, 42, 73, 117, 216

Victoria, Queen, 53
virtue: in classic philosophy, 33
Voyage to America (Chateaubriand), 3

Wallace, George, 162
War of 1812, 55
Washington, George, 54, 142
WASP establishment, 108–9
Watson, Bradley C. S., 169, 170, 172
Wattenberg, Ben, 216
Waugh, Evelyn, 91, 127
Web. *See* Internet
welfare class, 88
welfare state, 88, 97
Western civilization: liberalism as
the enemy of, 82; relationship of
democracy to, 82, 83

Western democracy: modern obsession
with rights, 173–74; origins in the
conflict between church and state,
37–40
Whitney v. California, 172
Wilson, A. N., 131
Wilson, Clyde, 55
Wilson, Edmund, 80
Wilson, Woodrow, 59–60, 64, 158, 195
Wolfe, Alan, 72, 219
Wood, Gordon S., 54–55
World War I: impact on democracy and
socialism, 46–47; national identity
and, 48; reaction to in peacetime
America, 60–61; Woodrow Wilson
and, 59
World War II, 48–49

Yanukovich, Viktor F., 207
Yushchenko, Viktor A., 207

Zakaria, Fareed, 200, 211, 212
Zimmermann Telegram, 193